Swiss Banking Secrecy and the US-Swiss Conflict Over Holocaust Claims

INTERNATIONAL RELATIONS IN ASIA, AFRICA AND THE AMERICAS

The series International Relations in Asia, Africa and the Americas is edited by the Centre for International Studies and Development of the Jagiellonian University in Kraków.

Edited by Andrzej Mania & Marcin Grabowski

Vol. 15

PETER LANG

Anna Pruska

Swiss Banking Secrecy and the US-Swiss Conflict Over Holocaust Claims

PETER LANG

Bibliographic Information published by the Deutsche Nationalbibliothek
The Deutsche Nationalbibliothek lists this publication in the Deutsche Nationalbibliografie; detailed bibliographic data is available in the internet at http://dnb.d-nb.de.

Library of Congress Cataloging-in-Publication Data
A CIP catalog record for this book has been applied for at the Library of Congress

Cover illustration: Courtesy of Tomasz Morawiec-Lanckoroński.

ISSN 2511-588X
ISBN 978-3-631-87281-9 (Print)
E-ISBN 978-3-631-88780-6 (E-PDF)
E-ISBN 978-3-631-88788-2 (EPUB)
DOI 10.3726/b20271

Peter Lang – Berlin · Bern · Bruxelles · New York · Oxford · Warszawa · Wien

This publication has been peer reviewed.

www.peterlang.com

To Michał

Table of Contents

List of Abbreviations 11

Introduction 13

Chapter 1. Swiss Banking Secrecy: Its Origins, Foundations and Legal Implications 27

1.1 The Swiss Banking System: A Historical and Contemporary Perspective 29

1.1.1 The Historical Foundations of Swiss Banking 29

1.1.2 Overview and Structure of the Contemporary Swiss Banking Sector 35

1.2 The Concept and the Customary and Legal Foundations of Swiss Banking Secrecy 40

1.2.1 Banking Secrecy in the United States 43

1.2.2 Protection of Banking Secrecy in Swiss Law 45

1.2.2.1 Swiss Constitution 45

1.2.2.2 Internal Bank Laws and Code of Conduct ... 45

1.2.2.3 Cantonal Laws 45

1.2.2.4 Swiss Civil Code and Swiss Code of Obligations 46

1.2.2.5 Swiss Criminal Code 47

1.2.2.6 Federal Act on Banks and Savings Banks (Banking Act) of 1934 48

1.3 Limits of Swiss Banking Secrecy Under Domestic and International Law 52

1.4 The Debate on the Origins of Swiss Banking Secrecy and the Role of the Conflict with the U.S. 55

1.5 Banking Secrecy and the Swiss Public Opinion 68

1.6 The Numbered (Anonymous) Accounts Controversy 69

1.7 Evaluation of the Role of Banking Secrecy in the Rise of the Swiss Financial Center 71

1.8 Conclusions 73

Chapter 2. Swiss Banking During World War II: The First Major Conflict with the United States 77

2.1 The Role of Swiss Banks in Gold Transactions with the Reichsbank 80

2.2 U.S. and Allied Measures to Restrict German Economic and Financial Expansion: The Swiss Connection. 83

2.2.1 Swiss Assets in the United States: U.S. Freezing Order, Suspicion and Criticism with Respect to the Conduct of Swiss Banks 83

2.2.2 Blacklisting 87

2.2.3 London Declaration of January 5, 1943 87

2.2.4 Declaration on Gold Purchases of February 22, 1944 88

2.2.5 The Safehaven Program and Bretton Woods Resolution No. VI 89

2.3 Escalation of Pressure: Negotiations and Impositions 92

2.3.1 The Currie Agreement 92

2.3.2 Allied Control Council's Vesting Decree: Public Law No. 5 94

2.3.3 The Puhl Affair 95

2.4 The Washington Accord 97

2.4.1 The Issue of Looted Gold During Washington Negotiations 99

2.4.2 The Provisions of the Washington Accord 105

2.4.3 Fulfillment of the Washington Accord 107

2.4.4 U.S.-Swiss Sentiments in the Aftermath of the Washington Accord 116

2.5 The Evaluation of Swiss Conduct During World War II in the Context of International Law: Legalism versus Morality 119

2.6 The Final Act: The Interhandel Case 123

2.7 Conclusions 130

Chapter 3. The Conflict Over Holocaust-Related Claims in the 1990s 137

3.1 Cold War Era Efforts to Resolve the Issue of Holocaust-Related Claims 140

3.1.1 Overview of Holocaust Compensation Efforts Before 1996 140

3.1.2 Legal Impediments 144

3.1.3 The Role of the Holocaust in the United States 146

3.1.4 Efforts to Settle the Dormant Accounts and Heirless Assets Issue Before the 1990s Conflict 147

3.2 The Development of the Conflict 152

3.2.1 The Initial Stage: Involvement of Jewish Organizations and the U.S. Congress 152

3.2.2 Independent Committee of Eminent Persons-Volcker Commission 157

3.2.3 Class Action Suits 160

3.2.4 The Bergier Commission 166

3.2.5 The Meili Affair 168

3.2.6 Diplomatic Blunders and the Holocaust Fund 170

3.2.7 The Eizenstat Report and the Involvement of the U.S. Government 172

3.2.8 Swiss Reaction to the Eizenstat Report 176

3.2.9 Holocaust Victims' Gold 178

3.2.10 Financial Sanctions 184

3.2.11 The Involvement of the U.S. State Department: Mediation of the Settlement 191
3.2.12 The Settlement 194
3.2.13 The Political Power Game 196

3.3 Holocaust Litigation: Its Distinctive Features and Historical Legacy 199
3.3.1 A Hybrid Legal Framework 200
3.3.2 The United States as Jurisdiction 201
3.3.3 Litigation and Banking Secrecy 201
3.3.4 The Role of the Judge in Class Actions 202
3.3.5 The Historical Legacy of Holocaust Litigation 203
3.3.6 International Legacy 205

3.4 Silent Bystander, Willing Accomplice or Righteous Neutral: The Role of Switzerland During World War II in the Light of the Conflict 207

3.5 The Debate on the Moral Ambiguity and Validity of Holocaust Restitution: How Legitimate Was the Final Outcome of the Conflict? 213

3.6 Conclusions 218

Concluding Remarks 225

Summary 237

Bibliography 239

Index of Names 257

List of Abbreviations

1MDB:	1Malaysia Development Berhad
AEOI:	Standard for Automatic Exchange of Financial Account Information in Tax Matters
AMLA:	The Federal Act on the Prevention of Money Laundering in the Financial Sector
BSA:	Bank Secrecy Act
BSAAG:	Bank Secrecy Act Advisory Group
BSI:	Banca Della Svizzera Italiana
CAA:	Competent Authority Agreement
CRS:	Common Reporting Standard
CTRs:	Currency Transaction Reports
DPA:	Deferred Prosecution Agreement
FATCA:	Foreign Account Tax Compliance Act
FATF:	The Financial Action Task Force on Money Laundering
FCPA:	Foreign Corrupt Practices Act
FFI:	Foreign Financial Institutions
FIAA:	Foreign Illicit Assets Act
FIFA:	Fédération Internationale de Football Association
FinCEN:	Financial Crimes Enforcement Network
FINMA:	Swiss Financial Market Supervisory Authority
FIU:	Financial Intelligence Unit
FSF:	Financial Stability Forum
GAF:	General Aniline and Film
GAO:	Government Accountability Office
GDP:	Gross Domestic Product
G-SIBs:	Global Systematically Important Banks
HIFCA:	High Intensity Money Laundering and Related Financial Crime Area
HIRE Act:	Hiring Incentives to Restore Employment ACT
IBF:	International Banking Facility
ICE:	Commission of Experts Switzerland – Second World War
ICEP:	Independent Committee of Eminent Persons
IGA:	Inter-Governmental Agreement
IGCR:	Intergovernmental Committee on Refugees
IMF:	International Monetary Fund

IRS:	Internal Revenue Service
ITSA:	Insider Trading Sanctions Act
KPC:	Kuwait Petroleum Corporation
KYC:	Know Your Customer
MCAA:	Multilateral Competent Authority Agreement on the Automatic Exchange of Financial Account Information
MLAT:	Mutual Legal Assistance Treaty
MLCA:	Money Laundering Control Act
MOU:	The Memorandum of Understanding
MROS:	Money Laundering Report Office of Switzerland
NPA:	Non-Prosecution Agreement
OECD:	Organisation for Economic Co-operation and Development
OFC:	Offshore Financial Center
PEP:	Politically Exposed Person
PIC:	Private Investment Corporations
PSI:	Permanent Subcommittee on Investigations
QIP:	The Qualified Intermediary Program
RFPA:	Right to Financial Privacy Act
RIAA:	Restitution of Assets Illicitly Obtained by Politically Exposed Persons
SAR:	Suspicious Activity Report
SBA:	Swiss Bankers Association
SBG:	Schweizerische Bankgesellschaft
SEC:	Securities And Exchange Commission
SESTA:	Swiss Criminal Code to the revised Stock Exchange Act
SFr:	Swiss Francs
SNB:	Swiss National Bank
SVP:	Swiss People's Party
TIEA:	Tax Information Exchange Agreement
TJN:	Tax Justice Network
U.S.:	United States of America
UBS:	Union Bank of Switzerland
UNCAC:	UN Convention against Corruption
UNCTAD:	UN Conference on Trade and Development
USA PATRIOT ACT:	The Uniting and Strengthening America by Providing Appropriate Tools required to Intercept and Obstruct Terrorism Act
WJC:	World Jewish Congress
WJRO:	World Jewish Resitution Organisation

Introduction

Until World War I, the relations between United States and Switzerland could be described as friendly. Often referred to as "sister republics"[1] the two countries shared common democratic values, historical experiences, and institutional features, as well as a sense of uniqueness with respect to their republican governments.

In 1776, the year when the United States Declaration of Independence was proclaimed, the Old Swiss Confederacy (Alte Eidgenossenschaft) had existed for almost five hundred years. The confederacy was a loose alliance of thirteen republican states called cantons. The contribution of the Swiss to the development of a republican form of government cannot be underestimated.

In eighteenth-century Europe, republics were an exception rather than the rule and the Swiss enthusiastically welcomed the creation of another republic in the "civilized world,"[2] even as far away, as another continent. The first American constitution – the Articles of Confederation and Perpetual Union was modelled on the Swiss confederacy of sovereign states.[3] The writings of Swiss professor and member of the Geneva Council of State, Jean Jacques Burlamaqui and his student Emmerich de Vattel exerted a major influence on the American Founding Fathers. In particular, Burlamaqui's works on natural law strongly resonated with Thomas Jefferson, providing him with counterarguments to the British constitutional doctrine of parliamentary sovereignty.[4] However, the absence of adequate central authority in the Swiss model became a source of stark criticism by the American Federalists, as they perceived it as rendering the governing of a state ineffective. Switzerland was criticized for its lack of competence and power at the center.

The constitution adopted by the U.S. in 1787 created a federal republic, a form of government which soon proved to be a reciprocal model for the Swiss, as the Constitution of 1848 transformed Switzerland into a federal state, with power divided between different levels of government. Separate legislative and judicial powers were established, as well as a seven-member executive – the Federal

1 Hutson, James H.: *The Sister Republics. Switzerland and the United States from 1776 to the Present*. Library of Congress: Washington, D.C. 1991, p. 66.

2 Ibid., p. 10.

3 Ibid., pp. 24–25.

4 Ibid., pp. 19–22.

Council. The basic principles governing the U.S. constitution were therefore adopted by the Swiss: bicameralism and federalism.

After the Civil War, U.S. local and state governments again turned to Switzerland for inspiration and adopted Swiss tools of direct democracy – the initiative and the referendum. By 1912, eighteen U.S. state governments had one or both these mechanisms in place. By 1918, five more states adopted similar instruments.[5]

Despite these strong common foundations of the two "sister republics" the relations between the U.S. and Switzerland were characterized by periods of strong tensions, which commenced during World War II and continued throughout the whole postwar period.

The major disagreements between the United States and Switzerland were connected to the concept of Swiss banking secrecy, which is defined in a most rigorous way compared to international standards practiced among developed countries worldwide.[6] This concept, firmly established in the Swiss financial sector has led to tensions between the two countries in numerous cases pertaining to money laundering, tax evasion, and other financial sector crimes, as well as in the context of Holocaust claims.

After World War II Swiss banking was associated in the U.S. with numbered bank accounts, safe deposit boxes full of gold and the proceeds of international crime hidden behind the bank secrecy laws of a tiny Alpine country. This view was in stark contrast to the desired Swiss self-representation of a politically stable state in possession of a highly developed economy and capital market, a stable and freely convertible currency, as well as professionally managed financial institutions, which offer world class financial services.

Throughout the post-war period, but particularly from the early 1960s until the early 1990s Swiss banks were accused by the U.S. authorities of facilitating illicit activities and enabling organized crime to pursue money laundering transactions as well as supporting violations in the U.S. financial sector. The two countries also engaged in numerous disputes over the practice of Swiss banking secrecy in relation to tax evasion and tax fraud. This misconduct by foreign nationals was greatly facilitated through Swiss banking practices. Since 2007, the bilateral relations between the two countries have been particularly strained by

---

5 Ibid., pp. 58–64.

6 Guex, Sébastien: "The Origins of the Swiss Banking Secrecy Law and Its Repercussions for Swiss Federal Policy". *The Business History Review* 74, No. 2, Summer 2000, p. 244.

this tax-related conflict and dominated by ongoing U.S. investigations into the involvement of Swiss banks in aiding U.S. taxpayers in tax evasion and tax fraud.

An extensive analysis of the conflicts between the U.S. and Switzerland pertaining to money laundering, violations of financial sector regulations and tax crimes will be the subject of a separate publication.

The purpose of this book is to examine in detail the relations between the United States of America and Switzerland in the context of Swiss banking secrecy and Holocaust related claims during the period from World War II until the end of the 1990s.

The first major conflict between the U.S. and Switzerland erupted during World War II and continued in its immediate aftermath. The character of World War II differed from World War I in that the former was a total war, whereby the U.S. policy was subordinated to the objective of eliminating the enemy, and the Swiss persistence to maintain its economic neutrality was met with much less understanding on the part of the U.S. and its Allies, than during World War I, when neutral Switzerland was determined to secure the supplies necessary for its survival and opposed any attempts at the economic blockade of Germany.[7]

This was also the first conflict of such magnitude between the two countries, where Swiss banking secrecy was the issue at stake. The rupture resulted from U.S. attempts to trace German funds suspected to be hidden in Swiss banks and the refusal of Switzerland to participate in the Safehaven program, which was designed to track down and block German assets and looted property in neutral countries, thereby preventing a potential resurgence of Nazi Germany via an economic recovery. These funds were later to be used for post war reparations.

But the Swiss persistently refused to provide any information on these issues to the Allies, on the grounds, that doing so would constitute a breach of trust and a violation of banking secrecy.

Throughout the war the Swiss also continued to purchase gold from the Reichsbank. The U.S. claimed that this gold was looted from the occupied countries, and by conducting gold transactions with Germany, Switzerland supported the Nazis by providing them with foreign currency necessary to pay for the imports of raw materials essential for the German war effort.

Following lengthy negotiations and a severe amount of pressure, the Swiss finally agreed to block German assets and provide a census of all German property in Switzerland. In May 1946, the Washington Accord was signed, whereby the

7 See Meier, Heinz K.: *Friendship Under Stress. U.S. Swiss Relations 1900–1950.* Herbert Lang & Co: Bern 1970, p. 291 for this argument.

Swiss government conceded to several provisions with the aim of resolving the impasse. However, the fulfillment of this Accord was carried out only partially and in 1952 a new solution was implemented.

The repercussions of the involvement of Switzerland in the purchasing of Reichsbank's gold as well as the safekeeping of German assets and the assets of the victims of Nazi Germany had profound consequences for U.S.-Swiss relations in the 1990s, fueling a major conflict over the dormant accounts of Holocaust victims.

In the 1990s, the U.S.-Swiss wartime conflict resurfaced with unexpected magnitude, when Jewish organizations raised questions about dormant Swiss bank accounts, which belonged to Holocaust victims, and the value of heirless assets on the books of Swiss financial institutions. The campaign for the restitution of these assets, assisted by the U.S. administration, not only resulted in a billion-dollar settlement financed by two largest Swiss banks, but also induced the Swiss to reexamine and reevaluate the wartime history of their country.

In each case when tensions could be observed in the relations between the U.S. and Switzerland, they took place in an economic context and were related especially to the role played by Swiss banks and their rigorous adherence to banking secrecy, a phenomenon firmly established in the legal system of Switzerland and comprehensively protected by various legal provisions. Therefore, this phenomenon is introduced and discussed in detail in Chapter 1 of this book. Swiss banking secrecy is placed both in a historical context, as well as in the context of the Swiss banking sector. The importance of banking for the Swiss economy is analyzed and the question, why banking secrecy became a central concept for the Swiss banking culture is addressed. The legal and customary foundations of banking secrecy are examined in detail, such as the Swiss Constitution, the Swiss Civil Code, the Swiss Code of Obligations, the Swiss Criminal Code, and the Banking Act of 1934, as well as internal bank regulations. The concept of financial privacy in the U.S. legal system is briefly presented to point out the key differences between the Swiss and American approaches to this concept. The limits of Swiss banking secrecy under domestic and international law are explored. An attempt is made to briefly evaluate, how important Swiss banking secrecy is for the Swiss banking sector and whether it is the major factor contributing to its success and competitiveness. Further, a detailed analysis of the discussion on the origins of Swiss banking secrecy is provided in this chapter and aimed to expose the myth that the Swiss have created around this concept, and how this myth was shaped by U.S. pressure. The final issues addressed here include an attempt to verify the acceptance for banking secrecy in the Swiss society and the role of Swiss banking secrecy in the development of the Swiss financial center.

Chapter 2 addresses the multidimensional root causes of the conflict over Holocaust claims, by discussing events which took place during World War II and in the immediate aftermath of the war. In particular, the role of the Swiss financial system and of the Swiss central bank in the economy of the Third Reich is analyzed and the gold transactions executed through Swiss banks are examined, as well as their impact on the financing of trade and the German war effort. During World War II about 80% of Reichsbank's gold passed through Switzerland. This gold included the reserves looted from occupied countries, as well as gold taken from Holocaust victims. The U.S. policy with respect to the gold issue was shaped not only by the need to compensate Nazi victims by using this gold for war reparations, but also by the fear of resurgence of German military power if these resources were to fall back into Nazi hands.

Chapter 2 explores the Allied efforts, led by the U.S., and aimed at reducing Reichsbank's transactions with the Swiss National Bank and through the Swiss banking system. Operation Safehaven, a program which was intended to track down German assets in neutral countries and prevent them from being re-used by the German power elites is also discussed here.

The Allied negotiations with the Swiss, which were led by the U.S are examined in detail. They focused on the liquidation of German external assets in Swiss banks and the return of looted gold purchased by the Swiss from the German Reichsbank and culminated in the signing of the Washington Accord on May 25, 1946. In the course of the fulfillment of this agreement, Swiss banks were obliged to lift banking secrecy with respect to the German asset holders, whose names were to be revealed to the Allies. However, this did not happen, since the provisions concerning the liquidation of German assets were never carried out. The Washington Accord was only partially implemented, and this fact, together with the issues which it left outstanding, had overwhelming consequences for the dispute between Switzerland and the United States in the 1990s. This chapter aims to evaluate the Washington Accord both from the Swiss and the U.S. perspective and investigates to what extent the strict adherence to banking secrecy influenced the Washington negotiations and their outcome.

The final section of Chapter 2 is dedicated to the U.S.-Swiss conflict over Interhandel, a Swiss based company, the assets of which were blocked in the U.S. during World War II. Although this dispute emerged before 1945, it nevertheless continued well into the post-war period, with Swiss banking secrecy playing in it a central role.

In Chapter 3, the conflict between the United States and Switzerland in the context of dormant accounts and assets belonging to Holocaust victims is analyzed in detail. The U.S.-Swiss conflict discussed in this chapter directly refers to

World War II and the role of Switzerland as the banker to the Third Reich, therefore it touches upon the events examined in Chapter 2 and their repercussions in the post war period.

Section 3.1 of this chapter examines the efforts to resolve the issue of dormant accounts and Holocaust assets during the Cold War era. These attempts were rather limited in their number and their effectiveness to bring a meaningful and permanent solution to the problem.

The fact that the issue of Holocaust claims had not been resolved immediately after the war, opened the door to claims of Jewish organizations in the 1990s and led to Swiss banks becoming a subject of intense scrutiny by the United States government.

In 1996, the U.S. Senate Banking Committee held hearings concerning dormant accounts and irretrievable Holocaust assets on the books of Swiss banks. On May 2, 1996, a Memorandum of Understanding was signed between the World Jewish Congress, the World Jewish Restitution Organization (WJRO) and the Swiss Bankers Association, which established the Independent Committee of Eminent Persons with Paul Volcker, former chairman of the U.S. Federal Reserve Board, as its head. The Volcker Commission, as it came to be known, conducted the largest bank audit in the history of world finance.

With the creation of the Volcker Commission special measures were introduced, which allowed to disclose information on accounts, which had been dormant since 1945. This procedure was characterized as a "special official audit" and allowed to circumvent the regulations concerning Swiss banking secrecy.

In 1996, Jewish plaintiffs submitted class action suits against three largest Swiss banks. The Swiss banks were accused of collaborating with the German Nazi regime by hiding assets which belonged to Holocaust victims and by laundering funds which were looted or stemmed from slave labor during World War II. As the conflict escalated throughout 1998 and the legal proceedings in the United States were in full swing, the U.S. authorities threatened Swiss banks with the use of economic sanctions. In 1999, the Swiss financial institutions finally agreed to a settlement, which imposed a payment of $1.225 billion to cover the claims to dormant accounts. These funds were later distributed for the benefit of Holocaust survivors and their heirs.

Chapter 3 provides a detailed analysis of the dynamics of this conflict, which involved Swiss banks on the one side and Jewish Organizations and the U.S. government on the other. The mechanisms of exerting pressure by the U.S. on both the Swiss banks and the Swiss government is discussed, including public relations measures and economic sanctions. The role of special commissions established during the conflict is analyzed, the Volcker Commission set up to investigate the dormant accounts issue, and the Bergier Commission, created to examine the history of Switzerland during World War II and the role played by its financial sector.

The so called Eizenstat Report and its impact is assessed in detail. In this report, prepared in 1997 by the U.S. Department of State, the Swiss were accused of being "the principal bankers and financial brokers for the Nazis."[8] The publication of the Eizenstat report led to a marked deterioration in the relations between the two countries.

This Chapter also examines the U.S. political mechanism, which has led to the involvement of different actors in the conflict, in particular the U.S. President, the U.S. government and administration officials, as well as political parties' representatives.

In Chapter 3, the role of banking secrecy as the main obstacle to solving the problem of dormant accounts before the U.S. intervention is investigated in detail. As a result of the conflict with the U.S. and the pressure of the U.S. administration the Swiss lifted for the first time the veil of banking secrecy on such a scale and enabled external access to Swiss bank accounts for the purpose of a comprehensive audit by the Volcker Commission. This chapter examines the extent to which the foundations of Swiss banking secrecy were weakened by U.S. policy and whether the conflict had an impact on its further practice.

Chapter 3 also includes an evaluation of the sources of U.S. economic pressure in the conflict, an analysis of the Swiss reaction to the U.S. official pressure and the attacks on the part of Jewish organizations, including a discussion of whether this reaction was appropriate, or whether it was possible to avoid an escalation of the conflict. The confrontation of the problem of the moral ambiguity of Jewish claims on the one hand with the concept of the right to compensation on the other is addressed in this chapter, in the context of the debate which took place within the Jewish community following the settlement with Swiss banks. Finally, the issue of how the conflict with the U.S. prompted the Swiss to reexamine their history and their conduct during World War II is addressed. Since the events of the 1990s brought about a lasting resolution of the Holocaust claims conflict for Switzerland, the analysis ends in this period and does not reach beyond the twentieth century.

This book is based on a dissertation defended at the Institute of Political Science and International Relations of the Jagiellonian University in Kraków, under

8 U.S. Department of State *U. Preliminary Study*, coordinated by Eizenstat, Stuart E., prepared by Slany, William Z., Washington, D.C.: Department of State, May 1997, p. 3.

the academic supervision of Professor Andrzej Mania, as the doctoral advisor, and Dr. Tomasz Pugacewicz as the doctoral co-advisor.

Swiss banking secrecy and its impact on U.S.-Swiss relations is placed in a historical, political, legal, and economic context, and in this sense the book provides a broad and comprehensive overview of the subject matter.

This book belongs to the field of political science, however, the specific subject matter it deals with requires reaching beyond this domain and applying an interdisciplinary approach, in line with the broad spectrum of the analyzed issues, which entail historical, legal, economic, and financial, as well as statistical aspects. This interdisciplinary approach is reflected in the methods applied during research.

The primary method which was employed is qualitative data analysis. This method includes case studies, text analysis and historical analysis.[9]

The approach adopted in this book involves the form of a case study, which allows for an in-depth examination of the relations between two countries in a specific context and over a certain period. This has in turn enabled a detailed explanation of how the events unfolded and how and why certain processes occurred, thereby contributing to the understanding of the historical, sociological, economic, political, and legal conditions of certain phenomena, as well as allowing to look at events through the different perspective of actors from these two countries. The collection, analysis, and interpretation of data, as complete, as possible, has permitted to observe long term processes, to identify patterns and categories, to discover relationships and conditions, to cultivate explanations, to extract interpretations of events, to develop critiques, and to verify the assumptions put forth in this book.

The comparative historical analysis approach which focuses on historically contextualized comparisons has enabled an understanding of the process of the development of Switzerland as a banking center and a tax haven.

Another key method applied in the book is the institutional and legal framework analysis. Using this method Swiss law is examined to provide insight into the regulatory foundations of Swiss banking secrecy and its limits.

In the course of investigating the Swiss and U.S. legal and institutional framework, the method of comparative legal analysis is applied, which allows to

9 For an analysis of qualitative research techniques and text and document-based techniques see for example Vromen, Ariadne: "Debating Methods: Rediscovering Qualitative Approaches". In: Marsh, David/Stoker, Gerry (eds.): *Theory and Methods in Political Science*. Palgrave Macmillan: Basingstoke, UK 2010, pp. 249–266.

juxtapose the domestic laws of two countries to determine how the same areas have been regulated.[10] Within this method the foundations of such key concepts as banking secrecy, tax evasion and tax fraud are analyzed and compared.

Since the topic of Swiss banking secrecy needs to be placed in the broader context of the Swiss financial sector, the Swiss tax haven and the general context of offshore jurisdictions, the applied methodology involves the unobtrusive research method of analyzing existing statistics. The sources used in the course of research include data provided by the World Bank, the Organization for Economic Co-operation and Development (OECD), the International Monetary Fund, the Swiss Bankers Association, various non-governmental organizations, as well as numerous other data sources. Quantitative methods applied in the research conducted by other scholars are also analyzed. This enables to provide a historical context for the argumentation, as well as to compare different results on the same issue. Statistical data is used for discussing the role of the Swiss banking system in the contemporary Swiss economy, to provide insight into the role of the Swiss National Bank and the Swiss financial sector during World War II, to assess the scale of offshore activities of Swiss banks and the extent of this phenomenon in the world. The analysis of statistical data is also crucial for addressing the problem of dormant accounts and heirless assets.

As regards the sources of data collected during research, various primary sources are the subject of examination and interpretation: government reports, official political statements and speeches, memoirs, court orders, official government press releases, documents issued by various government institutions and non-governmental institutions, or special commissions.

Secondary sources such as research papers in academic journals and books provide valuable input and insight into the many issues examined in this book.

The subject matter raised here became the topic of research primarily in Switzerland and in the United States. There is considerably more contribution from American scholars, but these publications tend to focus only on a narrow range of the issues explored in this book. Among the scope of Swiss publications one can find works that treat the subject matter more synthetically and comprehensively than U.S. sources.

---

10 Hopkin, Jonathan: "The Comparative Method". In: Marsh, David/Stoker, Gerry (eds.): *Theory and Methods in Political Science*. Palgrave Macmillan: New York 2010 and Adams, Maurice/Heirbaut, Dirk: *The Method and Culture of Comparative Law. Essays in Honour of Mark von Hoecke*. Hart Publishing: Oxford et al., Oregon 2014.

There is a number of studies of the Swiss financial system which include an analysis of Swiss banking secrecy and touch upon U.S.-Swiss relations in this respect, however, two volumes in particular deserve to be mentioned here. The first one is "Swiss Finance. Capital Markets, Banking, and the Swiss Value Chain,"[11] by financier Henri B. Meier, and two economists John E. Marthinsen and Pascal A. Gantenbein, which also provides insight into the political, legal, and economic factors that have contributed to Switzerland's leading position on the international financial markets. Another relatively comprehensive publication is by two professors from Romandy, Phillippea Braillard, and Henri Schwamm, entitled: "Place financière suisse. L'autre stratégie."[12] This book discusses the role of Switzerland as a financial center and tax haven and provides a broad analysis of the role played in its development by Swiss banking secrecy.

As regards research into the origins of Swiss banking secrecy, two Swiss historians should be mentioned in this context: Peter Hug and Sébastien Guex. Their pioneering work has helped to refute the myth about the idealistic motives behind the introduction of Article 47 (b) into the Swiss Banking Act of 1934.[13] Additionally, Sébastien Guex contributed with numerous publications to the research on the historical evolution of the Swiss financial center and historical perspectives on Swiss banking secrecy.

Another historian of Swiss origins, Heinz K. Meier, focused his research on U.S.-Swiss relations in the nineteenth and the twentieth centuries. His book

---

11 Meier, Henri B./Marthinsen, John E./Gantenbein, Pascal A.: *Swiss Finance. Capital Markets, Banking, and the Swiss Value Chain.* John Wiley & Sons, Inc.: Hoboken, New Jersey 2013.

12 Braillard, Philippe/Schwamm, Henri: *Place financière Suisse. L'autre stratégie.* Éditions Slatkine: Genève 2006.

13 Hug, Peter: "Eclairage. Les vraies origins du secret bancaire, démontage d'un mythe". *Le Temps*, 28.04.2000, retrieved 09.12.2017, from https://www.letemps.ch/opinions/eclairage-vraies-origines-secret-bancaire-demontage-dun-mythe, Hug, Peter: "Steuerflucht und die Legende vom antinazistischen Ursprung des Bankgeheimnisses: Funktion und Risiko der moralischen Überholung des Finanzplatzes Schweiz". In: Tanner, Jakob/Weigel, Sigrid (eds.): *Gedächtnis, Geld und Gesetz, Vom Umgang mit der Vergangenheit des Zweiten Weltkrieges.* Hochschulverlag: Zürich 2002, pp. 269–322, Guex, Sébastien: "The Origins…", pp. 237–266, Guex, Sébastien: "Place financière Suisse et secret bancaire au XXe siècle: ombres at pénombres". In: Froidevaux, Dominique (ed.): *La Suisse dans la constellation des paradis fiscaux.* Éditions d'en bas et COTMEC: Lausanne et al. 2002, pp. 54–79, and Guex, Sébastien: "Le secret bancaire a-t-il un avenir?". In: Froidevaux, Dominique (ed.): *La Suisse dans la constellation des paradis fiscaux.* Éditions d'en bas et COTMEC: Lausanne et al. 2002, pp. 171–182.

entitled "Friendship Under Stress. U.S.-Swiss Relations 1900–1950"[14] provides guidance to the understanding of the interactions between the two countries during World War II. Nonetheless, the point of view applied in this work corresponds to the Swiss perspective, which is why the examination of other publications is necessary to achieve a broader outlook on the discussed events.

The studies pursued by Marco Durrer, also a Swiss author, provide deeper insight into U.S.-Swiss relations in the context of the Swiss financial sector during World War II. Durrer, in particular, examines in detail the lengthy negotiations leading to the signing of the Washington Agreement of 1946, its fulfillment and implications.[15]

The research of the conflicts between Switzerland and the U.S. during World War II and in the 1990s in relation to the issues of looted gold, dormant accounts and assets of Holocaust victims could not be complete without referring to the reports prepared by three different commissions established to fulfill their particular purpose of analyzing certain aspects of Swiss conduct during World War II, known as the Bergier Report, the Volcker Report, and the Eizenstat Report. In 1996, under the guidance of Stuart Eizenstat, who was appointed by the U.S. President to investigate the role of Allied and neutral nations' dealings with Germany and the handling of Nazi assets, a special interagency working group consisting of American historians was established.[16] The research of this working group led to the publication of a comprehensive report, known as the Eizenstat Report, from the name of its main coordinator.[17]

In response to the Eizenstat Report, which presented the U.S. point of view on the events of World War II and Swiss policy during this turbulent time,

14 Meier, Heinz K.: *Friendship Under Stress…*

15 Durrer, Marco: *Die schweizerisch – amerikanischen Finanzbeziehungen im Zweiten Weltkrieg. Von der Blockierung der schweizerischen Guthaben in den USA über die "Safehaven" – Politik zum Washingtoner Abkommen (1941–1946).* Paul Haupt Verlag: Bern et al. 1984.

16 This interagency group included historians and experts from the following institutions: The U.S. State Department, The U.S. Treasury Department, U.S. Holocaust Memorial Museum, The Justice Department's Office of Special Investigations, the CIA, U.S. Army Center for Military History, National Security Agency and the Federal Reserve Bank of New York.

17 U.S. Department of State: *U.S. and Allied Efforts to Recover and Restore Gold and Other Assets Stolen or Hidden by Germany During World War II. Preliminary Study.* Coordinated by Eizenstat, Stuart E., prepared by Slany, William Z., Department of State, Washington, D.C. May 1997.

Switzerland established its own Independent Committee of Experts led by a respected Swiss historian Jean François Bergier. This body, known as the Bergier Commission, published several reports concerning different aspects of Swiss history during World War II, including its final report, in 2002.[18]

The Volcker Commission, named after its chairman and former head of the U.S. Federal Reserve Board, Paul Volcker, conducted the largest banking audit in history, which encompassed 254 Swiss banks. The Commission published the results of its enquiry in December 1999.[19]

American literature concerning the subject of litigation against Swiss banks and the compensation of Holocaust victims and their heirs for their material losses is quite voluminous. "Holocaust Restitution. Perspectives on the Litigation and Its Legacy", edited by Michael J. Bazyler and Roger P. Alford[20] is a collected edition which consists of different valuable articles on this subject matter. Michael J. Bazyler, an American professor of law is one of the leading experts in this area and has published numerous papers on Holocaust restitution.

A memoir published by Stuart Eizenstat,[21] the architect of the 1999 settlement, proved to be an interesting source of details on the negotiations between the United States and Swiss banks, and especially on the role of the U.S. administration in this process.

The arguments provided in this volume are greatly enriched by examining various non-scholarly sources, which despite a lack of academic research credential, nevertheless provided a broader framework for analyzing this topic. One such example is the widely quoted book written by T.R. Fehrenbach and published in 1966 under the title "The Gnomes of Zurich."[22] This popular work lifted the curtain on Swiss banking secrecy for the first time and contributed to raising a broader interest on this subject. At the same time, it was a source of many myths and inaccuracies connected with Swiss banking secrecy. Another interesting source is a book by an investigative journalist, Nicholas Shaxon, entitled

18 Independent Commission of Experts Switzerland – Second World War: *Switzerland, National Socialism and the Second World War. Final Report*, Pendo Verlag: Zürich 2002.

19 Independent Committee of Eminent Persons: *Report on Dormant Accounts of Victims of Nazi Persecution in Swiss Banks*. Stämpfli Verlag AG: Bern 1999.

20 Bazyler, Michael J./Alford, Roger P. (eds.): *Holocaust Restitution: Perspectives on the Litigation and Its Legacy*. New York University Press: New York et al. 2006.

21 Eizenstat, Stuart E.: *Imperfect Justice. Looted Assets, Slave Labor, and the Unfinished Business of World War II*. PublicAffairs: New York 2004.

22 Fehrenbach, T.R.: *The Gnomes of Zurich*. Leslie Frewin Publishers Limited: London 1966.

"Treasure Islands. Tax Havens and the Men Who Stole the World,"[23] which provides a behind the scenes account of the tax haven phenomenon.

A book by Norman G. Finkelstein, "The Holocaust Industry – Reflections on the Exploitation of Jewish Suffering,"[24] was a polemic and somewhat controversial voice in the debate on Holocaust compensation.

The issues connected with Swiss banking secrecy are on the one hand extremely interesting and at times even suspenseful, however, on the other, they are also controversial and quite sensitive for the Swiss. They need to be placed in the right context, and thoroughly researched. The specific character of the matter at hand may create temptation towards misinformation and distortion of facts, therefore even the examination of scholarly sources requires a good deal of common sense and careful determination to get to the bottom of the issues, which quite often are presented in a very subjective manner. For this reason, in each analyzed case, it was necessary to acknowledge different points of view and to compare them to achieve as broad and objective a perspective on this subject, as possible.

---

23 Shaxon, Nicolas: *Treasure Islands. Tax Havens and the Men who Stole the World*. Vintage Books: London 2012.

24 Finkelstein, Norman G.: *The Holocaust Industry. Reflections on the Exploitation of Jewish Suffering*. Verso: London et al. 2003.

Chapter 1. Swiss Banking Secrecy: Its Origins, Foundations and Legal Implications

Swiss banking law and policy grew up bent by the almost neurotic Swiss desire for personal privacy and by the determination of the individual to be left alone, not only by his neighbors but by his own government as well.[1]

The strong respect for privacy which lies at the root of the Swiss tradition of banking secrecy results from the fact that in Switzerland the citizens are the sovereign and the highest political authority in the country,[2] and therefore, the government has no right to disregard the privacy of the sovereign. Swiss banks operate in a country where confidentiality carries an immense legal and moral weight.

The regulative function of the government with respect to the financial system can be exercised without compromising banking secrecy, since financial information is passed by banks to the authorities in an aggregated form, without the need to reveal the details of relations with particular customers.

Banking secrecy both protects bank customers and enforces public confidence in banks, hence it has become the cornerstone of the Swiss financial sector. However, regardless of its role for the Swiss domestic economy, banking secrecy has been subject to criticism and challenge from outside Switzerland ever since the banking business began to thrive in this country. The criticism directed against banking secrecy, especially from the United States, has been particularly strong from the end of World War II.

Banking secrecy enjoys wide public support and recognition in Switzerland, as proven by surveys and unsuccessful political campaigns to limit it or abolish entirely. It is compatible with the principle of tax self-declaration and has not prevented the Swiss authorities from having an excellent tax collection record.

The protection of bank-client information has played an important role in the rise of the Swiss financial center to a global status. But it is by no means the only success factor. Other attributes, such as political and economic stability, a

---

1 Fehrenbach, T.R.: *The Gnomes…*, p. 41.

2 Federal Council: "Switzerland's Political System", retrieved 28.09.2016, from https://www.admin.ch/gov/en/start/federal-council/political-system-of-switzerland.html.

strong and freely convertible currency and a high quality of advanced banking services have played an important role in this process. Swiss banking business is based on trust, tradition, and stability, as much as on formal regulations pertaining to customer confidentiality. Switzerland is not an exception in terms of banking secrecy regulations. Austria, Belgium, Hong Kong, Liechtenstein, Luxembourg, Panama, Singapore, and Uruguay, just to provide a few examples, have introduced similarly strict banking secrecy provisions in their legislative systems, however, Switzerland is characterized by the longest history of persistent enforcement of these regulations, which renders them all the more credible and trustworthy.

The use of numbered accounts is not limited to Switzerland and the concept of banking secrecy is not endemic to the Swiss. Its history is as old as banking itself. But few countries, even those which tried to copy Swiss banking secrecy laws, have succeeded as the Swiss have, presumably due to the lack of such a strong national ethic or a hard-working, solid, and honest society, as well as a stable and consistent economic policy, all of them the defining traits of the Swiss.

Swiss banking secrecy laws were not passed to support criminal activity, money laundering or corruption, unfortunately they are often exploited precisely for these purposes, as numerous examples provided in the course of further analysis demonstrate.

Although Swiss banking secrecy will continue to protect Swiss citizens, its role in protecting the assets of foreign residents will likely subside, as Swiss banks and authorities succumb to external pressure and implement foreign and international legislation aimed at greater transparency and exchange of information.

This chapter provides a historical perspective on the development of the Swiss banking sector in the context of Swiss banking secrecy, as well as an overview of the contemporary banking business in Switzerland. The role of banks for the Swiss economy is discussed. The legal foundations of Swiss banking secrecy are analyzed, including the famous Article 47 of the Banking Act. Since banking secrecy is not an absolute right, its limits are examined both under domestic and international law. The debate surrounding the origins of Swiss banking secrecy is discussed in detail to help understand the moral component of the U.S.-Swiss conflict in relation to this concept. According to some historians, the tensions between the U.S. and Switzerland helped to fuel the humanitarian myth derived by Swiss banking circles, precisely in response to U.S. pressure on Swiss banking secrecy. Further, the support for banking secrecy among the Swiss public is briefly outlined in this chapter, and finally, the factors which are conducive to capital inflows into Swiss banks are examined, to pinpoint other strategic properties besides banking secrecy, which have contributed to the success of Switzerland as a leading banking center.

1.1 The Swiss Banking System: A Historical and Contemporary Perspective

Switzerland thus has none of the sources or tools of national power and prestige. But few nations have more prestige in the world at large, and few societies are more influential beyond their borders. The reason is not the superb Swiss watches or Swiss chocolate, both the world's best, or even the famed and genuine Swiss direct democracy [...]. It is Swiss money, of which the banks of Switzerland manage and control an immense amount.[3]

1.1.1 The Historical Foundations of Swiss Banking

Switzerland is located at the heart of Europe and commands access to alpine passes. In medieval times the country developed as a trading hub, with the German-Mediterranean trade route passing through Swiss towns. Commerce flourished, as did the wealth of the Swiss town merchants. The medieval trade fairs in Geneva, where merchants from Italian city states, German towns and French tradesmen offered their goods were also places of money exchange. Commercial lending developed, as did the first credit system and money changing facilities. It is fair to acknowledge that banking arrived in Switzerland by way of Italy, since the first bankers in Geneva were Italians. They possessed the necessary skills, including experience with the bill of exchange, the financial instrument which facilitated the evasion of the Catholic ban on usury[4] – the forbidden practice of charging an often excessive or abusive interest on loans.

When the teachings of religious reformers, John Calvin and Ulrich Zwingli, gained prominence in Swiss towns and led to the rise of Protestantism, the moral foundations for the development of banking were laid. A philosophy built upon the discipline of work emerged. Money was considered a reward from God and hard work was praised as leading to success and achievement. The Protestant work ethic supported material and financial accumulation, as opposed to spending and a state of sufficiency. It also offered a liberal interpretation of the

3 Fehrenbach, T.R.: *The Gnomes...*, p. 20.
4 Bauer, Hans/Blackman, Warren J.: *Swiss Banking: An Analytical History*. Macmillan Press: Basingstoke 1998, pp. 10–13.

Catholic ban on usury. The profession of a financier became a respected one, and Geneva evolved to become a major hub of the protestant banking network.[5]

Another marked phase in the initial development of Swiss banking can be dated back to the sixteenth century, when the first private banks were created. The Swiss economy generated a surplus of investable funds, resulting from a high savings rate and a relatively low demand for real capital investments. The mountainous region of Switzerland, inhospitable to agriculture, provided scarce opportunities for work and the male children of peasants turned to the profession of mercenaries to secure their income. Part of the payment they received for their services was retained by the city governments and this generated the surplus, which found its way to the banks of Geneva, to be used by protestant bankers for re-lending to the French court.[6]

In the seventeenth century, Switzerland, as a neutral country, provided refuge for Protestants during religious wars, it also provided refuge for their money. The influx of immigrants included bank specialists from France, and their skills helped build up the banking industry. During this period the private banks of Geneva provided financial services to the French court, in particular by lending money to the French kings to support their lavish spending habits.

The French Revolution brought about another influx of money belonging to the French nobility. The great banking families of Geneva emerged, most of them descending from French Huguenots.

The Swiss Constitution of 1848 specified, that the newly established federal government would be solely responsible for issuing money in Switzerland. Two years later the Federal Assembly introduced a single currency, the Swiss franc, to replace the twenty-five separate cantonal currencies and the 8000 different coins and notes in circulation at the time. This greatly facilitated the handling of money transactions.

Interestingly, until the mid-nineteenth century Switzerland was a poor country, one of the most inaccessible and unproductive in Europe. Together with the industrialization and the development of a railway system Switzerland embarked on a continuous path of stable economic growth, which has led it to become one of the wealthiest countries in the world.[7]

---

5 Ibid., pp. 49–51.

6 Ibid., p. 52.

7 See for example Studer, Roman: "When did the Swiss Get so Rich. Comparing Living Standards in Switzerland and Europe, 1800–1913". *Journal of European Economic History* 37, No. 2, January 2008, pp. 405–452 and Weder, Beatrice/Weder, Rolf: "Switzerland's Rise to a Wealthy Nation: Competition and Contestability as Key Success

The industrial revolution also accelerated the development of the Swiss banking industry. The concept of modern banking as we know it today was created in England, France and Holland, not in Switzerland. The Swiss private banks stored and exchanged money, but did not loan it. But in the mid-nineteenth century Switzerland needed a transportation system, a network of railroads such as the ones which emerged in other western European countries, which would provide a boost to the industrialization of the country, and this required credit. And one Swiss visionary had a dream and a very pragmatic idea how to make this dream come true. Alfred Escher, a Zurich merchant and a member of the newly established Federal Council,[8] wanted to build a great railroad system linking France and Austria through Switzerland, which would carry goods from Germany via the St Gotthard Pass down to Lombardy, with Zurich at the center of this railroad network.[9] However, such a project would need substantial financing and Escher set off to provide it through credit. During this period there were only two banks operating in Zurich, which with its 17,000 inhabitants was a rather provincial town, lagging behind Geneva, Basel, or Lausanne.

Alfred Escher decided to set up a new bank, modelled on the French bank Credit Mobilier, a bank created specifically to finance new industries such as railroads and manufacturing. But contrary to the French Credit Mobilier, which was entirely in the hands of a few individuals, the charter of the new Swiss Credit Bank (Kreditanstalt) assigned the control of the bank to Swiss citizens, and the bank was not permitted to issue bonds exceeding its subscribed capital. Half of the capital of the new institution was raised in Germany, without having to eschew control of the bank. Escher and a group of Swiss merchants and private bankers raised 3 million gold francs of the bank's capital, but the Zurich cantonal government refused to pay for the shares set aside for it. Therefore, these shares were added to the shares designated for the Swiss public. In 1856, 9000 shares in

---

Factors". In: Fosu, Augustin K. (ed.): *Development Success Historical Accounts from More Advanced Countries*. Oxford University Press: Oxford 2013, pp. 192–215. Such factors as internationalization, open and flexible markets, a high degree of competition as well as government efficiency and political stability contributed greatly to the development of the Swiss economy.

8 Swiss bankers were often involved in the government. In Switzerland, a country of merchants, bankers and businessmen this reflected a sense of duty and the social structure See Fehrenbach, T.R.: *The Gnomes*...,p. 42.

9 "Escher: The Founder of Modern Switzerland". Credit Suisse, retrieved 02.02.2016, from https://www.credit-suisse.com/us/en/articles/articles/news-and-expertise/2014/01/en/escher-the-founder-of-modern-switzerland.html.

the Swiss Credit Bank were offered to the public, worth 4.5 million gold francs. The success of the greatly oversubscribed public offering exceeded all expectations – the orders amounted to 436,539 shares at par value of 218,269,500 gold francs.[10]

In 1882, the Gotthard Tunnel resumed its operation. Zurich was now at the heart of Europe. It increased its population eleven-fold by 1900. Banks modelled on the Kreditanstalt were set up in all larger towns in Switzerland. The bankers became entrepreneurs, involved in the industrialization of the country. Banks also established the insurance industry. In 1863, Kreditanstalt, together with the Basler Handelsbank and the Helvetia General Insurance Company, created the Swiss Reinsurance Company, today known as Swiss Re, the world's second largest institution of this kind.[11] In 1870, Kreditanstalt's first foreign representative office was founded in New York City,[12] but it was not until 1964 that the bank obtained a full-service banking license from the U.S. authorities, which allowed the Swiss institution to accept customer deposits and involve in U.S. commercial banking activities.

The structure of the modern Swiss banking system was created mainly between 1850 and 1880. From the 1870s onwards, following the financial crisis of 1873 and the subsequent "long depression", a process of consolidation in the Swiss banking sector began. Bigger banks were thought to be less prone to failure. During this period the Commercial Bank of Basel, Swiss People's Bank and the Swiss Bank Corporation were created through mergers of smaller institutions.

In 1907, the Swiss National Bank (SNB) was set up and obtained a monopoly on the issuing of banknotes.[13] The Swiss central bank collected records on all Swiss banks, but all audits of Swiss banks by the central bank were kept a secret.

Despite these developments, Switzerland before 1914 was still lagging behind the major European banking centers of London, Paris, or even Amsterdam. Although a devastating event for Europe, World War I provided the turning point

---

10 See Iklé, Max: *Switzerland: An International Banking and Finance Center*. Dowden, Hutchinson & Ross Inc.: Stroudsburg (Pa.) 1972, p. 19 and Fehrenbach, T.R.: *The Gnomes…*, p. 36.

11 "Established 1863". SwissRe, retrieved 02.02.2016, from http://www.swissre.com/about_us/swissre_group/our_history/established_1863/?syr=1860&eyr=1869.

12 "Our Company". Credit Suisse, retrieved 12.06.2016, from https://www.credit-suisse.com/corporate/en/our-company.html.

13 Before the establishment of the SNB, there were numerous bank notes in circulation since cantonal banks and some private banks could issue bank notes. See Iklé, Max: *Switzerland…*, p. 34.

for Swiss banks, leading to a major boost for the financial sector. This process, beginning in the 1920s resulted from an actual lack of any change in the Swiss economic policy, as opposed to major new developments on the international arena. Switzerland as a neutral country did not participate in the war and managed to avoid all the post-war problems and economic turmoil, which the other European countries suffered. Their bankrupted governments established currency and capital restrictions, and isolationism became the new economic policy of the day, replacing the free market ideas of the pre-war period.

Meanwhile, the Swiss banks emerged from the war virtually intact and had grown too big to be able to flourish in the domestic market alone. The Swiss bankers were able to exploit their advantage in providing security among widespread monetary confusion. After World War I the Swiss franc was still convertible to gold, whereas the currencies of Germany, Austria, France, and Italy succumbed to inflation and hyperinflation, becoming worthless overnight. Switzerland did not impose foreign exchange or capital controls. Therefore, exchanging savings from national currencies to Swiss francs was the obvious solution to preserving their value and avoiding inflation for the nationals of the neighboring countries. "Frightened capital"[14] began flowing into Switzerland from 1920 onwards.

All the reasons for capital flight to Switzerland were provided by the regimes in post-war Europe: asset controls, excessive taxation, inflation and hyperinflation. Switzerland, on the other hand, provided a safe haven for European money, but it was not illegal money in today's sense of the word, these were the life savings of ordinary people, the wealth of entrepreneurs and of legitimate businesses.[15] Throughout the history of the Swiss banking sector, it was traditionally perceived as a safe haven from war, revolution, and all other forms of political upheaval, and a place of refuge from fiscal persecution and monetary instability for international capital.[16]

For German exporting corporations, having a Swiss bank account, where foreign exchange would be transferred, was standard practice. This allowed the German industry to accumulate hard-currency credits outside of Germany, bypassing war reparation demands, and laid solid foundations for the German industry, which later helped to fuel the German war machine.[17] For the Swiss, a moral aspect of accepting or not accepting the influx of foreign capital from

---

14 This term is used by Fehrenbach, T.R.: *The Gnomes…*, p. 66.

15 For these arguments see Guex, Sébastien: "Place financière…", pp. 5–47.

16 See Ibid., p. 56.

17 Fehrenbach, T.R.: *The Gnomes…*, p. 54.

other nations was non-existent, it was neither immoral, nor illegal. It was simply business.

The foreign governments tried to put a stop to this procedure by passing legislation, which rendered the possession of foreign accounts illegal, they blocked accounts of their citizens, they searched them at the boarders. But the Swiss were creative enough. Swiss bankers invented numbered accounts and used plain brown envelopes for correspondence with their foreign customers. Mail was carried by couriers across the borders and sent out using domestic stamps. The German, French and Italian governments applied diplomatic pressure on the Swiss, but without success. The Swiss authorities would not enforce foreign legislation and interfere in Swiss banking practices as long as the banks obeyed by Swiss domestic laws. In order to further protect their customers from their domestic tax authorities and increase the level of secrecy the Swiss introduced corporate structures, which served as a front for the true owners of the corporation's assets, whereby these assets could be based abroad, but under Swiss and international legislation they were considered Swiss.[18]

Towards the end of the 1920s and until the early 1930s, as a result of excessive lending and overexposure to German assets, combined with currency controls imposed by the German government, a banking crisis swept over Switzerland, causing many Swiss banks to fail.[19] A consolidation of the banking sector followed, which led to the formation of new banks, and simultaneously numerous other Swiss banks ceased to exist through acquisitions.

In 1934, the first federal banking law was passed, which introduced greater banking supervision and federal banking secrecy laws. Prior to the introduction of the Banking Act federal protection of banking confidentiality did not exist.

It seems a fair conclusion to state, that it is during the interwar period that the Swiss banks established themselves as equal members of the international financial system.[20]

After World War II the reputation of Swiss banking gained even greater prominence, with banking secrecy already enshrined in banking and criminal law, and as a result of the Swiss franc's persistent stability and convertibility, as opposed to rigid controls introduced by other countries. In simplified terms, it can be

18 Ibid., pp. 49–66.
19 Meier, Henri B./Marthinsen, John E./Gantenbein, Pascal A.: *Swiss Finance…*, p. 82.
20 Bauer, Hans/Blackman, Warren J.: *Swiss Banking…*, p. 209.

asserted, that the political turmoil of the twentieth century made Switzerland the banking center it is today.[21]

Traditionally, the Swiss banking sector was based on the principle of self-regulation. In the twenty-first century, however, banks became increasingly more regulated.

With the development of its banking industry, Switzerland became a major capital exporter and a major recipient of foreign funds, but until the 1950s Swiss banks did not pursue expansion abroad on a larger scale, and their international activities progressed without the need to form multinational institutions. This changed with the role assumed by Swiss big banks and their expansion into international markets.[22] Between 1950 and 2011 the share of assets of international customers held in Swiss banks increased from 8% to an average of 60% in the 2000s.[23] During this period Switzerland rose to become one of the world's leading financial centers.

1.1.2 Overview and Structure of the Contemporary Swiss Banking Sector

In 2015, the financial sector in Switzerland was responsible for 9.5% of GDP[24] and accounted for 14.2% of Swiss tax revenues. Swiss banks employed 169,000 skilled workers[25] and managed SFr 6656 billion, whereby 51.1% of these assets originated from abroad. This corresponds to 25% of the global cross-border asset management business, making Switzerland a global leader in this area.[26]

---

21 Allen, Matthew: "History bites back at Swiss private banking". *Swissinfo*, 22.02.2013, retrieved 14.11.2017, from http://www.swissinfo.ch/eng/roots-of-wealth_history-bites-back-at-swiss-private-banking/35033852.

22 For analysis of the early Swiss banks' foreign expansion see Cassis, Youssef: "Swiss International Banking 1890 – 1950". In: Jones, Geoffrey (ed.): *Banks as Multinationals*. Routledge: New York 2012, pp. 160–170.

23 Meier, Henri B./Marthinsen, John E./Gantenbein, Pascal A.: *Swiss Finance*..., p. 51.

24 This figure varies from year to year, for example in 2010 it amounted to 12%, see Swiss Bankers Association: *2015 Financial Centre Strategy*. 2010, retrieved 02.10.2016, from http://www.swissbanking.org/en/20100409-5000-finanzplatzstrategie_clean-nzw.pdf. The share of the financial sector in GDP for the U.S. is 7% (2014).

25 "Key Figures". Swiss Bankers Association, retrieved 11.10.2017, from http://www.swissbanking.org-/en/financial-centre/key-figures.

26 Swiss Bankers Association: *2015 Banking Barometer. Economic Trends in the Swiss Banking Industry*. September 2015, retrieved 14.06.2016, from http://shop.sba.ch/1100003_e.pdf, p. 22.

In 2014, two Swiss cities, Zurich and Geneva, were listed in the Global Financial Centers Index 2015 in place six, and thirteen, respectively. As regards bank assets per capita, they amount to $381,244 in Switzerland and for comparison $142.119 in Germany and $40.468 in the U.S. Bank assets expressed as a percentage of GDP equal 483% in Switzerland, and for comparison 346% in Germany and 84% in the United States.[27]

The two largest Swiss banks rank in place number 21 (UBS) and 35 (Credit Suisse) worldwide in terms of market capitalization.

However, private banking and wealth management are the financial services in which Switzerland excels, occupying the number one position globally. These services are rendered to so called high-net-worth-individuals on a more personal basis, typically via dedicated client advisors, as opposed to mass market retail banking. Financial advisors who specialize in private banking often manage an entire financial situation of a customer. In an international ranking of private banking, as measured by assets under management, six Swiss banks are listed among the top 20.[28] The largest Swiss bank, UBS was the world's top private banker in 2014, managing over $2.03 trillion.[29] To put this figure into perspective, in 2014 the GDP of Switzerland amounted to $701 billion[30] and the GDP of Italy was equal to $2.141 trillion. In 2014, Switzerland managed $2.7 trillion in wealth from abroad, or 25% of total global offshore wealth, defined as capital from investors with no Swiss tax domicile.[31]

In 2015, there were 275 banks in Switzerland. Following the classification of the Swiss National Bank, which divides banks into seven groups, taking into consideration their characteristics and activities, this included 2 big banks, 24

---

27 Nguyen, Duc-Quang: "Is Switzerland really the country of bankers?". *Swissinfo*, 18.09.2014, retrieved 20.10.2017, from http://www.swissinfo.ch/eng/by-the-numbers_is-switzerland-really-the-country-of-bankers-/40473658.

28 Ibid.

29 Cosgrave, Jenny: "UBS, Morgan Stanley private bank assets swell past $2trillion: Report". *CNBC*, 08.07.2015, retrieved 21.11.2017, from http://www.cnbc.com/2015/07/08/ubs-morgan-stanley-see-private-bank-assets-pass-2t.html.

30 "Switzerland". World Bank, retrieved 30.09.2017, from http://data.worldbank.org/country/switzerland.

31 Beardsley, Brent et al.: "Global Wealth 2015: Winning the Growth Game". Boston Consulting Group, 15.06.2015, retrieved 21.05.2017, from https://www.bcgperspectives.com/content/articles/financial-institutions-growth-global-wealth-2015-winning-the-growth-game/?chapter=2.

cantonal banks, 63 regional and savings banks, 118 foreign banks, 1 Raiffeisen Group Bank, 7 private banks and 60 "other banks".

The two Swiss big banks, UBS AG and Credit Suisse AG are classified as global systematically important banks (G-SIBs) by the Financial Stability Board and the Basel Committee on Banking Supervision.[32] Systematically important financial institutions, which include global systematically important banks and global systematically important insurers are "financial institutions whose distress or disorderly failure, because of their size, complexity and systemic interconnectedness, would cause significant disruption to the wider financial system and economic activity."[33] The failure of such an institution might cause a financial crisis, therefore they are considered too big to fail, and are subject to stricter capital and liquidity requirements.[34]

UBS and Credit Suisse together cover 48% of the balance sheet total of all banks in Switzerland. They are universal banks, involved both in commercial, as well as investment activities, and operate globally in all areas of the banking business.[35] Credit Suisse was founded in 1856 in Zurich. Union Bank of Switzerland was established in 1854 and grew in time via acquisitions of smaller banks. The big bank UBS was created via the merger of Union Bank of Switzerland and Swiss Bank Corporation in 1998, becoming Europe's largest financial institution.

Cantonal banks were created as each canton opted for its own "national Bank". The first cantonal bank was founded in the Canton of Geneva in 1816 and the last one in the Canton of Valais in 1917. Most cantonal banks are state owned, and they conduct operations in their respective cantons, which are also responsible for the liabilities of these banks. The most important activity of cantonal banks is the extension of mortgage loans.[36] The Zürcher Kantonalbank – the

---

32 Financial Stability Board (FSB): *2015 Update of list of globally systematically important banks (G-SIBs)*, 03.11.2015, retrieved 13.09.2017, from http://www.fsb.org/wp-content/uploads/2015-update-of-list-of-global-systemically-important-banks-G-SIBs.pdf.

33 Financial Stability Board (FSB): *Reducing the moral hazard posed by systemically important financial institutions: FSB Recommendations and Time Lines*, 20.10.2010, retrieved 15.06.2016, from http://www.fsb.org/wp-content/uploads/r_101111a.pdf.

34 "Adressing SIFIs". Financial Stability Board, retrieved 12.06.2017, from http://www.fsb.org/what-we-do/policy-development/systematically-important-financial-institutions-sifis/.

35 Swiss Bankers Association: *2015 Banking Barometer...*, p. 5.

36 For a discussion of the role of cantonal banks see Bär, Hans J./Albrecht Daniel U.: *The Banking System of Switzerland.* Schulthess Polygraphischer Verlag AG: Zurich 1975, pp. 10–12.

largest cantonal bank is classified as a systematically relevant financial institution from November 1, 2013.[37] This bank also conducts business on the international markets.

The Raiffeisen Group is a network of 312 independent Raiffeisen banks,[38] organized in the form of a cooperative, with locations all over Switzerland. It is the third largest bank group in Switzerland, classified as a systematically relevant financial group since June 2014. The Raiffeisen Switzerland cooperative acquired Notenstein Private Bank in 2012, as its 100% subsidiary.[39] The role of the Reiffeisen Banks is similar to that of credit unions in the U.S.: the idea is to use the resources of the local population to finance credit to the members of the cooperative.[40]

The foreign banks category includes the branches of foreign banks and foreign-controlled banks, which cater for customers abroad and are active mostly in the field of investment banking. They are incorporated under Swiss law, but over 50% of their ownership must be held by persons or companies domiciled outside of Switzerland, or branches of foreign banks.[41]

Private banks are focused on wealth management, and they conduct business in Switzerland and abroad. They are the oldest Swiss financial institutions and the most unusual by legal standards prevailing worldwide. Swiss private banks have traditionally occupied an important position in both the Swiss financial sector and on the international stage, by controlling and supervising a vast amount of wealth, despite a lack of precise statistical data on the scale of these activities.[42] Their key distinguishing feature is that these banks are not incorporated. Private banks are organized as sole proprietorships, partnerships, or limited partnerships, whereby the owners of these banks are made personally liable for the financial obligations of these institutions, to the full extent of the banker's entire private fortune. Private banks are not required to build reserves, or to publish or report their balance sheets or any other financial data to the Swiss National Bank. In effect, there are no credible estimates of their scale of business, including their assets, or the number of clients they serve, and therefore the private banks are underrepresented in the official statistics. They have large off-balance sheet activities, which are difficult to evaluate due

37 Swiss Bankers Association: *2015 Banking Barometer…*, p. 5.
38 As of the end of 2014.
39 Swiss Bankers Association: *2015 Banking Barometer…*, p. 6.
40 Bär, Hans J./Albrecht, Daniel U.: *The Banking System of Switzerland*, pp. 23–24.
41 Meier, Henri B./Marthinsen, John E./Gantenbein, Pascal A.: *Swiss Finance…*, p. 71.
42 For an attempt to estimate the extent of the private banks' financial activities see Bär, Hans J./Albrecht, Daniel U.: *The Banking System…*, p. 32.

to lack of appropriate data. They are predominantly located in Geneva, Zurich, and Basel. In the beginning of the century, there were over 200 private banks in Switzerland, this number decreased to 60 in 1964, and further, to only 13 in 2012.[43]

"Other Banks" include stock exchange banks, consumer credit banks, commercial banks, investment management specialists and other types of financial institutions, which cannot be classified under the other specified bank categories.[44]

The Swiss Bankers Association is the most important organization in the banking sector. It is a professional organization of the finance industry, which represents the interests of Swiss banks in relations with the Swiss government, the Swiss regulators and law makers as well as the governments of other states.[45] The SBA also cooperates with the Swiss National Bank and the Swiss government in the negotiations of international treaties and agreements, which have an impact on the Swiss banking industry.[46] It was founded in Basel in 1912, as a trade association, and today it has 300 institutional members. One of its primary aims is to promote the image of Switzerland as a financial center on the international arena.

The core values of the Swiss financial center as seen through the eyes of the Swiss Bankers Association are:

1. Stability, which includes political, legal, monetary and currency stability, as well as neutrality in foreign policy.
2. Universality, which stands for the comprehensive offer of products and services, diversification of financial services and global approach of the banking business.
3. Responsibility, which refers to the approach of the players in the financial center including the fulfillment of due diligence obligations, risk awareness and the protection of financial privacy.
4. Excellence, which stands for professional, innovative, and high-quality services, as well as a client-oriented approach.[47]

Banking is Switzerland's most important service industry and one of the most important sources of foreign exchange. The high productivity and the relatively

---

43 Meier, Henri B./Marthinsen, John E./Gantenbein, Pascal A.: *Swiss Finance…*, pp. 73–74.

44 Swiss Bankers Association: *2015 Banking Barometer…*, p. 6.

45 "Portrait". Swiss Bankers Association, retrieved 15.10.2017, from http://www.swissbanking.org/en/bankers-association/about-us/mission.

46 Bär, Hans J./Albrecht, Daniel U.: *The Banking System…*, p. 40.

47 Swiss Bankers Association: *The Financial Centre: Engine of the Swiss Economy*. April 2016, retrieved 15.09.2017, from http://www.swissbanking.org/en/20130715-fp_motor_der_schweizer_wirtschaft.pdf.

low employment in the banking sector are the factors behind the large share of banking in the Swiss GDP. Switzerland is one of the most intensively banked countries in the world, with one bank office per 3150 inhabitants.[48]

1.2 The Concept and the Customary and Legal Foundations of Swiss Banking Secrecy

Bank secrecy law is only one category among the various financial privacy laws and vehicles, which include also other means of protection of bank customers such as bank structures and legal forms (including for example numbered accounts, trusts and corporate vehicles) as well as impediments and blocking statues, which prohibit the production of documents for a foreign authority or the compliance with foreign government orders.[1]

Many developing countries have adopted bank secrecy laws as a means of fostering economic development. Switzerland, in addition, perceives bank secrecy laws as a means of protecting financial assets from confiscation, in line with the Swiss policy of providing a safe haven for individuals persecuted by political regimes. Therefore, banking secrecy laws in the Swiss case embody both national economic objectives, as well as reflect a deeply held conviction of certain moral superiority.[2] Although bank secrecy in Switzerland originated in customary law, it has been codified and is now statutory.

Banking secrecy is by no means a phenomenon unique to Switzerland. The first documented secrecy provisions were adopted in the statutes of the Banco Ambrosiano Milano of 1593, where the punishment for violating secrecy was the withdrawal of the banking license. The German Hamburger Bank adopted a similar clause in 1619 whereby banking secrecy entered the practice of German banks. Many other jurisdictions protect financial privacy to a varying extent, including using criminal sanctions: Panama, Luxembourg, Liechtenstein, Denmark, Austria, Finland, Mexico, Norway, Portugal, Sweden, Turkey, Singapore, and Hong Kong are the most widely quoted examples.[3] Swiss banking privacy

---

48 The data is for 2011, see Meier, Henri B./Marthinsen, John E./Gantenbein, Pascal A.: *Swiss Finance…*, p. 40.

1 See for example Jones, C. Todd: "Compulsion Over Comity: The United States' Assault on Foreign Bank Secrecy." *Northwestern Journal of International Law and Business* 12, No. 3, Winter 1992, pp. 459–464.

2 This issue will be examined in detail further in this Chapter.

3 See Capitani, Werner de: "Banking Secrecy Today". *University of Pennsylvania Journal of International Business Law* 10, No. 1, 1988, pp. 60–61 and Palan, Ronen/Murphy, Richard/Chavagneux, Christian: *Tax Havens: How Globalization Really Works…*

legislation is often perceived as being unique, in that its violation is coupled with criminal sanctions, and although Switzerland is not the only country which protects bank secrecy with criminal penalties, the Swiss system of protecting bank secrecy can be considered unrivaled in the world as it spans over many legal provisions and various legal acts.[4] No other country has proved to be as strongly attached to the principle of banking secrecy, which causes such widespread criticism and public condemnation abroad.

The protection of privacy of bank customers was introduced in Switzerland gradually. As the banking sector developed, the protection of banking secrecy evolved from a customary practice of Swiss banks, into regulations protected by civil law, to be finally encoded in the Banking Act of 1934, and protected by severe penalties resulting from criminal law provisions. Despite the prevailing common perception in Switzerland, which assigned the protection of banking secrecy a sense of moral purpose, some researchers point to it being specifically engineered to fuel the Swiss tax haven. In line with this explanation banking secrecy was not strengthened by Swiss law to protect the private sphere of individuals as a means of guaranteeing them a fundamental freedom, but rather it was aimed at safeguarding shady activities of individuals and corporations.[5] Notwithstanding the purpose of its codification, Swiss banking secrecy has become an inseparable part of the Swiss banking culture.

Interestingly, despite being protected by numerous legal provisions the term "banking secrecy" lacks a formal definition in Swiss law. In its broadest capacity it is generally understood to cover all aspects of the banker – client relationship, unless they are public knowledge.[6] The banking secret can be interpreted as an extension of the professional secret, as in case of all the professions, where a disclosure of personal information is a necessity, inherent in the nature of the professional relationship, such as in case of a lawyer, doctor, or clergyman, and referred as far back as the Roman Law principle of "actio iniuriarum" or the infringement of personality rights.[7] In this respect banking secrecy can be defined

4 For this argument see Grassi, Paolo S./Calverese, Daniele: "The Duty of Confidentiality of Banks in Switzerland: Where It Stands and Where It Goes – Recent Developments and Experience – The Swiss Assistance to, and Cooperation with the Italian Authorities in the Investigation of Corruption among Civil Servants in Italy (The "Clean Hands Investigation): How Much Is Too Much". *Pace International Law Review* 7, No. 2, April 1995, pp. 331–334.

5 Guex, Sébastien: "Le secret…", pp. 171–182.

6 Capitani, Werner de: "Banking Secrecy Today…," p. 61.

7 For a discussion along these lines see Bär, Hans J./Albrecht, Daniel U.: *The Banking System*, p. 57.

"as the banker's particular obligation, inferred from private law protection of the personality, to treat confidentially the secret facts learned in his professional capacity."[8] Swiss bank secrecy laws provide statutory protection for the relationship between the banker and the client, which is accompanied by criminalizing the breach of secrecy of the information obtained in the course of such a relationship.

To understand the tensions between Switzerland and the U.S. in the context of Swiss banking secrecy, it is important to point out the differences in the attitude with respect to an individual's privacy in common law countries, such as the U.S. and civil law countries, as exemplified by Switzerland.

In civil law countries, the protection of privacy is considered a basic personality right, in line with such prerogatives as the safeguarding of physical and intellectual integrity and liberty of action and can be traced back to Roman law. The protection of privacy is often guaranteed by the constitution, as is the case of Switzerland.

In common law countries, in turn, the general personality right to privacy is less developed and not as firmly established by legal provisions.

The confidentiality of the professional relationship, such as that of a clergymen, doctor or lawyer is protected in common law countries, but not to the same extent as in civil law countries. In the common law countries, the breach of professional secrecy is followed by disciplinary sanctions, whereas in civil law countries it is usually considered a crime. This difference in the legal approach towards the right to privacy and the professional confidentiality obligation is also reflected in the attitude of Switzerland and the U.S. with respect to banking secrecy.

In the U.S., the relationship between a bank and its customer is considered confidential. However, this duty of discretion is only an implied obligation of the bank to keep secret the details of its relation with the customer. U.S. banks must disclose information about accounts and customer transactions, if ordered to do so by the U.S. authorities, including courts and tax authorities.[9]

---

8 For this definition see Meyer, Bernhard F.: "Swiss Banking Secrecy and Its Legal Implications in the United States". *New England Law Review* 14, 1978, p. 5 and Luescher M.: *Das Schweizerische Bankgeheimnis in Strafrechtlicher Sicht.* Schulthess Polygraphischer Verlag: Zürich 1972, p. 5.

9 For a discussion of the difference in the approach to privacy in common law and civil law countries and its implications for the protection of banking secrecy in the U.S. and Switzerland see Meyer, Bernhard F.: "Swiss Banking Secrecy…," pp. 18–81.

In Switzerland, a civil law country, financial privacy is an integral part of personal rights, surpassing the interest of the government in various instances. The bank-customer relationship is confidential and protected by criminal sanctions in the same way as other professional relationships of trust. Despite a lack of specific secrecy laws in the form of an independent legal statute, banking secrecy in Switzerland is comprehensively protected throughout the Swiss legal system by a variety of individual provisions including the Civil Code, as an elementary personality right, the Code of Obligations, as a contractual duty of the banker, and by various articles of the Criminal Code. The various provisions aimed at protecting banking secrecy in the U.S. and Switzerland will be discussed in detail below.

1.2.1 Banking Secrecy in the United States

U.S. Constitution

The fundamental constitutional rights to privacy in the U.S. include only highly personal issues such as the freedom of choice in marital, sexual, and reproductive matters.

U.S. Common Law

The U.S. Common Law regarding the contractual relationship between the bank and its client provides that the bank owes an implied contractual duty to its client not to disclose customer information to third parties except for the following: 1) disclosures required by law, 2) disclosure required by duty to the public, 3) disclosure required by bank interests, 4) disclosure with the explicit or implied consent of the customer.

U.S. Federal Rules of Civil Procedure

The U.S. Federal Rules of Civil Procedure allow for civil discovery of private financial information, unless the information is not privileged and is relevant to the subject matter involved.

Bank Secrecy Act (BSA)

The name of this act is misleading in that it provides for exactly the opposite, namely includes provisions regarding mandatory record keeping and reporting requirements on the part of U.S. banks.

This U.S. legislation was shaped by evidence presented to the U.S. Congress, which demonstrated that the obligatory reporting of financial transactions by financial institutions was an important factor in the fight against white collar and organized crime. This resulted in enacting the Bank Secrecy Act. The U.S.

authorities may ban a foreign bank from operating on the territory of the United States if such a bank is convicted of a criminal violation under the BSA.

Right to Financial Privacy Act (RFPA)

In 1978, the Congress enacted the Right to Financial Privacy Act to protect the privacy of bank depositors in the United States. This law was passed eight years after the BSA was enacted and provides for procedural safeguards, as opposed to a substantive financial privacy law. The Act requires a financial institution to notify the client before passing banking information to government authorities in response to their request. However, in certain cases the RFPA requires banks in fact not to notify the customers of such a request.[10] The purpose of the RFPA is to provide the client with the possibility to challenge the government's inquiry.[11]

Although the RFPA does not provide any enforceable right to privacy, it nevertheless imposes a procedural requirement upon a federal agency, which needs to provide a formal written agency request, a grand jury subpoena, a judicial subpoena, an administrative subpoena or summons, a search warrant, or a customer authorization, before it can have access to account information.[12] The RFPA does not provide financial privacy, nor does it protect any financial privacy interests, furthermore it only applies to federal agencies. State and local agencies are not obliged to comply with this regulation.[13]

To sum up this brief analysis of the U.S. legal stance on bank-customer confidentiality: if the U.S. government is seeking to obtain personal financial information, it can generally do so. Banking secrecy in the scope and form as practiced and secured by Swiss law does not exist in the United States.[14]

---

10 12 U.S. Code § 3409 – Delayed Notice.

11 Rutledge, G. Philip.: "Bank Secrecy Laws: An American Perspective". *Dickinson Journal of International Law* 14, No. 3, p. 607.

12 Stauter, Robert Louis: "Swiss Bank Secrecy Laws and the U.S. Internal Revenue Service – Are the Swiss to Blame for Tax Dollars That the U.S. Internal Revenue Service Cannot Collect When U.S. Citizens Hide Their Money in Swiss Banks". *Case Western Reserve Journal of International Law* 20, No. 2, 1988, pp. 623–641.

13 Eldridge, James E.: "The Bank Secrecy Act: Privacy, Comity, and the Politics of Contraband". In: *North Carolina Journal of International Law and Commercial Regulation* 11, No. 3, 1986, p. 681 for a discussion of the shortcomings of the RFPA.

14 Rutledge, G. Philip: "Bank Secrecy Laws…", pp. 610–611.

1.2.2 Protection of Banking Secrecy in Swiss Law

1.2.2.1 Swiss Constitution

The Swiss Constitution grants fundamental rights to all Swiss citizens, including the right to privacy of personal information. Article 13 "Right to privacy" states the following: "1. Every person has the right to privacy in their private and family life and in their home, and in relation to their mail and telecommunications. 2. Every person has the right to be protected against the misuse of their personal data."[15]

Article 27 refers to economic freedom, which is guaranteed by the Constitution and includes, in particular, the freedom to "pursue a private economic activity."[16] Since banks deal with private information, the provisions of the Constitution protect their customers and they are obliged to abide by the same principles of confidence and trust as lawyers, notaries or doctors.

1.2.2.2 Internal Bank Laws and Code of Conduct

Banking secrecy was part of the Swiss banking tradition and the internal code of conduct of Swiss banks from the very beginning of the development of the banking industry in Switzerland. Swiss banks were recognized for "consistently, persistently, and aggressively defending confidential customer information,"[17] even prior to the introduction of the famous Banking Act of 1934.

1.2.2.3 Cantonal Laws

Provisions regarding privacy were enshrined in cantonal laws alongside the provisions regarding civil and commercial rights. In 1713, the Great Council of Geneva introduced the requirement to maintain customer records, but explicitly forbade banks the disclosure of customer information to third parties, unless approved by the Council. The regulations regarding financial privacy differed from canton to canton, which complicated the enforcement of privacy laws.[18]

---

15 See Article 13 "Right to privacy" of the Federal Constitution of the Swiss Confederation, of 18.04.1999 (Status as of 14.06.2015), Federal Council, retrieved 15.08.2016, from https://www.admin.ch/opc/en/classified-compilation/19995395/201506140000/101.pdf.

16 See Article 27 of Ibid.

17 Meier, Henri B./Marthinsen, John E./Gantenbein, Pascal A, *Swiss Finance…*, p. 99.

18 Ibid., p. 100.

1.2.2.4 Swiss Civil Code and Swiss Code of Obligations

Swiss law assigns a high priority to privacy, which is recognized as an integral part of the personal rights. Article 28 of the Swiss Civil Code, enacted in 1907, specifies that "any person whose personality rights are unlawfully infringed may petition the court for protection against all those causing the infringement."[19] The protection of the banking secret is not directly mentioned, but rather is derived from the interpretation of Article 28, which grants any person, whose privacy is violated, the right to undertake legal action. Article 28 induces a general obligation not to interfere with the private life of other people, which includes information related to economic affairs, including financial information. Also, legal entities are protected within the scope of Article 28 of the Civil Code.

Articles 41 and 49 of the Swiss Commercial Code deal with the civil consequences of illegal acts and provide a legal basis for liability, creating the option of suing the bank, or its individual employees for damages.[20] Article 41 of the Swiss Commercial Code of Obligations states the following:

> 1. Any person who unlawfully causes loss or damage to another, whether willfully or negligently, is obliged to provide compensation. 2. A person who willfully causes loss or damage to another in an immoral manner is likewise obliged to provide compensation.[21]

Article 49 of the Swiss Commercial Code specifies that:

> 1. Any person whose personality rights are unlawfully infringed is entitled to a sum of money by way of satisfaction provided this is justified by the seriousness of the infringement and no other amends have been made. 2. The court may order that satisfaction be provided in another manner instead of or in addition to monetary compensation.[22]

Paragraph 2 of Article 398 of the Swiss Commercial Code states: "2. The agent is liable to the principal for the diligent and faithful performance of the business entrusted to him." This provision deals with contract law and agency

---

19 Article 28 of the Swiss Civil Code of 10.12.1907 (Status as of 01.01.2018), Federal Council, retrieved 03.05.2018, from https://www.admin.ch/opc/en/classified-compilation/19070042/2018-01010000/210.pdf.

20 Grassi, Paolo S./Calverese, Daniele: "The Duty of Confidentiality of Banks in Switzerland…", p. 338 and p. 353.

21 Federal Act on the Amendment of the Swiss Civil Code (Part Five: The Code of Obligations) of 30.03.1911 (Status as of 01.07.2015), Federal Council, retrieved 28.10.2017, from https://www.admin.ch/opc/en/classified-compilation/19110009/201507010000/220.pdf.

22 Ibid.

relationships. Both the duty of care and the obligation of faithful execution of services, as set forth in §2 of Article 398, establish the legal basis for the duty of confidentiality of banks, whereby a breach of the mandate contract assigns to the principal both the right of termination of the contract, and the right to compensation for damages.[23]

1.2.2.5 Swiss Criminal Code

Article 162 of the Swiss Criminal Code states:

> Any person who betrays a manufacturing or trade secret that he is under a statutory or contractual duty not to reveal, any person who exploits for himself or another such a betrayal, is liable on complaint to a custodial sentence not exceeding three years or to a monetary penalty.[24]

This article prohibits the disclosure of confidential business information. Punitive measures in the form of imprisonment or fine can be applied to a person who obtains information in the course of employment and breaches the confidentiality provision of Article 162 for his own benefit, or for the benefit of other parties.

Further, Article 273 of the Swiss Criminal Code on economic espionage states the following:

> Any person who obtains a manufacturing or trade secret in order to make it available to an external official agency, a foreign organisation, a private enterprise, or the agents of any of these, or, any person who makes a manufacturing or trade secret available to an external official agency, a foreign organisation, a private enterprise, or the agents of any of these, is liable to a custodial sentence not exceeding three years or to a monetary penalty, or in serious cases to a custodial sentence of not less than one year. Any custodial sentence may be combined with a monetary penalty.[25]

Article 273 specifically criminalizes the revealing of trade or business secrets to a foreign party or foreign governmental agency. This provision also refers to

---

23 Grassi, Paolo S./Calverese, Daniele: "The Duty of Confidentiality of Banks in Switzerland…", p. 339.

24 See Article 162 of the Swiss Criminal Code of 21.12.1937 (Status as of 01.01.2017), Federal Council, retrieved 03.05.2018, from https://www.admin.ch/opc/en/classified-compilation/19370083/201701010000/311.0.pdf.

25 See Article 273 of the Swiss Criminal Code of 21 December 1937.

the offence of passing information to foreign fiscal or currency authorities, as the Swiss Federal Court repeatedly confirmed.[26]

Article 320 of the Swiss Criminal Code[27] specifies the penalties for disclosing secret information by members of authority or public officials. This provision therefore also refers to officials of the Swiss banking supervisory body. The penalty is limited to up to three years of imprisonment, or a monetary penalty. The crime of breach of official secrecy remains an offence also following the termination of employment of the official in his position. However, the official is not liable to any penalty in the case when he has disclosed secret information with the written consent of his superior authority.

As there is no statute of limitations on the enforcement of the Swiss Criminal Code, its effect extends beyond the duration of an employment contract and its violations can be prosecuted after the employment relationship has ceased.[28]

1.2.2.6 Federal Act on Banks and Savings Banks (Banking Act) of 1934

As discussed in previous paragraphs, before the adoption of the federal banking law Swiss banks were required to maintain customer confidentiality within the scope of the Civil Code and the Commercial Code of Obligations, but the remedies available in case of violations of professional secrecy could be applied only if a customer took legal action against the bank. Banks were subject only to civil liability for damages for a breach of the banking secret and Swiss courts ruled that the adherence to secrecy was an implied contractual obligation on the part of the bank.[29]

The connection to criminal law was first made with the codification of banking law by means of the Federal Act on Banks and Savings Banks, commonly known as the Banking Act of 1934. The breach of banking secrecy was made a state crime. By introducing this law, the disclosure of bank secrets was subject to punishment, even without a specific complaint on the part of the bank customer, and thereby the political authorities

26 Meier, Walter: "Banking Secrecy in Swiss and International Taxation". *The International Lawyer* 7, no. 1, January 1973, p. 19.

27 Swiss Criminal Code of 21 December 1937.

28 Meier, Henri B./Marthinsen, John E./Gantenbein, Pascal A.: *Swiss Finance…*, p. 101.

29 Meyer, Hermine Herta: "Banking Secret and Economic Espionage in Switzerland". George Washington Law Review, No. 23, 1955, p. 288.

emphasized its protection as essential for not only private, but also public interest.[30]

Article 47 of the Banking Act explicitly links any breach of banking secrecy to the Swiss Criminal Code, stating as follows:

> 1 Punishable with imprisonment for up to three years or a fine is who:
> A.
> Discloses a secret which has been entrusted to him in his capacity as an institution, employee, agent or liquidator of a bank, as an institution or employee of an audit firm, or which he has exercised in this capacity;
> B.
> To such an infringement of professional secrecy;
> c.2
> A secret disclosed under letter a is disclosed to other people or used for himself or another.
> 1 bis
> Penalty of up to five years or a fine shall be penalized whoever gains an asset advantage by virtue of an action under paragraph 1 (a) or (c)
> 2 Anyone who acts negligently will be fined up to 250,000 francs.
> 3 … 4
> 4 The breach of professional secrecy is also punishable after the termination of the official or business relationship or professional practice.
> 5 The Federal and cantonal provisions on the obligation to report and the obligation to provide information shall remain reserved to an authority.
> 6 Prosecution and assessment of the acts under this provision shall be the responsibility of the cantons. The general provisions of the Criminal Code 5 apply.[31]

---

30 Grassi, Paolo S./Calverese, Daniele: "The Duty of Confidentiality of Banks in Switzerland…", p. 336.

31 Own translation from the German original version:
"Mit Freiheitsstrafe bis zu drei Jahren oder Geldstrafe wird bestraft, wer vorsätzlich:
a. ein Geheimnis offenbart, das ihm in seiner Eigenschaft als Organ, Angestellter, Beauftragter oder Liquidator einer Bank, als Organ oder Angestellter einer Prüfgesellschaft anvertraut worden ist oder das er in dieser Eigenschaft wahrgenommen hat;
b. zu einer solchen Verletzung des Berufsgeheimnisses zu verleiten sucht;
c.[2] ein ihm nach Buchstabe a offenbartes Geheimnis weiteren Personen offenbart oder für sich oder einen anderen ausnützt.
1bis Mit Freiheitsstrafe bis zu fünf Jahren oder Geldstrafe wird bestraft, wer sich oder einem anderen durch eine Handlung nach Absatz 1 Buchstabe a oder c einen Vermögensvorteil verschafft.[3]
2 Wer fahrlässig handelt, wird mit Busse bis zu 250 000 Franken bestraft.
3 …[4]
4 Die Verletzung des Berufsgeheimnisses ist auch nach Beendigung des amtlichen oder dienstlichen Verhältnisses oder der Berufsausübung strafbar.

The federal law, therefore, provides specific penalties for the violation of the banking but it fails to offer a definition of this secret.

The original provision, the famed Article 47 (b) was altered to adjust the penalty levels to modern circumstances, whereupon the imprisonment limit was increased from 6 months to three years and if the breach of banking secrecy is associated with a pecuniary benefit, the prison sentence is limited to 5 years. The fine for negligence was raised from 10,000 to 250,000 Swiss francs.

Two important implications result from Article 47 of the Banking Act. The first is that a Swiss banker is punishable for any violation of bank secrecy, whether it occurs in Switzerland, or abroad, and the second is that only Swiss judicial authorities are endowed with the power to lift Swiss banking secrecy.[32]

The violation of banking secrecy is an ex officio offence (German: Offizialdelikt), meaning that it is an offence prosecuted by virtue of office. The injured party does not have to file a request to the authorities for the crime to be prosecuted, this is done quasi automatically by the Swiss state prosecutor. The ex officio qualification emphasizes the public interest in the pursuit of any breach of banking secrecy, and an implied government assurance to protect an individual's privacy.[33] Even an unsuccessful attempt to induce a person to disclose confidential information is subject to punishment. This provision is aimed at protecting bank employees from third party's pressure to provide such information.

Paragraph 4 of Article 47 specifies that a violation of banking secrecy is subject to punishment also beyond the termination of the official duty or professional relation.

The final two paragraphs of Article 47 refer to the Federal and cantonal provisions on the duty to testify by a witness and to provide information to an official, which remain valid in the case of banking secrecy. The aim of these paragraphs

---

[5] Vorbehalten bleiben die eidgenössischen und kantonalen Bestimmungen über die Zeugnispflicht und über die Auskunftspflicht gegenüber einer Behörde.

[6] Verfolgung und Beurteilung der Handlungen nach dieser Bestimmung obliegen den Kantonen. Die allgemeinen Bestimmungen des Strafgesetzbuches[5] kommen zur Anwendung". See Bundesgesetz über die Banken und Sparkassen (Bankengesetz, BankG) vom 8. November 1934 (Stand am 1. Januar 2016), Federal Council, retrieved 28.10.2017,
from https://www.admin.ch/opc/de/classified-compilation/19340083/201601010000/952.0.pdf.

32 Aubert, Maurice: "The Limits of Swiss Banking Secrecy under Domestic and International Law". *Berkeley Journal of International Law 2,* No. 2, Fall 1984, pp. 273–297.

33 Meier, Walter: "Banking Secrecy…," p. 18.

is to ensure that in certain cases other legal provisions can take precedence over banking secrecy, and to emphasize that banking secrecy does not enjoy an absolute legal protection. Article 47 does not specify the overriding provisions, which supersede banking secrecy. These have to be found in specific Federal and cantonal laws. The cantons have the authority to prosecute and judge the violations of Article 47.

The famed Article 47 of Banking Law, despite being the most important element of the protection of Swiss banking secrecy, nevertheless constitutes just one layer of this broad legal defense mechanism enshrined in various acts of law such as the Swiss Constitution, Swiss Civil Code, Commercial Code of Obligations, Swiss Penal Code, and Swiss Banking Act.

The Federal Act on Banks and Savings Banks includes yet another provision connected to the protection of banking secrecy. The Swiss Financial Market Supervisory Authority, FINMA is responsible for the regulation of the financial system and by Article 23 of the Banking Act[34] it is endowed with the power to withdraw a bank's license if a serious breach of legal obligations occurs. A breach of banking secrecy would constitute such a case and the supervisory authority could prevent the bank from conducting business in Switzerland, on the grounds that it failed to guard customer confidentiality.[35]

The Swiss banking law does not create a new professional obligation, but rather it reinforces the long-established practice and the protection provided to a bank customer by private law. The fact that banking secrecy is first and foremost of a private law character has important implications for the limitations of banking secrecy in Swiss law. Due to the supremacy of public law over any private law obligation in civil law countries, banking secrecy will be superseded by any disclosure obligations as specified by public law.[36]

---

34 See Article 13 of the Bundesgesetz über die Banken und Sparkassen (Bankengesetz, BankG) vom 8. November 1934 (Stand am 1. Januar 2016), Federal Council, retrieved 28.10.2017,
from https://www.admin.ch/opc/de/classified-compilation/19340083/201601010000/952.0.pdf.

35 Aubert, Maurice: "The Limits...," pp. 273–297 and p. 275.

36 Meyer, Bernhard F.: "Swiss Banking Secrecy...," p. 27.

1.3 Limits of Swiss Banking Secrecy Under Domestic and International Law

The purpose of banking secrecy is the protection of the customer and not the bank, and as banking secrecy is primarily of private law nature, it is the bank customer who is the master of the banking secret. The account holder must receive any information concerning his own account and may also permit the bank to provide this information to third parties. Banking secrecy can therefore be waived through the personal authorization of the bank customer at any time, but unless the customer explicitly waives his right, the confidentiality of the bank-customer relationship is presumed.

Banking secrecy is subject to explicit constraints under Swiss law, as it can be overridden by the provisions of Swiss domestic law and by international treaties. Swiss banking secrecy cannot be invoked in criminal proceedings to override the duty to testify. Hence, it can be lifted in various criminal proceedings, crimes, and misdemeanors, which today include money laundering, corruption, insider trading, manipulation of stock exchange rates and tax fraud, as defined by Swiss law. Lifting of banking secrecy may also occur in certain cases in divorce proceedings, inheritance matters, as well as in debt collection and bankruptcy proceedings. Banking secrecy may also be lifted in cases of international assistance in criminal matters, as specified in international treaties, as well as certain administrative or civil matters, provided, that the conditions defined by the respective Swiss laws, as well as international treaties signed by Switzerland are fulfilled.

There are a number of cases, in which Federal and cantonal laws supersede the Federal rule on banking secrecy. The banker cannot refuse to testify, or produce evidence in criminal proceedings, as lawyers, notaries, physicians, or clergy can. Only a judge can waive the obligation to disclose a professional secret in certain cases, where the interests of the person involved not to disclose the information outweigh other interests. In civil trials the procedure for lifting banking secrecy varies from canton to canton. In some cantons, banking secrecy is not regarded as professional secrecy in this respect.[37]

In case of inheritance laws, the principle of direct succession applies, whereby all rights of the deceased pass to the heirs and they become immediate joint owners of the estate. A bank is obliged to disclose the information with respect to the estate to the heirs. Thus, upon furnishing proof of being an heir under

37 For a discussion of cantonal laws in the context of Swiss banking secrecy see Aubert, Maurice: "The Limits...," p. 282.

the will, an individual can receive information about a deceased person without violating banking secrecy, but this disclosure is generally limited to their estate and excludes details of a private and personal nature, which are not necessary to establish the claim to the estate.[38]

Banking secrecy does not protect bank customers in proceedings for the enforcement of debts: a debtor cannot hide assets under the shield of bank secrecy. The bank is required to furnish all necessary information pertaining to the debtor's assets in debt collection proceedings. In case of bankruptcy, information on all assets of the bankrupt person is passed to the official receiver, the trustee in bankruptcy, or the liquidator of a company.[39]

In general, the provisions protecting banking secrecy apply also to subsidiaries, or branch offices of foreign banks in Switzerland. These entities are obliged not to reveal any information on their clients to their parent company, head office or auditors, unless they are one of the organs of the bank, listed in its articles of incorporation. A foreign resident, who serves on the board of directors of a Swiss subsidiary of a foreign bank is also subject to Article 47 of the Banking Law and cannot reveal any information to any third parties, including foreign authorities, affiliates, or the parent bank.[40] In certain cases, however, the disclosure of customer information from the subsidiary to the foreign parent bank might be necessary. For example, when a customer applies for a large credit, he is required to sign a waiver on banking secrecy, allowing for his identity to be revealed to the foreign bank. A branch of a foreign bank does not have an independent legal personality and the foreign parent bank is liable for all debts of the branch. Such a parent bank must have direct control over the branch's assets and therefore access to all the customer information, which is essential for branch control.[41] Nevertheless, the internal legal obligations and disclosure requirements of foreign states do not have the power to overrule Swiss law and authorize or legitimize the provision of secret information to foreign authorities by foreign-controlled banks in Switzerland.[42]

The Swiss tax system is based on the principle of self-assessment and tax authorities are unable to obtain assessment data on taxpayers directly from

---

38 Ibid., p. 278.

39 Ibid., pp. 278–279.

40 Mueller, Kurt: "The Swiss Banking Secret: From a Legal View". *The International and Comparative Law Quarterly* 18, No. 2, April 1969, pp. 363–364.

41 Aubert, Maurice: "The Limits…," pp. 276–277.

42 Meyer, Bernhard F.: "Swiss Banking Secrecy…," p. 36.

banks. In certain cases, however, tax claims can result in the judicial lifting of banking secrecy. The Swiss law distinguishes between two different types of tax offences: tax evasion and tax fraud. Tax evasion includes incomplete tax reporting, whereby certain income or assets are missing from the tax return. In cases of tax evasion, the tax authorities act within the limits of standard administrative procedure and cannot obtain information from banks directly. Tax fraud includes the submission of fraudulent financial documents with the intention to avoid paying taxes. Tax fraud can be prosecuted within the scope of administrative procedure or criminal procedure. In the latter case the judge has the right to lift banking secrecy. The fact, that in line with Swiss law banking secrecy protects bank customers with Swiss accounts in cases of tax evasion, has become a source of major debate and conflict with other countries.

Only Swiss judicial authorities are endowed with the power to lift Swiss banking secrecy and foreign officials are not permitted to conduct independent investigations in Switzerland.[43] Assistance to foreign authorities can be granted within international agreements such as Mutual Legal Assistance Treaties.

In 1983, a Federal Law on International Assistance in Criminal Matters, adopted by the Swiss Parliament, came into force. It facilitates assistance to countries, which do not have an international agreement with Switzerland. According to this law, Swiss authorities have the right to refuse assistance in cases of tax evasion. As regards tax fraud, assistance may be granted only with respect to offences, which are recognized as tax fraud according to Swiss law. This law lifts banking secrecy when the request for information pertains to a crime, which is subject to punishment both in the foreign country and in Switzerland.[44]

The duty of confidentiality of banks can be lifted within the scope of international treaties, however the cases in which this can occur are subject to various limitations.[45]

Switzerland concluded treaties on mutual assistance in civil and criminal matters with a number of countries, including the United States. The U.S.-Swiss Treaty on Mutual Legal Assistance in Criminal Matters included a provision regarding the refusal to testify if under the law in either State, the witness has the right to refuse a testimony. This provision represents an exceptional privilege aimed to satisfy the Swiss professional secrecy legislation against the compulsory

43 See Article 271 of the Swiss Criminal Code of 21 December 1937.

44 Aubert, Maurice: "The Limits...," p. 286.

45 For a list and discussion of these limitations see Grassi, Paolo S./Calverese, Daniele: "The Duty of Confidentiality of Banks in Switzerland...", pp. 355–358.

testimony in the U.S. courts and has no known counterpart in any international agreement signed with a foreign country by the United States.[46]

The confidential relationship between the bank customer and the banker creates the foundation of the Swiss banking business. The strong position of the Swiss banking sector on the world stage is based upon the tradition of banking secrecy, which attracts capital from abroad and fuels both the financial and industrial growth of Switzerland[47] and Swiss authorities and Swiss banks have gone to great lengths to maintain this tradition, especially when it was attacked from abroad, this included creating and nurturing myths regarding the reason, why banking secrecy was encoded in Swiss law. The following section explores in detail the origins of the famed Article 47 of the Banking Act and the influence, that the conflict of Swiss banks with the U.S. might have had on this issue.

1.4 The Debate on the Origins of Swiss Banking Secrecy and the Role of the Conflict with the U.S.

"When the bill was introduced in Parliament (Federal Assembly) the article concerning criminal punishment for secrecy violations passed without material discussion as all representatives understood the need for better protection of financial privacy and of the Jewish people."[48] This is an example of a typical reference to the plight of the Jews and the need to protect their assets from confiscation by the German Nazi government which appears in the context of discussing the origins of Swiss banking secrecy and persistently prevails throughout both popular and scientific literature on Swiss banking secrecy since the 1960s.

After World War II, the Swiss financial circles have nurtured such myths pertaining to the origins of Swiss banking secrecy, placing its roots in the Swiss humanitarian tradition of protecting personal freedoms from government abuses and the tradition of granting political asylum. These values extended via banking secrecy to the protection of private property rights. The humanitarian and moral aspects of banking secrecy will be subject to further scrutiny in later chapters, as they were raised in every conflict between Switzerland and the U.S., which involved the financial sector; therefore, it is necessary to pinpoint the key arguments in the debate over the origins of this phenomenon and verify the Swiss claims to moral righteousness in this regard.

46 Aubert, Maurice: "The Limits…," p. 290.
47 For this argument see Bär, Hans J./Albrecht, Daniel U.: *The Banking System…*, p. 60.
48 For this quote see Meyer, Bernhard F.: "Swiss Banking Secrecy…," p. 26.

Banking secrecy in Switzerland has a long tradition. It was incorporated into cantonal law as early as the eighteenth century, when Switzerland's self-governing cantons codified the already practiced culture of discretion towards aristocrats and royalty who entrusted Swiss banks with their money. Since the sixteenth century, the Swiss economy generated a surplus of savings which were put to the use of private banks. The trade of banking in Switzerland flourished throughout the seventeenth century, when Swiss financial institutions supplied the capital needed to finance the French Court. The service provided to the French kings had to be done with the utmost discretion and therefore contributed to creating the foundations of banking secrecy in Switzerland.[49] In 1713, the Great Council of Geneva adopted banking regulations which required the maintenance of customer data, at the same time prohibiting the release of this information by banks without the approval of the Great Council.

Swiss banking secrecy was therefore not introduced in 1934, its origins are much older. The Swiss Banking Act of 1934 merely consolidated and fortified regulations pertaining to banking secrecy, which were already a common practice within the Swiss banking sector.

What triggered this transition from banking secrecy being a part of the Swiss banking culture and being protected solely by civil law, to such strict and explicit protection as safeguarded by Article 47 of the Swiss Banking Act? The consensus among Swiss historians is still to be reached on this issue. However, the common misperception which prevails to this day about the origins of Swiss banking secrecy refers to laws passed in 1933 in Nazi Germany, which forced domestic residents to disclose all their foreign assets and enabled the confiscation by the regime of foreign-held assets of Jewish residents. The Swiss banking secrecy law was introduced in 1934, supposedly in order to protect Jewish assets deposited in Swiss banks from being expropriated back to Germany. This myth was fabricated by the Swiss banks themselves in the 1960s and officially endorsed by the Swiss Federal Council in 1970.[50] It is still widespread in Swiss society, as well as popular media and scientific publications worldwide.

A 1955 article by Hermine Herta Meyer states, that the motivation for the implementation of the Banking Act in 1934 was the international banking crisis in the early 1930s, which created demand for increased supervision of the banking sector in Switzerland. Meyer further quotes the references to the espionage by foreign powers, which were made by Swiss legislative bodies during the debates

49 Meier, Henri B./Marthinsen, John E./Gantenbein, Pascal A.: *Swiss Finance…*, p. 38.
50 Guex, Sébastien: "The Origins…", p. 265.

on the new legislation. These references, as Meyer claims, pointed to the fact that the major purpose of Article 47 was to safeguard Swiss banks against such activities and to prevent the repatriation of funds held by Germans in Switzerland, as a result of Nazi spying. There is no mention of the Jewish issue in this context.[51]

Already in 1977, Christoph Buechenbacher rejected the prevailing claim, that the introduction of Swiss bank secrecy was a result of the persecution of Jews in Nazi Germany. He pointed to provisions regarding banking secrecy as being well rooted in both the Swiss legal system and common practice. The codification of the banking law in 1934 was a result of a bank crisis, which occurred in the 1930s and the aim of the new legislation was to introduce regulations on the protection of creditors, internal bank organization, liquidity, capital requirements, and so forth. The enacting of the Federal Act on Banks and Savings Banks merely created favorable circumstances to codify provisions regarding banking secrecy, already well established in the Swiss banking culture.[52]

In 1982, Nicholas Faith, a British journalist, vehemently refuted the theory about the "generous Swiss gesture" towards the Jews, whereby the Swiss supposedly "rushed through a special provision to prevent bankers and their employees from cooperating with the Nazi efforts."[53] Faith points to the fact that there is no proof to this theory in any credible sources and the prevalence of the myth owes to "a total lack of historical curiosity" on the part of the Swiss and the rest of the world. The myth, as Faith suggests, provided the Swiss with "a flag of morality which they could wrap securely round themselves when they were accused of harboring criminals of every nationality and description and of facilitating their nefarious activities."[54] Faith stressed the fact that there is no historically

---

51 See Meyer, Hermine Herta: "Banking Secret...," pp. 284–327, p. 290 and pp. 311–312. Moreover, in her paper Meyer discusses the enactment of the Federal Act Concerning the Protection of the Security of the Federation (the so-called Espionage Act) which was passed in June 1935 to prevent the infiltration of the Swiss economy and society by foreign powers as well as to protect foreign individuals from obduction. Meyer points to the same background, namely fascist spy activities, as leading up to both to the 1935 legislation and the writing of Article 47 into the Banking Act of 1934. See Ibid., pp. 302–313.

52 Buechenbacher, Christoph: *Tatsachen über das schweizerische Bankgeheimnis*. Nova-Press AG: Zürich et al. 1977, pp. 77–80.

53 Faith, Nicolas: *Safety in Numbers. The Mysterious World of Swiss Banking*. Hamish Hamilton: London 1982, pp. 73–80.

54 Ibid., p. 49.

authenticated source of the Swiss myth, despite the existence of extensive literature on the subject of Swiss banking secrecy.[55]

The Banking Act of 1934 was enacted as a result of a banking crisis in Switzerland in the first years of the 1930s, as Faith explained. Its aim was to provide regulations of the banking industry and protect the banks and their customers from bankruptcy, insolvency, and other failings in the banking system. Provisions regarding banking secrecy were encoded in Swiss banking law as a response to the Basler Handelsbank affair, which is discussed in detail below and which triggered calls to the defense of banking secrecy in the Swiss press. Attempts by foreign authorities to undermine banking secrecy had to be prevented, as they posed a threat to the Swiss economy. Switzerland, confronted with the policies of other European states such as Germany, France or Czechoslovakia, which tried to subjugate banking secrecy to accommodate their fiscal authorities, was obliged to safeguard banking secrecy as a shield from external infringement.[56] In addition, a number of rulings of the Swiss Supreme Court eroded banking secrecy, by allowing for disclosure of certain personal information, stating that secrecy was not a legal obligation, but rather a matter of custom and common practice of bank employees. Therefore, to protect this custom, in particular from foreign intervention, banking secrecy needed strengthening by law and this occurred in the form of Article 47(b) of the 1934 Banking Act.[57] Faith provides a thorough analysis of these developments, which finally led to the codification of banking secrecy in Swiss law.

Peter Hug, a Swiss historian, pointed to two crucial phases in the creation of the Swiss myth, both of them connected with events in the United States.

The first step was taken in 1959, when the President of Union Bank of Switzerland, the predecessor of today's UBS AG, Alfred Schaefer, in his speech to the Society of the Friends of Switzerland in the U.S. referred to the Swiss humanitarian tradition of protecting property rights, which was strengthened by banking secrecy. This humanitarian argument was raised in response to the allegations of the U.S. authorities and the U.S. public. In the 1950's, the U.S.–Swiss relations were strained by an ongoing conflict over Interhandel, a Swiss-based holding company, formerly called IG Chemie. The assets of Interhandel, a chemical giant, remained blocked in the U.S. after World War II under allegations that the company served as a turntable for covered Nazi operations and was later used to

55 Ibid., p. 51.
56 Ibid., p. 76.
57 Ibid., pp. 76–77.

transfer Nazi capital abroad into neutral countries. In 1956, the Swiss government intervened in the conflict of the company with the U.S. to prevent the encroachment of the U.S. authorities upon Swiss banking secrecy. This so called Interhandel Affair will be discussed in detail in Chapter 2.

In 1958, a U.S. Senator, Ohlin D. Johnston, construed a link between the Interhandel Affair, Cold War and Swiss banking secrecy. Johnston alleged that Swiss banking secrecy was a facade for concealed Soviet operations in Switzerland. Although in the 1960s the significance of the Interhandel problem gradually diminished on the public relations front and was finally resolved by the Kennedy administration in 1965, it succeeded to pollute the image of banking secrecy in the U.S. public opinion for years to come.

In the late 1950s, the criticism against Swiss banking secrecy in the U.S. increased. Banking secrecy was blamed for aiding tax evasion, for facilitating the so-called proxy fights, which were used as a strategy for taking over companies against the consent of the management, and for the infiltration of U.S. companies by Soviet capital. It was in response to these allegations that the moral righteousness argument was raised by Schaefer in defense of Swiss banking secrecy.[58]

Further, Hug put forth a theory that in 1966, in a second step in the creation of the myth, the Swiss bankers invented the legend about the intended protection of Jewish assets through the codification of banking secrecy, as a reaction to the increased hostility they faced in the United States in the 1960s. The attacks against Swiss banks were initiated by Robert M. Morgenthau, District Attorney for the Southern District of New York, who accused the banks of aiding U.S. citizens in tax evasion as well as facilitating white collar crime.[59] Hug points out that

58 See Hug, Peter: "Steuerflucht…," p.273 and Vogler, Robert U.: *Swiss Banking Secrecy: Origins, Significance, Myth.* Association for Financial History: Zurich 2006, p. 76.

59 The investigations conducted by Morgenthau's office further led to congressional hearings on foreign bank secrecy, which commenced in December of 1968. Switzerland was portrayed as the main culprit in facilitating illegal activities via the use of secret accounts in Swiss banks. The Myth must have been well established at this point. It is quoted in the first statement of the hearings, made by Fred M. Vinson, Assistant attorney General: "The Swiss contend, and not without some historical justification, that these laws were created to protect legitimate business secrets and to prevent certain piratical governments from plundering their own citizens. As an example, they cite their refusal to cooperate with Adolph Hitler's regime in its campaign to locate and seize private assets owned by German Jews and deposited in Swiss banks". See U.S. Congress, House of Representatives: *Legal and Economic Impact of Foreign Banking Procedures on the United States: Hearing Before the Committee on Banking and Currency*, 90th

the idea that Swiss banking secrecy was introduced to protect Jews persecuted by the Nazis in the years preceding World War II, and to protect their assets from being confiscated, first appeared in a book by T.R. Fehrenbach "The Gnomes of Zürich". Fehrenbach's explanation was later reprinted in a bulletin published by Credit Suisse in November 1966 and promptly reproduced by a number of journals specializing in law, fiscal affairs, and economics. This Swiss myth, in line with Hug's interpretation, was instrumentalized by Swiss bankers and used to feed a positive public relations campaign, especially oriented towards the United States, where a law directed against the abuse of Swiss secret accounts was under debate.[60] The Swiss were bashed for their unwillingness to sign bilateral tax treaties that included a clause on administrative assistance in case of tax evasion. The factors which were conducive to popularizing the myth and helped to fuel its significance in the 1960s included the increased worldwide interest in Nazi crimes and Jewish suffering following the Auschwitz trials in Germany and the Eichmann trial in Jerusalem, which in turn led to the sensitization of the public with respect to issues surrounding the plight of Jews during World War II.[61]

Swiss bankers have therefore used the argument that banking secrecy was introduced to prevent Nazi spies from seizing Jewish assets in Switzerland in order to gain the moral higher ground. It was a smart maneuver, according to

---

Congress, 2nd Session, 09.12.1968, U.S. Government Printing Office: Washington, D.C. 1968, p. 6.

60 For this argument see Hug, Peter: "Eclairage...". Already in 1958, the New York Regional Office of the Internal Revenue Service investigated the use of secret Swiss accounts for the purpose of tax evasion. Both a congressional investigation and a tightening of U.S. legislation was recommended, but neither was pursued. In the 1960s Robert Morgenthau Jr, U.S. Attorney for the Southern District of New York, conducted investigations into illegal use of secret foreign accounts and faced challenges in pursuing cases where foreign banks were involved, as they were beyond the reach of the U.S. justice. Morgenthau established a special unit to investigate securities fraud and testified before the House Banking and Currency Committee chaired by Wright Patman, which launched an investigation on this issue. The Committee proposed a bill, which would restrict tax evasion and violation of securities trading laws with the help of secret accounts abroad This issue is explored in detail in Chapter 3. See "Secret Swiss Bank Accounts: Uses, Abuses, and Attempts at Control". *Fordham Law Review* 39, No. 3, 1971, p. 505 and Sheehan, Neil: "White House Backs Curbs On Use of Swiss Accounts". *New York Times*, 03.03.1970, retrieved 12.03.2018, from https://www.nytimes.com/1970/03/03/archives/white-house-backs-curbs-on-use-of-swiss-accounts-nixon-backs-bill.html.

61 Hug, Peter: "Steuerflucht...", p. 20.

Peter Hug, who claims that an argument in support of banking secrecy, based on the integrity of Swiss bankers, placed Swiss banks on a pedestal from which it was difficult to remove them.[62] This explanation for introducing Article 47 into banking law was easily acceptable and instantly understandable, in contrast to the real, economic origins of banking secrecy regulations in Switzerland.

Ironically, a similar argument in support of banking secrecy, namely the need to protect assets from falling into the wrong hands, was raised throughout the post-World War II period by the Swiss, to justify the inability of banks to reveal the identity of Jewish owners of Swiss bank accounts, who perished in the Holocaust, and to return their assets to the Jewish heirs, in response to requests by individuals, the state of Israel and Jewish organizations. As a result of immense U.S. pressure, Swiss banking secrecy was lifted in this case only in the late 1990s.

Sébastien Guex, another Swiss historian, claims that the rigorous approach to banking secrecy regulations as specified in the Swiss Banking Act was ultimately triggered by a scandal involving the Basler Handelsbank, known as the Paris Affair.

In October 1932, a Paris branch of the Swiss bank Basler Handelsbank was searched by French authorities. The seized documents revealed that the Basler Handelsbank actively aided French customers in tax evasion, thereby circumventing French tax law. The amount in question was exorbitant, with the value of assets estimated at over one billion French francs. French authorities established a list of names involved in the scandal, which comprised over 1,000 customers, including prominent French politicians, generals, judges, clergy, and industrialists, such as for example the Peugeot brothers.[63] The search extended to two other Swiss banks. A legal suit was filed against Basler Handelsbank and its assets in France were frozen, as well as the assets of two other Swiss banks.[64] The French authorities requested an investigation into French accounts of the Basler Handelsbank in its headquarters. The two directors of the Bank, which were enquired about the activities of the bank refused to cooperate and were imprisoned for two months. All these measures were applied to force the Basler

62 Quite a similar argument, that the myth about the provenance of banking secrecy offers the Swiss banks a "flag of morality" is provided by Faith, Nicolas: *Safety in Numbers...*

63 These figures are provided in Meier, Henri B./Marthinsen, John E./Gantenbein, Pascal A.: *Swiss Finance...*, p. 110; however, Palan, Ronen/Murphy, Richard/Chavagneux, Christian: *Tax Havens...*, p. 121, claim their research produced much higher figures: ten notebooks containing the names of 2000 French citizens were found at the sight, who placed 2 billion francs with the bank.

64 Guex, Sébastien: "The Origins...", p. 249.

Handelsbank to lift banking secrecy and provide access to the bank books for French tax inspectors. In November 1932, France requested a mutual assistance treaty with Switzerland, however this proposal was rejected by the Swiss government. The Swiss newspapers outraged by these events distributed information about a French campaign against Swiss banks.[65] During the whole investigation, Swiss federal authorities unconditionally rejected any judicial cooperation with the French authorities. Swiss business circles perceived the French response as aimed at undermining, or even destroying the Swiss financial center and, in the aftermath of the Paris Affair, the Swiss financiers called for a legal reinforcement of banking secrecy.[66] The Swiss authorities regarded the affair as an attack on the Swiss tradition of banking secrecy and more broadly, on the national sovereignty of Switzerland.[67] Moreover, this scandal could have led to the downfall of the Swiss financial center, which was dependent upon capital stemming from fiscal evasion, if the Swiss would have yielded to French pressure. The introduction of the new legislation undoubtedly helped to encourage confidence in the Swiss banking sector and led to an increase of banking business in the years immediately following the enacting of the Article 47 of Swiss Banking Law.[68]

Sébastien Guex points to the fact that the Swiss Federal Council provided for a first draft of the new banking law in February of 1933, not even a month after Hitler's rise to power, whereby an article on banking secrecy was already contained in this document. Despite undergoing numerous changes, before being finally ratified, the Banking Act of 1934 included the provision on banking secrecy in an unaltered form, compared to the draft version proposed in February 1933.[69]

From 1931, the Nazi regime passed a number of laws and regulations which allowed for the confiscation of assets held by German citizens abroad. The law, passed in June 1933, obliged all German residents to disclose all their foreign assets and the law passed in July enabled the confiscation of Jewish assets held outside of Germany.[70] The chronology of the drafting of the secrecy provision to

---

65 Ibid., p. 251.

66 Ibid., p. 251.

67 Ibid., p. 251.

68 For an argument along these lines also see Hug, Peter: "Eclairage…".

69 Guex, Sébastien: "The Origins…", p. 244.

70 "Gestez über die Einziehung volks- und staatsfeindlichen Vermögen vom 14. Juli 1933", (Reichsgesetzblatt 1, 1933, p. 479). Official Website of the Claims Resolution Tribunal of the Holocaust Victim Assets Litigation against Swiss Banks and other Swiss Entities, retrieved 18.05.2017, from http://crt-ii.org/_nazi_laws/_lpdfs/19330714.pdf.

be included in the Banking Act, and the passing of the Nazi laws therefore clearly refute the claim that the German anti-Jewish legislation was the driving force behind the Swiss secrecy provision.[71]

Robert U. Vogler, a Swiss historian, who also was a researcher and archivist at the Swiss National Bank, also admits that the catalyst for the introduction of the 1934 law was neither Hitler's rise to power, nor the Nazi regulations introduced in Germany. Such an interpretation is contradicted by the actual sequence of events which took place.

However, as regards the role played by the Paris Affair in the enacting of banking secrecy in the Banking Law of 1934, Robert U. Vogler, contrary to other scholars does not share the view that it was an incident, which was decisive in any way. Basler Handelsbank encountered difficulties already in 1931 due to its exposure to the German market and the Paris Affair was merely an additional strain for the bank. Basler Handelsbank might have suffered reputational damage, but there was no direct link between the problems of the bank and the debate on enacting strong banking secrecy provisions into the Swiss legislation.[72]

Vogler instead provides an explanation along the lines of the concept put forth by Buechenbacher. Banking secrecy regulations were prompted by the global financial crisis at the beginning of the 1930s and its broad implications for the Swiss banking system. The Swiss banks were seriously affected by the German banking crisis of 1931. Between 1930 and 1935, the total assets of eight major Swiss banks decreased by more than a half. Five major banks had to be restructured and the Swiss Volksbank and Banque d'Escompte Suisse both received direct financial aid from the federal government. Between 1930 and 1939 a total of 60 Swiss banks were taken over or were forced to close business.[73]

Robert U. Vogler points to the fact that the banks in Switzerland opposed the introduction of banking law until 1933 and the "catalyst" responsible for accelerating the political process and leading to the enacting of the Banking Law was the crisis suffered by the Swiss Volksbank, which had to be rescued by the Federal Government.[74] The bail out of the Volksbank could have been justified to the public only by taking steps to avoid similar problems in the future, such as the introduction of stronger banking supervision in a codified banking law. This

71 This argument is also brought up in Meier, Henri B./Marthinsen, John E./Gantenbein, Pascal A.: *Swiss Finance…*, p. 109.

72 Vogler, Robert U.: *Swiss Banking Secrecy…*, pp. 22–23.

73 Ibid., pp. 11–12.

74 Ibid., pp. 24–25.

explanation tends towards viewing the codification of banking secrecy as being only a by-product of a new banking legislation which was passed as a response to the general consensus for the need of introducing formal controls in response to a banking crisis.[75]

The process which led to the explicit legal protection of banking secrecy in Switzerland was not straightforward and many convoluted factors contributed to the final outcome, namely the codification of Article 47 (b) in the Swiss Banking Law.

Sébastien Guex discusses other factors which may have played a role in encoding banking secrecy in a federal law.

With the adoption of the Swiss Constitution of 1848, by means of which a league of sovereign states converted to create a federal state, various powers were distributed over different levels of government. In the course of this distribution, direct taxation remained at the discretion of individual cantons, whereas indirect taxation was placed in the hands of the central government. The formation of tax privileges in Switzerland resulted from the competition among the various cantons, and from this rivalry, combined with the practice of banking secrecy, Switzerland gradually emerged as one of the world's first offshore centers.[76]

Tax increases in various European countries at the turn of the twentieth century offered Swiss banks a chance of gaining a competitive advantage over well-established financial centers such as London, Paris, and Berlin. Foreign residents were offered a possibility to evade domestic taxation, by allocating their assets in Switzerland. As a result, banking secrecy gained an unprecedented level of importance for the economy. A common banking practice became crucial in attracting foreign capital inflows to Switzerland, thereby playing a key role in the international competition for capital on the financial markets. Advertising campaigns in neighboring countries promoted Switzerland as a tax haven for wealthy Europeans.[77]

---

75 Interestingly, calls for increased state control and regulation protecting bank customers were made even before World War I. A draft law was written in 1916 by Professor Julius Landmann. But this draft legislation contained no mention of banking secrecy. The proposal was criticized for leading to excessive state intervention and for allowing far reaching inspection of banks by the federal government including the breach of professional confidentiality. Such a state-controlled banking industry could potentially lead to the withdrawal of funds by foreign customers. See Ibid., pp. 12–13.

76 For a detailed account of this process see Palan, Ronen/Murphy, Richard/Chavagneux, Christian: *Tax Havens…*

77 Guex, Sébastien: "The Origins…", pp. 241–242.

In the aftermath of World War I, further massive increases in taxation in led to an influx of French, Italian, Austrian and German capital to Swiss banks. Attracted by moderate taxes, political stability, and neutrality, and last but not least, by a culture of banking secrecy, foreign depositors massively escaped domestic fiscal burdens and located their assets in Switzerland. The capital flight from domestic economies did not gain the approval of French, Belgian, Italian or German authorities, and pressure on the Swiss to lift banking secrecy was repeatedly exercised by the governments of these countries.[78] The strengthening of banking secrecy provisions could be seen in this broader economic context, as a measure designed to protect Swiss banks from the intervention of foreign governments, which attempted to gain access to bank records of their citizens, thereby undermining the credibility of Swiss banking as a whole, and discouraging the inflow of foreign assets to Switzerland. The Paris Affair can be seen as a specific manifestation of the argument put forth by Sébastien Guex, that the reinforcement of banking secrecy occurred in response to external threats and in defense of Swiss economic benefits.[79] The new secrecy provisions were intended to improve confidence in the Swiss financial sector and send a clear message to the outside world that Swiss banking secrecy would be safeguarded against any attempts at encroachment by any foreign powers.

A similar explanation, which connects the codification of secrecy legislation to the need to thwart foreign intervention in the Swiss financial sector, refers to espionage activities by German and French economic spies. These espionage activities were carried out in an effort to curb tax evasion of the citizens of France and Germany and intensified in the 1930s. The secret agents of the neighboring countries resorted to all sorts of elaborate tricks in order to extract information about their citizens' assets in Swiss banks. The acts of bank espionage represented an infringement of Swiss sovereignty and therefore contributed to the codification of banking secrecy according to Robert U. Vogler and T.R. Fehrenbach. Foreign deposits were protected with restrictive provisions against revealing professional information by bankers, and the Swiss banker was protected against foreign pressure with not only a moral, but also a legal code, by which he was now obliged to abide.[80]

78 Ibid., pp. 241–242.

79 Ibid., pp. 247–252.

80 See Vogler, Robert U.: *Swiss Banking Secrecy...*, p. 19 and Fehrenbach T.R.: *The Gnomes...*,pp. 72–73 and pp. 76–77.

Sébastien Guex considers the introduction of Article 47 in the Banking Law to also be a counter measure advocated by Swiss bankers, threatened with increased banking supervision. The Swiss authorities, pressured by the middle class and the powerful Swiss Farmers' Union, planned for a new banking law which would include provisions concerning the general oversight of the financial system. In exchange for endorsing the concept of banking supervision, Swiss bankers demanded explicit legal restrictions with respect to banking secrecy to be incorporated into the new law, in order to protect access to individual account information from any party, including the federal officials. Bankers feared that the weakening of banking secrecy provisions by allowing for inspection of customer information would cause a withdrawal of both Swiss and foreign deposits, leading to a capital flight on a greater scale. Therefore, increased bank supervision as foreseen by the proposed Banking Law was explicitly linked to the tightening of banking secrecy to accommodate the fears of the banking circles and gain their support for the drafted legislation.[81]

Finally, Sébastien Guex points to the rise of the socialist movement as a factor, which also contributed to the strengthening of bank secrecy provisions in Swiss legislation. The Socialist Party, which represented the interests of Swiss workers, was vehemently opposed to banking secrecy, since it prevented fiscal authorities from effectively combatting fiscal fraud. During the interwar period the Socialists campaigned for the loosening of this practice and the introduction of a federal tax on income and property. The issue was raised again in 1932 in an initiative which collected a substantial number of signatures. Despite it being finally rejected, the initiative raised the concerns of the banking circles. In the beginning of the 1930s, the socialist movement won in several cantons and fears reemerged that reforms regarding the limitation of banking secrecy and taxes might be enacted at a cantonal level. The enacting of the new Banking Law at a federal level would prevent such cantonal reforms from being implemented, as the federal status of the new legislation would have to take precedence.[82]

The interpretations of the origins of Swiss banking secrecy have evolved from explanations emphasizing humanitarian reasons, to purely economic ones. Until the end of the 1990s the prevailing line of interpretation was that banking secrecy was legally secured in 1934 in the context of the rise of political insecurity in Western Europe before World War II, as a means of protecting foreign victims of authoritarian regimes and their assets from economic espionage and

81 Guex, Sébastien: "The Origins…", pp. 246–247.
82 Ibid., pp. 254–256.

confiscation, and in particular it was a remedy introduced for the protection of Jewish assets from the Nazis and the German Jews from persecution by Nazi Germany. This "humanitarian" interpretation gained widespread popularity and was readily embraced by Swiss banks and subsequently repeated in numerous academic and non-academic publications. The "myth" was cultivated as a useful tool in the defense of banking secrecy against international criticism – the humanitarian trump card was played to counterbalance the negative side effects of the Swiss banking practice, such as the protection of criminal assets and facilitation of money laundering.

As Peter Hug pointed out, the legend about the origin of banking secrecy allowed Swiss bankers to justify their adherence to this practice by means of moral superiority, instead of by their economic interests, which were the real motive behind it. The propagation of the myth achieved its purpose, presumably exceeding by far the expectations of its inventors – a critique of Swiss banks and banking secrecy was for many years perceived as an unethical attack on the Swiss nation and the superior Swiss moral values.[83]

The debate concerning the origins of Swiss banking secrecy gained momentum only following the U.S.-Swiss conflict regarding heirless assets and dormant accounts of Holocaust victims. Swiss historians, within the framework created by the special commissions which were designated with the task of reexamining Swiss wartime history, began to evaluate documents and search archives for the ultimate truth about the origins of Article 47 (b) of the Swiss Banking Act. Just as the U.S.-Swiss conflict precipitated this interest, it also was discovered to be the primary explanation behind the creation of the "banking secrecy myth".

Following the conflict surrounding dormant accounts of Holocaust victims in the late 1990s, a new line of research with a critical approach to interpreting the origins of Swiss banking secrecy emerged, with contributions from historians such as Sébastien Guex and Peter Hug. In line with this interpretation Swiss banking secrecy was established firmly in Swiss banking law primarily to facilitate the practice of tax evasion by foreign citizens. Just as the myth about the humanitarian origins of banking secrecy helped to protect and defend banking secrecy against foreign powers, the exposure of the myth, and the accusations of following a purposeful strategy to create it on the part of the Swiss banks strengthened the perception of Switzerland as a tax haven and helped to fuel

83 Hug, Peter: "Steuerflucht…," pp. 269–322.

international pressure on Switzerland to abolish banking secrecy, as part of the efforts to curb tax evasion which intensified after 2000.[84]

1.5 Banking Secrecy and the Swiss Public Opinion

The Swiss people strongly value personal liberties. The individual right to privacy is considered a fundamental concept of democracy, and therefore, the Swiss public opinion has been always overwhelmingly supportive of financial privacy and its specific manifest in the form of banking secrecy. It is also not without significance, that the concept of banking secrecy is recognized as being a key success factor for the development of the Swiss financial sector.

In September 2000, the Swiss Bankers Association published a survey, which revealed that 80% of the Swiss supported the concept of banking secrecy, but would lift it in cases involving money laundering or plundering of assets. Another survey conducted in the same year found that 60% of the Swiss wanted banking secrecy abolished in case of tax fraud, and 80% of the public supported Swiss cooperation with other countries in tax evasion investigations.[85]

In 2015, the results of another survey commissioned by the Swiss Bankers Association were published, whereby the respondents were asked what role they assign to bank-client secrecy. Banking secrecy is viewed first and foremost as a means for private individuals and companies to protect their financial privacy by 38% of the respondents, 21% of the surveyed see its most important role in protecting from the state, and 23% claim that it protects tax evaders abroad. Only 8% of the surveyed perceive banking secrecy primarily as a tool for tax evaders who live in Switzerland. For the first time the survey inquired whether tax information relating to Swiss bank customers should be exchanged within Switzerland in the future, and if yes, how this should be accomplished. This question pertained to the domestic exchange of information. The current Swiss regulation still enjoys the highest level of support at 41% but 21% of the surveyed stated that taxpayers should be able to decide in favor of, or against a direct exchange of information between their bank and the tax authorities. An overwhelming majority of the Swiss (85%) are in favor of having their financial privacy protected

84 For this argument see Emmenegger, Patrick: "The Politics of Financial Intransparency…," p. 160. However, the humanitarian explanation is still firmly rooted in publications in reference to the origins of Swiss banking secrecy.

85 "Banking secrecy loosing 'sacred' status among Swiss public". *Swissinfo*, 14.09.2000, retrieved 03.12.2017, from http://www.swissinfo.ch/eng/banking-secrecy-losing--sacred--status-among-swiss-public/1657958.

from third parties. This result spans across all age groups and political orientations, but the approval rating is the highest in the group of 18 to 29-year-olds, with 89% of respondents supporting this concept. However, 72% of participants in the survey believe that the protection of privacy will decrease in the future.

As regards the view of the Swiss people on the role of banks in the Swiss economy, 51% regard it as one of the heavyweights of the Swiss economy, 35% consider it to be fairly important, and only 3% perceive it to be unimportant. In the Italian-speaking cantons of Switzerland, 70% of the surveyed consider banks to be very important.[86]

The results of the survey prove, that there is still firm support for the concept of banking secrecy among the Swiss public.

Any change in the Swiss legislative framework on banking secrecy would require approval by the Swiss Parliament, and if a request for a referendum would be submitted, the approval of the majority of the voters would be required.

In 1978, a people's initiative was launched by the Swiss Socialist Party. The initiative included the following proposals: 1) lifting banking secrecy in specified cases of tax evasion, and in cases of foreign exchange-control regulations, 2) introducing the requirement for banks to publish full financial statements and empowering the Swiss Parliament with the authority to analyze these statements, 3) limiting bank involvement in direct financing of the economy, and 4) introducing the requirement to insure savings deposits. In an address to the Swiss Parliament in August 1982, the Swiss Federal Council recommended the rejection of the popular initiative. A counter proposal was not submitted for consideration. The Swiss voted on the initiative on May 20, 1984 and rejected it with an overwhelming majority of 73% of votes against the proposal.[87]

1.6 The Numbered (Anonymous) Accounts Controversy

The Swiss numbered accounts also called "secret accounts", or anonymous accounts, have become notorious for their association with criminal activity. They have fueled the myth of Swiss banking secrecy in public imagination, by featuring

86 "Survey 2015: Banks make significant reputational gains, protection of privacy central, but bank-client confidentiality in Switzerland viewed in differentiated manner". Swiss Bankers Association, 26.03.2015, retrieved 26.10.2017, from http://www.swissbanking.org/en/medienmitteilung-20150326.

87 See Aubert, Maurice: "The Limits...," pp. 296–297, for a detailed discussion of this initiative.

in spy stories and embezzlement scandals. They appear often in popular culture in connection with crime, corruption, and money laundering.

In fact, there is no legal difference between regular and numbered accounts in Switzerland. There is a procedural difference in one single respect, namely the number of bank employees, who have access to all the customer information. The true identity of the numbered account owner is known only to a small number of senior bank officials.

The numbered account is in fact a "coded account,"[88] whereby the account is identified by a code number, or a code name, as opposed to regular bank accounts identified by the true name of the account holder. The customer's name does not appear on the bank statements, instead a number and/or a code name is used. Apart from this one distinctive feature numbered accounts require the same verification procedure and duty of diligence, as any other bank relationship with a Swiss financial institution. Upon opening the account all the required information must be provided, such as the identity of the bank client and the beneficial owners. Numbered accounts are subject to the same legal protection with respect to banking secrecy as ordinary accounts.

Numbered accounts nevertheless do provide an additional level of protection from a potential breach of secrecy: the documents pertaining to the bank customer are placed in a safe in the bank, only a limited number of authorized bank employees have access to these documents and there is no database, which matches the name of the account holder and the account number.[89] Numbered accounts can be useful in cases of divorce, inheritance, or simply, when anonymity is required in bank relations with celebrities. The fees associated with numbered accounts are higher than those charged for regular accounts.

Numbered accounts are common practice not only in Switzerland, but also in Austria, Luxembourg, Monaco, and Liechtenstein. Historically, numbered accounts were introduced in Switzerland in the period between the two World Wars as a means of protecting bank customers from France and Germany from the scrutiny of their respective governments. There is no evidence pointing to numbered accounts as a Swiss invention. They were used in Italy and Austria already before World War I.[90]

---

88 Meyer, Bernhard F.: "Swiss Banking Secrecy…," p. 28.

89 "Numbered Accounts Profit from Bank Crisis". *Swissinfo*, 08.02.2010, retrieved 02.12.2017, from http://www.swissinfo.ch/eng/numbered-accounts-profit-from-bank-crisis/8256858.

90 Vogler, Robert U.: *Swiss Banking Secrecy…*, p. 55.

1.7 Evaluation of the Role of Banking Secrecy in the Rise of the Swiss Financial Center

Throughout the twentieth century, Switzerland has built an efficient and competitive banking sector. The answer to the question, to what extent this success can be attributed to the unique role played by banking secrecy remains rather ambiguous. The rise of Switzerland to become a world class financial center should not be explained solely by the phenomenon of banking secrecy. State-regulated financial markets, unpredictable currencies, foreign exchange restrictions and various regulatory limitations hindered the expansion of the world economy from the 1930s well into the post-World War II years. During this period many Europeans transferred their assets to Switzerland, lured by its traditional neutrality and the resulting political stability, the solid reputation of its banking system, a stable economy, its accessibility in the center of Europe, a lack of foreign exchange controls and last but not least, a strong currency.

Clearly, a number of factors have played an important role, leading to the buildup of trust in the Swiss financial institutions. Presumably, the most important of them is a feature rarely experienced by European countries in the twentieth century, namely Switzerland's over 150 years of political stability and legal security. The stability of the legal system is connected to the security of the right to ownership and the freedom to dispose over assets. Political stability is reflected in the frequency of the change of political stance and ruling cabinets as well as civil or political unrest and the occurrence of dictatorships. Political instability increases regulatory risk, leading to higher legal insecurity. Since the liberal revolutions of 1848, Switzerland has enjoyed political and legal stability unparalleled by international comparisons.[91]

The Swiss franc has remained a stable currency over the long term and today enjoys the reputation of the hardest of the major world currencies. Switzerland did not experience the waves of inflation and hyperinflation, which tore through European economies in the period between the two world wars. In fact, the Swiss economy remained quite immune to inflation, including in the post-World War II period. Even the unfavorable interest rate differential between the Swiss franc and other currencies, which dominates from World War II until the present day, was not a deterrent for foreign investors, presumably due to the fact that

91 For a detailed analysis of factors such as political stability, economic stability, monetary stability and free convertibility of the Swiss currency and their contribution to the rise of the Swiss financial center see Ibid., pp. 30–51.

a long-term investment in Swiss francs offered better protection from a breakdown in value than an investment in other major European currencies or the U.S. dollar. The convertibility of the Swiss franc was guaranteed for decades, and it was one of the few currencies to remain freely convertible during World War II. The Swiss franc remained a freely convertible currency in the period after 1945, whereas many other countries maintained various currency restrictions well into the 1980s. The Swiss franc consistently occupies one of the top places among the world's most actively traded currencies, due to it being a popular "neutral" safe haven currency.[92] Its global trading volume is out of proportion to the Swiss domestic market.[93] The Swiss franc enjoyed a substantial long-term appreciation relative to all major European currencies since the 1920s, after Switzerland left the Latin Currency Union.[94] The Swiss exit from the Latin Currency Union marked the beginning of Switzerland's role as a major financial center. The Swiss franc consistently appreciated in value following every major international turmoil, including financial, economic, terrorist, or even weather-related crises.[95] Therefore, the confidence in the Swiss currency, as being a safe and reliable one played a major role in the development of the Swiss financial center, and in its role as a safe haven for foreign assets.

The Swiss financial center is not a stand-alone phenomenon, but is instead tied inseparably to the rest of the Swiss economy. Today, banks and insurance companies are a part of a well-functioning organism which consists of trading corporations, the international art market, the tourism sector, but also prestigious private schools and universities, as well as law firms, which have specialized in catering to the affluent customers of Swiss banks, be it private persons

92 The five most frequently traded currencies (so called majors) are: the U.S. dollar, the euro, the pound sterling, the Japanese yen, and the Swiss franc, see "Currencies Traded in the Forex Market". ForexTraders, 03.11.2016, retrieved 15.03.2017, from http://www.forextraders.com/forex-analysis/forex-fundamental-analysis/currencies-traded-in-the-forex-market.html.

93 For example, in April 2010 the turnover of the Swiss franc amounted to only 6.4% of the global activity, but the daily volume equaled 54% of the annual Swiss GDP. See Meier, Henri B./Marthinsen, John E./Gantenbein, Pascal A.: *Swiss Finance…*, p. 210.

94 Switzerland was a member of the Latin Currency Union between 1865 and 1927 together with France, Belgium and Italy. The Union was later joined by Spain, Greece and Romania, Bulgaria, Montenegro, Venezuela, Serbia and San Marino. It was a bimetallic union, a combined gold and silver standard with a gold-to-silver ratio of 15.5 to 1. For details of this argument see Ibid., pp. 213–214.

95 See Ibid., p. 219 for a list of these events.

or international corporations. This broad extent of economic interrelations differentiates the Swiss financial center from other countries, which have specialized in providing financial services and fiscal incentives to foreigners, such as Panama, or the Principality of Monaco.[96]

The long-lasting stability of Swiss banks and the financial industry as a whole played a part in creating a positive image for Switzerland as a financial center. There have been regional perturbations, especially in the 1930s, but the reputation of Swiss banks never suffered a profound international crisis before the 1990s. Swiss banks are also famous for their high level of professionalism and the quality of services offered by their employees.

Institutional investors are the big customers of banks today and they are not especially interested in banking secrecy, instead they assign a high value to a professional and efficient service, performance, and other factors, which were already discussed here.

Banking secrecy is a major factor, but nevertheless only one of the many factors that played a role in establishing the success of the Swiss banking industry.[97]

1.8 Conclusions

Swiss banking secrecy is deeply rooted in the Swiss banking tradition and enjoys public support, as proven by various surveys and unsuccessful campaigns to abolish it.

Banking secrecy in Switzerland has a long history. It was incorporated into cantonal law as early as the eighteenth century, when Switzerland's self-governing cantons codified the already practiced culture of discretion towards the aristocrats and royalty, who entrusted Swiss banks with their money. Since the sixteenth century Swiss economies generated a surplus of savings which were put to the use of private banks. The trade of banking in Switzerland flourished throughout the seventeenth century, when Swiss financial institutions supplied the capital needed to finance the French Court. The service provided to French kings had to be done with the utmost discretion, and therefore, contributed to create the foundations of banking secrecy in Switzerland. In 1713, the Great

96 For this argument see Guex, Sébastien: "Place financière…", pp. 62–64.

97 A similar argument was brought up by Werner de Capitani: "Today, strict bank secrecy is not enough to make a country an important financial center. […] bank secrecy […] will continue to add to the attractiveness of any reputable financial center". See Capitani, Werner de: "Banking Secrecy Today…," pp. 69–70.

Council of Geneva adopted banking regulations which required the maintenance of customer data, at the same time prohibiting the release of this information by the banks without government approval.

The concept of banking secrecy is protected by numerous provisions within the Swiss legal framework. General provisions referring to the rights to privacy of personal information were incorporated into the Swiss Constitution, as well as the Swiss Civil Code of 1907, which grants any person, whose privacy is violated the right to undertake legal action. Internal bank laws and code of conduct, cantonal laws, the Swiss Civil Code, the Swiss Code of Obligations and the Swiss Criminal Code also include provisions aimed at protecting financial privacy.

Until 1934, the breach of banking secrecy was subject to civil, rather than criminal law sanctions. The connection to criminal law was first made with the codification of banking law, by means of the Federal Act on Banks and Savings Banks, commonly known as the Banking Act of 1934.

The famed Article 47 (b) of the Banking Act explicitly links any breach of banking secrecy to the Swiss Criminal Code. The original provision was altered to adjust the penalty levels to modern circumstances, whereupon the imprisonment limit was increased from 6 months up to three years and the fine for negligence was raised from 10,000 to 250,000 Swiss francs.

The development of Swiss banking gained a boost as a result of the turmoil and the uncertainty of the first half of the twentieth century. The tax increases in various European countries before World War I and in the 1920s provided Swiss banks with an opportunity of obtaining a competitive advantage over well-established financial centers such as London, Paris, or Berlin. This was to be done by offering foreign residents a possibility to evade domestic taxation, by allocating their assets in Switzerland. As a result, banking secrecy gained an unprecedented level of importance for the economy – this common practice became crucial in attracting foreign capital inflows to Switzerland, therefore playing a key role in international competition for capital on financial markets. A campaign was started to promote Switzerland as a tax haven for wealthy Europeans.

The aftermath of World War I saw massive increases in taxation in France, Italy, and Germany, and this in turn led to an influx of foreign capital to Swiss banks. Attracted by moderate taxes, political stability and neutrality, and last but not least, by the culture of banking secrecy, foreign depositors massively escaped domestic fiscal burdens and located their assets in Switzerland. The capital flight from domestic economies did not win the approval of French, Belgian, Italian, or German authorities, and pressure on the Swiss to limit banking secrecy was exercised.

After World War II, as the international expansion of Swiss banks developed, Switzerland rose to become the world's major financial center.

Today, the Swiss banking sector is of key importance to the Swiss economy, consistently accounting for about 10% of the Swiss GDP. Switzerland is a global leader in private banking and wealth management with $2.7 trillion of offshore assets under management, which accounts for 25% of the total global offshore wealth.

Switzerland is not the only country in the world to protect banking secrecy by law, however, it is considered a pioneer in this respect. The comprehensive legal protection granted to banking secrecy in Switzerland, as well as the strong attachment to this principle by both Swiss banks and the Swiss public, are unrivalled in the world.

The protection of banking secrecy in Switzerland stands in stark contrast to the status that banking secrecy enjoys in the United States, where banks have to disclose information about accounts and customer transactions, if compelled to do so by the U.S. government, notably the U.S. tax authorities, and U.S. courts.

Swiss banking secrecy is not an absolute right and can be overridden by the provisions of Swiss domestic law, as well as by international treaties. It can be lifted in numerous criminal proceedings which involve money laundering, insider trading and cases of tax fraud, but not tax evasion. The instances in which Swiss law allowed to lift Swiss banking secrecy have been a major source of conflict with the United States.

Swiss banks have disseminated a myth pertaining to the origins of Swiss banking secrecy. This myth referred to the concept of Switzerland as a refuge for foreign assets and to the laws passed in June 1933, in Nazi Germany, which enabled the seizure of foreign-held assets of German Jews. Banking secrecy was supposedly introduced in Switzerland to protect Jewish assets deposited in Swiss banks from being revealed to and confiscated by Nazi authorities.

However, this myth does not stand up to the facts. The driving force behind the introduction of the Banking Act of 1934 was not Hitler's rise to power and the Nazi regulations introduced in Germany, but rather the world financial crisis in the beginning of 1930s and its implications for the Swiss banking system.

The Swiss Federal Council provided for a first draft of the new banking law in February 1933, whereby an article on banking secrecy was already contained in the document. Despite undergoing numerous changes, before being finally ratified, the Banking Act of 1934 included the provision on banking secrecy in an unaltered form, compared to the draft version proposed in February 1933.

The humanitarian explanation advocated by Swiss banking circles has been scrutinized and questioned by Swiss historians in the early 2000s. Peter Hug has suggested that the myth was invented in response to attacks on the Swiss banking practice by the United States in the 1960s. In fact, Swiss banking secrecy was not introduced in 1934, but merely strengthened by encoding it in the Banking Law of 1934 and fortifying by the provisions of the Criminal Code, since by this time the practice of Swiss banking secrecy was already deeply rooted in the Swiss banking culture. The reasons behind the reinforcement of banking secrecy and the adoption of criminal sanctions to punish its violations were purely economic. The strong legal protection of banking secrecy rendered Swiss banks attractive for capital stemming from fiscal evasion and allowed the Swiss banking sector to flourish and gain a competitive advantage over other well established financial centers. However, the humanitarian explanation, readily endorsed by banks and authorities in Switzerland, provided both legitimacy and respectability to banking secrecy. It was much harder to attack a practice, which was invented to support such a noble cause.

Although banking secrecy has played an important role in the development of the Swiss banking sector, it is not the only success factor. Political and economic stability and legal security, the continuous convertibility of the Swiss currency, as well as the high quality of banking services provided by Swiss banks have all contributed to the international success of Swiss banking.

However, it is Swiss banking secrecy which has become the most widely known, albeit a notorious feature of the Swiss banking culture, and not least due to the policy of the United States. It has been the subject of conflicts and debates and held accountable for facilitating all manner of illegal activities. Swiss banking secrecy has poisoned relations between Switzerland and the United States during and after World War II. The conflicts in which it has played a major part are discussed in the following chapters of this book.

Chapter 2. Swiss Banking During World War II: The First Major Conflict with the United States

The hottest places in hell are reserved for those who in a time of moral crisis preserve their neutrality[1]

In this chapter, the first major conflict between the U.S. and Switzerland, which erupted during World War II is examined in the context of Swiss banking secrecy.

During the war Swiss banks facilitated the settlement of transactions and the transfer of gold, currencies, and commodities for Nazi Germany, thereby acting as clearinghouses within the wartime financial system. This was due to two major reasons: first of all, the Swiss franc remained the only internationally convertible currency throughout the entire war, and secondly its value remained strong by international comparison. And since the Nazi regime required a steady supply of foreign currency to furnish exports essential for maintaining Germany's war

1 "Here sighs and lamentations and loud cries were echoing across the starless air, […] And I – my head oppressed by horror – said: "Master [Virgil], what is it that I hear? Who are those people so defeated by their pain?" And he to me: "This miserable way is taken by the sorry souls of those who lived without disgrace and without praise. They now commingle with the coward angels, the company of those who were not rebels, nor faithful to their God, but stood apart. The heavens, that their beauty not be lessened, have cast them out, nor will deep Hell receive them – even the wicked cannot glory in them."
Dante Alighieri, Divine Comedy, Inferno (Hell). Based upon this quote from Dante's work was one of President John F. Kennedy's favorite citations, as quoted above, which emphasizes and exacerbates the message embedded in Dante's masterpiece, namely that those who in this world have never taken a side neither with evil nor with good occupy a special place of infamy and are denied the moral dignity of a place even in hell itself. This citation is used as a motto of this chapter to emphasize the U.S. stance on the policy of neutrals during World War II. See "John F. Kennedy's Favorite Quotations: Dante's Inferno". John F. Kennedy Presidential Library and Museum, retrieved 23.05.2018, from https://www.jfklibrary.org/Research/Research-Aids/Ready-Reference/JFK-Fast-Facts/Dante.aspx.

effort, this was provided for by exchanging the Reichsbank's[2] gold for Swiss francs in Switzerland. The gold that the Reichsbank accumulated during the war came from various sources, including sources outside of Germany, primarily from national gold reserves of the occupied countries. In addition to seizing public gold reserves, as of the early 1930s the German government pursued a policy intended to increase its gold holdings by restricting the possession of gold and by confiscating privately owned gold of initially German citizens and later also the citizens of the occupied states.

At the same time when the German Reichsbank conducted its gold affairs, individual Germans and German corporations prepared for imminent defeat in the war by allocating their assets in foreign countries, including the neutral states, thereby protecting them from seizure by the Allies. The Swiss financial sector served either as an intermediary or the ultimate destination for the assets of German citizens. At least this was the prevailing conviction among the U.S. policy makers, in particular of the Department of Treasury under the leadership of Henry Morgenthau.

In response to Allies' fears that the German assets including gold and flight capital of German companies and private persons would be used for financing another war and would not be made available for reparations and the reconstruction of Europe after the end of hostilities the U.S. devised the Safehaven Program. This Program stipulated that the German assets in neutral countries such as Switzerland should be tracked down and placed at the disposal of post-liberation authorities. This idea was inconsistent with the Swiss policy stance on financial privacy, and private ownership of assets, which had to be safeguarded regardless of the political considerations of the belligerents. Therefore, the Swiss authorities persistently refuted the Allied demands to provide a census of German assets deposited in Swiss banks and to turn them over to the Allies. The Swiss also refused to cease trading gold with Germany.

The issue of the gold trade between Switzerland and Germany, and in particular the question of the provenance of this gold, which the Allies believed was looted, as well as the problem of German assets in Switzerland was the subject of intense disputes between Switzerland and the U.S. during the war and immediately thereafter. The attempt to resolve these differences culminated in signing the Washington Accord in May 1946.

---

2 The Reichsbank was the Central Bank of Germany from 1876 to 1945. Established from the Bank of Prussia, it was a privately owned bank but was under government management.

However, the provisions of the Washington Accord were not fulfilled by the Swiss and the discussions between the U.S. and Switzerland continued until 1952, when the treaty was replaced by a new contractual set up.

In this chapter, the role of Swiss banks and in particular the Swiss National Bank in the gold trade with the German Reichsbank is examined in detail. Further, the various U.S. measures employed to restrict German economic expansion are discussed in the context of the impact of this policy on Swiss interests. The U.S. negotiations with the Swiss authorities are analyzed, which failed to provide sufficient results in inducing the Swiss to accept the principles of the Safehaven Program. The conflict over German assets in Switzerland was to be resolved by the Swiss and the Allies in the course of negotiations, which were held in 1946 in Washington, and these negotiations are examined in detail, including the aspect of Swiss trade in looted gold, which in fact dominated the talks between the parties. The final outcome of these arduous negotiations, the Washington Agreement, and the main stumbling blocks in its fulfillment are researched, as well as its implications for the U.S.-Swiss relations in the immediate post-war period. Last but not least, an attempt is made to outline the different points of view on the evaluation of Swiss conduct during World War II, taking into consideration both legal and moral aspects, which were raised in this debate. Above all, the U.S. has invoked the argument of the higher moral ground of the Allies and the immoral approach of neutral Switzerland during the course of the events of World War II. Equally strong accusations were made in the 1990s, when the issues examined in this chapter became the subject of renewed interest of scholars and politicians on both sides of the Atlantic.

As a preventive measure, in 1941 the U.S. administration declared frozen all assets of continental European countries, which were deposited in the United States. This move was driven by the need to protect the financial resources which belonged to countries invaded by Germans from being seized by the Nazi government and in case of Switzerland also in part by fears of the exploitation of Swiss banking secrecy and the infiltration of the Swiss banking system by the Nazis. This move was another source of conflict as it was met with resentment on the part of the Swiss. The conflict escalated when, by the provisions of the Washington Agreement, the U.S. was compelled to release Swiss assets blocked in the United States, but failed to do so with respect to the shares of certain private corporations, which were perceived by the U.S. to be in fact concealed German property. This issue is examined in detail in the final section of this chapter using the most prominent example of the U.S.-Swiss custodial conflict, namely the case of Interhandel, which was finally resolved by the Kennedy administration as late as 1963.

2.1 The Role of Swiss Banks in Gold Transactions with the Reichsbank

As a result of the world economic crisis and the monetary policy of the 1930s, the regime of Hitler did not manage to accumulate sufficient gold reserves in the pre-war period to finance the imports necessary for the German war effort.

Therefore, the gold, which the Nazis robbed from central banks of the occupied countries and the victims of the Nazi regime played a decisive role in the financing of the purchases of strategic goods that were essential for the German war effort, including raw materials for the arms industry as the payments for raw materials such as wolfram, iron ore and chrome purchased from Portugal, Spain, Sweden, and Turkey were executed in foreign currency.[1]

The neutral countries, being among the primary suppliers of raw materials indispensable for the German industrial manufacture, did not accept payments in German Reichsmarks. They wanted to be paid in an international currency which would be convertible. Settling transactions in U.S. dollars was possible until the summer of 1941, but after the U.S. started its policy of blocking enemy assets it was no longer an option. The use of Swiss francs remained the only viable solution for the German state to finance the needed imports of goods and raw materials and the Reichsbank purchased Swiss francs by paying for them with gold. For example, when the need for imports of wolfram from Portugal increased considerably, the demand for foreign currency to pay for these imports also grew and the Reichsbank turned to Swiss banks for their hard currency. The gold with which the Reichsbank paid for Swiss francs was stored in Swiss banks in the form of reserves. The Portuguese exporters on the other hand exchanged their Swiss francs into escudos and thus the Swiss francs were stored in the Portuguese Central Bank in the form of currency reserves. Whenever these currency reserves were excessive, they were in turn exchanged for gold at the Swiss central bank. But the Swiss National Bank, which was obliged to maintain a certain level of gold to cover the exchange rate of the Swiss franc in circulation, was not prepared to part with its gold reserves and proposed to the Reichsbank to sell escudos directly in exchange for gold. The Swiss National Bank took over the role of intermediary from Swiss banks and became the most important trading partner for the Reichsbank's gold transactions [2] and the central connecting link for the German wartime payments.

---

1 Steinberg, Jonathan: *Die Deutsche Bank und ihre Goldtransaktionen während des Zweiten Weltkrieges*. C.H. Beck Verlag: München 1999, p. 17.

2 Ibid., pp. 18–19.

In a German document from June 3, 1943, Walther Funk, the Minister of Economics of the Third Reich and the President of the Reichsbank admitted that he could not forego exchanging gold for currencies in Switzerland longer than two months,[3] without imposing a risk on the German economy, which was totally dependent upon imports of raw materials. Gold was indispensable for their acquisition, and the balancing of clearing transactions was impossible without gold. Switzerland took over the role of the clearinghouse for such transactions, thereby becoming indispensable for the German economy.

The Reichsbank delivered $387.8 million worth of gold to the Swiss National Bank and $56.3 million to Swiss commercial banks. Swiss banks received in total $444.1 million, making Switzerland the most important recipient of German gold.[4] The Reichsbank also shipped gold to the Bern depot of the SNB, this gold was not purchased by the Swiss central bank, but rather was recorded as a deposit on the accounts of other central banks. From this depot the Reichsbank sold gold to other central banks and commercial banks in Portugal, Sweden, Romania, Slovakia, Spain, the Bank of International Settlements, and Swiss commercial banks. The SNB did not appear as the purchaser in these transactions, but the depot merely served as a convenient transition point.[5]

In addition to executing gold transactions via the SNB, the German central bank shipped gold directly to Swiss commercial banks. The seizure of the Reichsbank's records by the U.S. occupying forces enabled them to put the amount of these transactions into perspective. According to American calculations in 1946, gold valued at about $20.3 million, or SFr 87.3 million,[6] was delivered to Swiss commercial banks between mid-1940 and May 1945. This was the estimate quoted in the negotiations preceding the signing of the 1946 Washington Agreement. However, a review of the Reichsbank's records by the Bergier Commission estimated the value of gold deposited in Swiss commercial banks to be closer to 61 million USD. The discrepancy in the figures can be partially explained by the different timelines applied for the calculation. The Allies' calculation begins in mid-1940 and does not take into consideration the substantial deposits of gold

3 Durrer, Marco: *Die schweizerisch…*, p. 314.

4 Independent Commission of Experts Switzerland – Second World War: *Switzerland and Gold Transactions in the Second World War, Interim Report*, Bern July 1998, retrieved 12.01.2017, from https://www.uek.ch/en/publikationen1997-2000/golde.pdf, p. 39 and p. 44.

5 See Ibid., pp. 36–37, p. 53, and p. 55, the value of this gold amounted to SFr. 470 million.

6 The exchange rate used here is 1:4.3.

made until the first half of 1940. The date of 30 April 1940 was chosen by the Allies as the starting point for Allied claims for the restitution of gold by Switzerland, and 30 June 1940 was chosen as a starting point for the calculations.[7]

During the first two years of the war the Reichsbank executed gold transactions in Switzerland predominantly via commercial banks. However, by the end of 1942 the Swiss Federal Council centralized the trading of gold between Switzerland and all foreign parties via the SNB.[8] The Swiss National Bank requested the Reichsbank to channel all gold deliveries through the Swiss central bank. The request stemmed from the fact that the Swiss gold reserves declined steadily, which in turn undermined the Swiss exchange rate policy.

The handling of the gold business epitomizes the pedantry and brutal efficiency of the Nazi regime. Part of the gold which passed though the hands of the German and Swiss bankers did in fact originate from concentration camp victims. In April 1945, the Allies found a secret depot set up by the Reichsbank in a mining tunnel in Thüringen, Germany. In the depot, there were sacks full of personal items, such as spectacle frames and wedding rings. Evidence was found that looted dental gold was routinely melted into standard bars of gold, acknowledged with a receipt, weighted, and certified and finally used as a means of payment for imports and other war expenditures. Gold was also smelted from wrist watches, fountain pens and other precious items.[9] The issue of gold looted from concentration camp victims would come back fifty years after the war with astounding media coverage and become a crucial argument in the debate between the Swiss and the U.S. Government in the second half of the 1990s. This conflict, including the problem of the so-called victim gold, is examined in detail in Chapter 3.

---

7 Independent Commission of Experts Switzerland – Second World War: *Gold Transactions in the Second World War: Statistical Review with Commentary: A Contribution to the Conference on Nazi Gold London, 2–4 December 1997*, Bern December 1997, retrieved 04.02.2017, from https://www.uek.ch/en/publikationen1997-2000/dec97-e.pdf.

8 Independent Commission of Experts Switzerland – Second World War: *Switzerland and Gold Transactions…*, p. 159 and p. 191.

9 Steinberg, Jonathan: *Die Deutsche Bank…*, p. 10.

2.2 U.S. and Allied Measures to Restrict German Economic and Financial Expansion: The Swiss Connection.

2.2.1 Swiss Assets in the United States: U.S. Freezing Order, Suspicion and Criticism with Respect to the Conduct of Swiss Banks

Even before the U.S. entered World War II it introduced specific measures of economic warfare and one such measure, with the most profound consequences for the U.S – Swiss relations, was the blocking of funds of other countries, a step taken with the aim of preventing the Nazis from using financial resources accumulated in the U.S. to finance the German military campaign.

Switzerland was only one of over thirty countries, the assets of which were blocked by the U.S. during World War II.[10] By Executive Order 8785 of June 14, 1941,[11] the Roosevelt administration declared frozen all assets of continental European countries. The primary purpose of the American financial blockade was to protect the assets and financial resources, which belonged to the countries invaded or occupied by Germany, but were accumulated in the United States, from being seized by the invaders.

The assets, after being frozen, were subject to licensing, whereby their owners could apply for a license and retrieve the assets under the supervision of the Treasury Department. In the case of Switzerland, a considerable amount of the frozen assets was held in anonymous numbered accounts and, in line with the Swiss banking secrecy law, the Swiss banks refused to reveal the identity of the owners, despite pressure from the U.S. Treasury. As a result, the Swiss accounts were treated as enemy assets by the United States.[12]

This issue was particularly critical to Swiss bankers due to the fact, that out of 5 billion Swiss francs frozen in the U.S. roughly 2 billion belonged to French citizens. Had the names of these asset holders been revealed, they would have reached French fiscal authorities and in accordance with French law the funds would be subject to heavy taxation, in compliance with French fiscal regulations, whereas the owners might have been prosecuted for tax fraud. In the eyes of the

10 Durrer, Marco: *Die schweizerisch*, p. 19.

11 Roosevelt, Franklin D.: "Executive Order 8785 Freezing the Assets of Certain European Countries", 14.06.1941.

12 Meier, Heinz K.: *Friendship Under Stress…*, p. 279.

Swiss this would have definitely constituted a major blow to the credibility of Swiss banking.[13]

There were numerous arguments supporting the freezing of Swiss funds.

The Swiss assets in the U.S. could be seized by the Germans in case of an invasion of Switzerland. Moreover, Germany maintained access to the dollar market via Swiss banks, as it continued to process direct banking transactions via the neutral states, and Switzerland in particular. Whereas direct deposits of the Reichsbank in the U.S. were limited, the German central bank executed its dollar transactions on the foreign exchange markets of the neutrals, including Switzerland. The Reichsbank closed its account with the National City Bank in New York, where its largest bank deposit was held, and transferred the funds to the Swiss Bank Corporation. It was also suspected that the Axis assets could be moved to the neutral countries, which proved to be a justified claim, as in the months following the blockade of Swiss assets in the U.S. the American embassy in Bern received information from the Swiss banking circles that senior officials from the axis countries opened numbered bank accounts in Switzerland, immediately following the outbreak of the war, which were denominated in U.S. dollars, but later exchanged to gold or Swiss francs.[14]

Despite a lack of absolute unanimity within the U.S. political circles,[15] the decision to include Switzerland in the blockade was finally made, following the concerns of the Treasury Department about the attitude of Swiss financial institutions. The Swiss banking sector was perceived to be out of proportion to the Swiss economy and the success of Swiss banking was interpreted as being a direct result of Swiss banking secrecy laws and the widespread use of the structure of omnibus accounts. The Treasury Department also feared that the nationals of the Axis countries would sell their interests in assets blocked in the U.S. to the Swiss voluntarily, or under pressure, and that these funds could in turn be made available to the Axis powers. The U.S. officials were concerned about the possible infiltration of the Swiss banking system by the Nazis. Finally, the U.S. Justice Department suspected that Swiss banks were used as intermediaries by Germany to move funds to the U.S. and Latin America.[16]

---

13 Guex, Sébastien: "The Origins…", p. 264.

14 Durrer, Marco: *Die schweizerisch*, p. 31.

15 The Department of Treasury led by Henry Morgenthau strongly supported the concept, whereas the Department of State headed by Cordell Hull was in strong opposition to the Treasury's stance on this issue. See Ibid., pp. 32–33.

16 U.S. Department of State: *U.S. and Allied Efforts To Recover and Restore Gold and Other Assets Stolen or Hidden by Germany During World War II…*, pp. 4–5.

In 1941, the U.S. Department of Treasury led by Henry Morgenthau ordered a thorough investigation of the activities of Swiss financial institutions and Swiss corporations in the United States. The investigation was conducted from Fall of 1941 until Summer of 1943 and produced a document entitled "Final Report: Swiss Bank Investigation". The report pointed to the role played by Swiss banks in managing refugee capital, which was invested to a large extent in the United States. The beneficial ownership of this capital was concealed in line with the practice of Swiss banking secrecy, which was criticized as running counter to U.S. law. The Swiss policy of discretion and customer anonymity raised suspiciousness and the Department of Treasury assumed that the Swiss banks were hiding the beneficiaries of Swiss accounts in the U.S. from U.S. authorities.[17] One such example of Swiss secrecy severely criticized in the report were the so called omnibus or collective accounts, which pooled together the assets of more than one customer and were held in one bank in the name of another bank and not in the name of the bank customers.[18]

A further issue which came under criticism was the power of disposition, which was a means of protecting customers of Swiss banks against the U.S. blocking measures, introduced before the launch of the U.S. freeze on Swiss funds. The powers of disposition allowed the banks under certain explicitly specified circumstances to transfer or overwrite assets in the accounts of Swiss banks in the U.S. to third parties, which had no contact with Switzerland, and thereby could not be affected by the freeze. The Department of Treasury investigation had shown that from 1940 until June 14, 1941, the date of the decree on the freezing of Swiss assets in the U.S., all branches of Swiss banks in New York prepared and accepted such powers of disposition. The Treasury saw in this procedure a clear intention to circumvent the freezing order on the part of Swiss financial institutions.[19]

Finally, banks, in case of withdrawals, were obliged to fill out so called TFR-300 Reports, which provided information on ownership structure and beneficiaries. Swiss bank subsidiaries provided false data in filling out these forms and they circumvented them in case of transactions pertaining to collective accounts.[20]

17 Durrer, Marco: *Die schweizerisch...*, pp. 123–124.
18 Ibid., p. 125.
19 Ibid., pp. 127–128.
20 Ibid., pp. 4–5.
Ibid., pp. 123–124.
Ibid., p. 125.
Ibid., pp. 127–128.

The Department of Treasury had reasons enough to suspect that the purpose of such measures, undertaken by Swiss banks was to cover up German interests in the United States. Whereas the Swiss banks mainly strove to ensure that their customers had access to their own assets under any circumstances, and they were prepared to go to great lengths to safeguard this principle.

Despite the U.S. freezing of Swiss assets, owing to the maintenance of trade in foreign exchange and gold by the Swiss central bank, the Swiss franc became one of the most important international currencies, not only for the neutral states, but also the belligerent parties.

This unilateral U.S. decision placed the SNB in a difficult position due to the blocked access to Swiss gold inventories in the United States. From one day to the next, the share of frozen gold reserves had risen from 25% to 65%. Since the SNB was obliged to convert dollars from the private sector, the portion of frozen currency reserves would still increase. The SNB therefore introduced dollar controls, by concluding in September 1941 a gentlemen's agreement with the Swiss banks, whereby the SNB would accept only those dollars remaining from the settlement of import and export transactions at the official rate. The SNB therefore introduced two categories of conversion – the goods dollars, used for trade which were convertible and financial dollars, which were not. The Swiss franc-dollar exchange rate was thereby split between a rate for goods dollars and a rate for financial dollars, which was considerably lower. As a result of this policy the Swiss importers were able to buy cheaply the so-called financial dollars on a free-floating money market which emerged outside of the banking system and the New York Stock Exchange. Financial dollars could not be converted at the SNB at the preferred official exchange rate. As the SNB expected imports and exports to be roughly equal, it hoped to accept only relatively low amounts of dollars.[21]

The dollar management policy of the Swiss was met with strong disapproval of the American authorities. The Department of Treasury saw in this measure a lack of political trust.[22] The Swiss defended their position claiming that if the

---

Ibid., pp. 129–130.

21 For a discussion of the Swiss management of dollar holdings following the U.S. blockade Independent Commission of Experts Switzerland – Second World War: *Switzerland and Gold Transactions…*, pp. 141–144; and Crettol, Vincent/Halbeisen, Patrick: *Monetary policy background to the gold transactions of the Swiss National Bank in the Second World War.* Zürich, Swiss National Bank, May 1999, retrieved 05.05.2017, from https://www.snb.ch/en/mmr/reference/gold_transactions_ww2/source/gold_transactions_ww2.en.pdf, p. 24.

22 Durrer, Marco: *Die schweizerisch*, p. 308.

U.S. would have eased its freezing policy, it would have allowed Switzerland to reduce its surplus of U.S. dollars without the need to resort to such measures.

Although since 1943 the Swiss provided the Allies with Swiss francs for their payments, the Allies nevertheless criticized the Swiss for favoring Germany in financial matters and supplying the Third Reich with Swiss francs on credit, whereas the U.S. and Great Britain were denied sufficient quantities of the Swiss currency, despite offering immediate exchange for dollars and gold.[23]

The widespread suspicion towards Swiss banks in the U.S. during World War II only led to further exacerbating the existing differences. The American enquiry into the conduct of Swiss banks in the U.S. following the blockade of Swiss assets pointed to a clear violation of the U.S. Freezing Order and U.S. procedures by the Swiss banks and provided arguments for the Treasury Department to support its policy stance with respect to the Swiss.

2.2.2 Blacklisting

Another measure of trade control introduced by the U.S. shortly after the Executive Order No. 8785 was the blacklisting of persons and companies which engaged in business with the Axis countries. U.S. firms were prohibited from trade with the entities listed on the "Proclaimed List of Certain Blocked Nationals". The British government introduced a similar measure called the Statutory List. The Proclaimed List included 1100 Swiss persons and 1330 Swiss companies.[24] The blacklisting of Swiss persons and firms was an important means of exercising pressure on the Swiss government throughout the wartime negotiations. Both policies: blacklisting and the freezing of Swiss assets were discontinued after the signing of the Washington Accord of 1946, which is discussed in detail in subsequent sections of this chapter.

2.2.3 London Declaration of January 5, 1943

In July 1942, the British initiated the idea of warning the Axis powers and the neutrals that the Allies would not recognize any seizure of property in the occupied territories. A joint declaration was to be issued as a formal warning against the dispossessions performed by the Axis countries.

---

23 Independent Commission of Experts Switzerland – Second World War: *Switzerland and Gold Transactions...*, p. 145.

24 Meier, Heinz K.: *Friendship Under Stress...*, p. 279.

On January 5, 1943, the Inter-Allied Declaration Against Acts of Dispossession Committed in Territories under Enemy Occupation and Control was signed. The document, also referred to as the London Declaration, stated that "the Governments making this Declaration and the French National Committee reserve all their rights to declare invalid any transfers of, or dealings with property, rights and interests of any description whatsoever which are, or have been, situated in the territories which have come under the occupation or control, direct or indirect of the Governments with which they are at war, or which belong, or have belonged to persons, including juridical persons, resident in such territories."[25] The signatory nations committed to do all that was in their power to expropriate all the seized assets. Despite having made no explicit reference to the gold dealings with the Germans, the U.S. Treasury Department hoped that this declaration would have a deterring effect on the neutrals and their purchases of looted gold from the Reichsbank.[26]

2.2.4 Declaration on Gold Purchases of February 22, 1944

Since 1943, the neutral states were repeatedly warned by the Allies that after the war they will be made accountable for their gold and capital transactions with the Axis powers. Taking into consideration the pre-war German official reports of its gold reserves, which in 1938 amounted to 70.8 million Reichsmarks[27] and the scale of the German trade with the neutral states, financed through gold sales, it became apparent to the Allies that the gold used by the Reichsbank was certain to have been looted from occupied countries.

On February 22, 1944, the U.S. Treasury Secretary Morgenthau issued a declaration in which the looting of gold by the Nazis was explicitly mentioned and condemned, as well as the policy of gold trade with the Germans by the neutrals.[28]

---

25 "Inter-Allied Declaration against Acts of Dispossession Committed in Territories under Enemy Occupation of Control (with covering Statement by His Majesty's Government in the United Kingdom and Explanatory Memorandum issued by the Parties to the Declaration) London, January 5. 1943". London Declaration, H. M. Stationery Office: United Nations 1943.

26 U.S. Department of State: *U.S. and Allied Efforts To Recover and Restore Gold and Other Assets Stolen or Hidden by Germany During World War II…*, pp. 6–7.

27 Independent Commission of Experts Switzerland – Second World War: *Switzerland and Gold Transactions…*, p. 25. One U.S. dollar was worth approximately 4.2 Reichsmarks. This would put the Reichsbank gold holdings at less than 20 million USD.

28 "[…] the United States Government formally declares that it does not and will not recognize the transference of title to the looted gold which the Axis at any time holds or has disposed of in world markets. It further declares that it will be the policy of the

The transfer of ownership rights to looted gold acquired in world markets would not be recognized by the United States. This warning, known as the Gold Declaration, was officially passed on to Switzerland and initiated a hardline approach on the gold issue towards the neutrals on the part of the Allies, who followed the U.S. policy stance on this issue. Subsequently, the U.S. estimates of German gold holdings in the pre-war period were revised downwards making the trade in looted gold even more apparent.

2.2.5 The Safehaven Program and Bretton Woods Resolution No. VI

The Safehaven Program originated in the U.S. Foreign Economic Administration,[29] where a small group of policymakers designed an operation to thwart German industrial and commercial power.[30] This project was a response to the

---

United States Treasury not to buy any gold presently located outside of the territorial limits of the United States from any country which has not broken relations with the Axis, or from any country which after the date of this announcement acquires gold from any country which has not broken relations with the Axis, unless and until the United States Treasury is fully satisfied that such gold is not gold which was acquired directly or indirectly from the Axis powers or is not gold which any such country has been or is enabled to release as a result of the acquisition of gold directly or indirectly from the Axis powers". See U.S. Department of State: "Concern of the United States over enemy attempts to secrete funds or other assets in neutral countries: Inception of the Safehaven program: Circular Telegram: The Acting Secretary of State to Certain Diplomatic and Consular Officers, Washington, February 22, 1944" by Stettinius Jr., Edward. In: *Foreign Relations of the United States: Diplomatic Papers, 1944, General: Economic and Social Matters, Volume II*. U.S. Government Printing Office: Washington, D.C. 1967. Office of the Historian Website, retrieved 17.12.2016, from https://history.state.gov/historicaldocuments/frus1944v02/d161.

29 The Foreign Economic Administration was established in 1943 to centralize the foreign economic functions of numerous preceding U.S. governmental agencies. This agency was abolished in September 1945. See "Records of the Foreign Economic Administration". National Archives, retrieved 02.04.2016, from https://www.archives.gov/research/guide-fed-records/groups/169.html#169.1.

30 The FEA memorandum which outlined the Safehaven objectives was sent to the Department of State and the Department of Treasury on 5 and 17 May 1944. After a bureaucratic struggle between the two departments the State Department emerged as the principal agency responsible for Safehaven. See Steury, Donald P.: "The OSS and Project SAFEHAVEN: Tracking Nazi Gold". *Studies in Intelligence*, No. 9, Central Intelligence Agency, Center for the Study of Intelligence: Summer 2000, retrieved 27.02.2016, from

U.S. government's fears of a revival of German aggression resulting from German economic capacity which could be recovered from capital and resources accumulated abroad. The gold and assets looted in occupied countries by the Nazis and safely located in foreign countries, including the neutrals, would have served this purpose well. To prevent such a resurgence of Nazi Germany, a special program was devised in Washington.

The Safehaven Program, as it came to be known, since its main purpose was to deny any safe haven for Nazi looted assets, was designed primarily to track down German assets in neutral countries and prevent them from being re-used by the Nazis. It was aimed not only at preventing the escape of tangible assets to neutral countries but also the escape of German Nazi leaders and strategic personnel with industrial know how. The neutral states were pressured by the U.S. not to grant asylum to Axis political and business leaders.[31]

Moreover, as the war progressed, the issue of providing funds for the rebuilding of Europe became increasingly important and German gold and assets, when hidden abroad, could not be used for war reparations. Safehaven therefore also served the purpose of making German assets available for war indemnities and the rehabilitation of Europe. The Allies also feared a German economic infiltration of the neutral states and therefore the final principal aim of Safehaven was to restrict German economic influence abroad. It was irrelevant whether it concerned private or state-owned assets.[32]

During the United Nations Monetary and Financial Conference at Bretton Woods, New Hampshire, on July 1–22, 1944 the U.S. submitted a draft of a resolution,[33] which called for action by the neutral countries to prevent the disposition or the transfer of assets or gold which belonged to occupied countries or their citizens, as well as the concealment of such assets.[34]

---

https://www.cia.gov/library/center-for-the-study-of-intelligence/csi-publications/csi-studies/studies/summer00/art04.html.

31 Meier, Heinz K.: *Friendship Under Stress…*, p. 336.

32 For an analysis of the strategic goals of Safehaven see Durrer, Marco: *Die schweizerisch*, pp. 132–134ff; and U.S. Department of State: *U.S. and Allied Efforts To Recover and Restore Gold and Other Assets Stolen or Hidden by Germany During World War II…*, p. 15.

33 This draft built upon a proposal from the Polish delegation to strive cooperation of the neutrals in blocking and liquidating Axis funds within their territories, and using them for reparation payments. See Lorenz-Meyer, Martin: *Safehaven: The Allied Pursuit of Nazi Assets Abroad.* University of Missouri Press: Columbia, Missouri 2007, p. 42.

34 During the Bretton Woods Conference in addition to resolution Number VI a Resolution Number V was passed, which called for the abolition of the Bank of International

The final text of the draft was adopted on July 22, at the Plenary Session of the Conference as Resolution Number VI. The Resolution was implemented to discourage the liquidation of property looted by the Germans and to foster locating and tracing the ownership of such assets, as well as taking the appropriate measures to restore the assets to their rightful owners. The neutral governments were called upon to take all the necessary steps to prevent the transfer of enemy assets such as looted gold, currencies, art objects, securities, and other ownership titles through their territories or territories subject to their jurisdiction and to place these assets at the disposal of the post-liberation authorities.[35] The Resolution therefore encompassed the basic goals of the U.S. Safehaven Program.

As it was a conference of the 44 wartime coalition nations, the neutral states were not invited to participate in drafting the Bretton Woods Resolution. The Swiss Federal Council, upon being informed about the Resolution, remained silent and continued to remain so throughout the following months.[36]

On August 7, 1944, the Department of State telegraphed to Bern, informing the Swiss that the U.S. government expected the adjustment of the Swiss policy in line with the Gold Declaration of February 22, 1944.[37]

The determination to pursue the goals outlined by Safehaven and embodied in the Bretton Woods Resolution No. VI was further expressed in a comprehensive document prepared by the U.S. interdepartmental Executive Committee on Economic Foreign Policy. The document entitled "United States Proposal for Allied Economic Policy Toward Neutral Countries" was approved by President Roosevelt, and for the first time included a far-reaching demand that the neutral countries implement measures which would recognize Allied authority over all enemy assets, which were to be found within the jurisdiction of the neutral countries.[38]

Settlements since its financial transactions with Germany violated the concept set forth by the Safehaven program. Finally, the BIS was not dissolved.

35 Meier, Heinz K.: *Friendship Under Stress…*, p. 338.

36 Ibid., p. 339.

37 Durrer, Marco: *Die schweizerisch*, p. 144.

38 See U.S. Department of State: "Memorandum by the Secretary of State to President Roosevelt, Washington, December 29, 1944" by Edward Stettinius Jr. In: *Foreign Relations of the United States: Diplomatic Papers, 1944, General: Economic and Social Matters, Volume II*. U.S. Government Printing Office: Washington, D.C. 1967. Office of the Historian Website, retrieved 17.12.2016, from https://history.state.gov/historicaldocuments/frus1944v02/d108 and Meier, Heinz K.: *Friendship Under Stress…*, p. 339 for a commentary.

With the conclusion of the Washington negotiations in 1946 the U.S. files on the Safehaven project were closed and reopened only 50 years later by a new generation of government historians striving to get to the bottom of the Nazi gold issue.[39]

2.3 Escalation of Pressure: Negotiations and Impositions

2.3.1 The Currie Agreement

Throughout the war the Allies insisted on a total ban on both Swiss exports to Germany[40] and the granting of transit rights. Towards the end of 1944 the Swiss suggested that a joint Anglo-American delegation should come to Bern to discuss the outstanding trade and transport issues. On February 13, 1945, Lauchlin Currie, who headed the U.S. Mission to Switzerland, arrived in Bern.

The U.S. Mission had three key objectives: to persuade the Swiss to completely cease trading with Germany, to stop any remaining transit traffic across Switzerland between Germany and Northern Italy via the Swiss Alps for the purpose of preventing German shipments by rail to German-controlled Italian factories, and finally, Currie was also instructed to explore the Safehaven goals during the discussions with the Swiss, and pursue the implementation by the Swiss of the Bretton Woods Resolution No. VI.[41]

The first breakthrough happened almost immediately and provided great, albeit false, hopes for the Americans. On February 16, 1945, the Swiss Federal Council issued a freezing order on all German assets in Switzerland. This would have been a first major concession on bank secrecy since Article IX of this decree permitted the Swiss Clearing Office, a governmental agency, which supervised all wartime trade between Switzerland and Germany, to obtain from Swiss banks information which would allow to determine the rightful owners of the property.

After three weeks of intensive negotiations, the Swiss signed a final agreement with the Allies on March 8, 1945. The document, known as the Currie

---

39 Steury, Donald P.: "The OSS...".

40 Switzerland exported such strategic items to Germany as: ammunition, locomotives, automobiles, diesel engines, machinery, 40% of the total power supply of southern Germany, aluminum and aluminum products. By 1943, in total nearly 30% of all Swiss exports went to Germany. See U.S. Department of State: *U.S. and Allied Efforts To Recover and Restore Gold and Other Assets Stolen or Hidden by Germany During World War II...*, p. 24 and p. 26.

41 Meier, Heinz K.: *Friendship Under Stress...*, p. 342.

Agreement or the Bern Agreement, meant yielding to all the major points of the allied Safehaven policy. The Swiss authorities agreed to make a census of all assets of persons falling under Swiss blocking decrees (this took into consideration primarily German assets), and to cease purchasing gold from Germany, except for the amounts required to finance the German diplomatic services. The Swiss also agreed to prevent the cloaking of assets of the persons falling under Swiss blocking decrees and agreed to assist in the restoration of the looted property. Currie was satisfied with the effect of his mission. No reference to the Bretton Woods Resolution No. VI was made in line with the Swiss request, as the Resolution used the term "enemy" and the introduction of such terminology would question Swiss neutrality.[42]

The initial success of the Currie Mission was soon overshadowed by the practical problems of the interpretation and implementation of the Currie agreement. The Swiss would not reveal the information on the census of German assets and the details regarding transactions with the Germans. By signing the Currie Agreement, the Swiss consented to make a census of German assets but they were only prepared to use it for their own purposes. Switzerland would follow Allied demands in its own way, "in full harmony with its rights as a sovereign power, keeping in mind always its international obligations to individuals and states alike."[43]

Within the scope of the Currie Agreement the Swiss committed to identify foreign assets blocked in Switzerland, but the process was delayed, among other reasons due to the necessity of identifying bank customers by their names. This procedure, being in conflict with the practice of banking secrecy, encountered strong internal opposition.[44] In September and October 1945, the U.S. urged Switzerland to complete the census of German assets and expressed its dissatisfaction with the general lack of cooperation of the Swiss authorities.[45] Finally, on November 14, 1945, the Swiss Compensation Office[46] submitted a report of its investigation.

42 For a detailed account of the Currie Agreement see Ibid., pp. 342–344.

43 For this quote see Meier, Heinz K.: *Friendship Under Stress…*, p. 344.

44 D Durrer, Marco: *Die schweizerisch*, p. 243.

45 U.S. Department of State: *U.S. and Allied Efforts To Recover and Restore Gold and Other Assets Stolen or Hidden by Germany During World War II…*, p. 34.

46 The Swiss Compensation Office or Swiss Clearing Office (German: Verrechnungsstelle) was founded in 1934 to manage payments between Germany and Switzerland.

The process of collecting the data was arduous, the data was tampered with, company assets were depreciated and manipulated with accounting tricks. Only a few names of leading Nazi officials were to be found on the lists.[47]

The tensions between Switzerland and the U.S. over the fulfillment of the Currie Agreement and the Allied Safehaven Program continued until the end of 1945.

During the discussions with the Swiss, as the problem of German assets remained unresolved, the U.S. officials working in the Treasury Department demanded that the Allies gain complete control over these assets to prevent them from being used for financing the revival of German economic and war power or the development of atomic energy.[48]

2.3.2 Allied Control Council's Vesting Decree: Public Law No. 5

The U.S. targeted neutral Switzerland as one of the key areas of German financial and economic expansion. The German assets in Switzerland, which the Foreign Economic Administration estimated towards the end of the war to total $300 million, were to be put under Allied control and later used to provide reparation payments and reconstruction funds for war-ravaged countries. These estimates were based on intelligence collected by the Treasury and War Departments in occupied Germany.[49]

At the initiative of the U.S. a draft of a vesting decree, which would place German assets in neutral states under the control and disposition of the Allied Control Council was proposed during the Potsdam Conference which lasted from July 16 to August 1, 1945. During the conference Stalin relinquished all Soviet claims to gold found by the Allies in Germany. The British opposed the vesting decree on the grounds that the neutrals would question its foundations in international law. The U.S. on the other hand feared that unless such a decree was adopted, the neutral countries would seize German assets for their own use.[50] Due to a lack of unanimity the U.S. proposal was not enacted during the Potsdam Conference.

---

47 Durrer, Marco: *Die schweizerisch*, p. 247.

48 U.S. Department of State: *U.S. and Allied Efforts To Recover and Restore Gold and Other Assets Stolen or Hidden by Germany During World War II…*, p. 34.

49 Meier, Heinz K.: *Friendship Under Stress…*, p. 348.

50 U.S. Department of State: *U.S. and Allied Efforts To Recover and Restore Gold and Other Assets Stolen or Hidden by Germany During World War II…*, pp. 51–52.

In August 1945, the U.S. government requested the right of ownership or control of all German assets in Switzerland. The authority over all enemy assets was to be held by the Allied Control Council as the de facto government of Germany. The Swiss Federal Council declined this request, which according to the Council had no legal foundations.

Finally, on October 30, 1945, the Allied Control Council passed a Vesting and Marshalling Decree, which established a German External Property Commission, and granted it all titles and rights to German property outside of Germany, owned by German citizens. The Decree became Law No. 5 of the Allied Control Council. But the Swiss Federal Council further refused to recognize the rights of ownership or control of the Allies over German property in Switzerland.[51] To resolve this impasse, the U.S. government proposed a meeting in Washington to discuss the disputable issue. The negotiations initially planned for one week lasted for over two months and were not dominated by the issue of German assets, but instead focused on the polarizing problem of gold looted by the Nazis from occupied countries and sold to the Swiss National Bank.

2.3.3 The Puhl Affair

The gold issue was one of the key concerns of the Allies, who were certain that Germany could not have had at its disposal sufficient gold holdings to conduct the gold trades, which it executed during the war and that the vast majority of the gold purchased by the Swiss National Bank from the Reichsbank was looted. The Allies, led by the U.S., defended their position claiming that after the war they would not accept any gold which was purchased from Germany, since this gold had to be returned to its rightful owners.[52]

U.S. Senator, Harley M. Kilgore, chaired hearings of the War Mobilization Subcommittee of the Senate Military Affairs Committee set up to investigate German schemes and capacity to a new attempt at conducting a world war. In June 1945, Kilgore presented to the Subcommittee in Washington the contents of four letters sent by Emil Puhl, the Vice President of the German Reichsbank and the architect of the grand scheme of the German gold trade to his superior, Walther Funk, the President of the Reichsbank and Minister of Economics of the Reich. The letters were sent in March and April 1945, that is in the period

51 Meier, Heinz K.: *Friendship Under Stress…*, pp. 350–354.
52 Durrer, Marco: *Die schweizerisch*, p. 201.

immediately following the Currie Agreement.[53] The letters clearly indicated that Puhl managed to strike yet another deal with the Swiss and sell three tons of gold only a month before the end of World War II. The letters were revealed at a time when Switzerland was arguing that it fulfilled the Currie Agreement and rejected any U.S. claims to the contrary.

Puhl's letters clearly exposed the fact, that Switzerland was practicing a double standard with respect to the Allies. The purpose of Puhl's visit in Switzerland was to maintain unobstructed financial channels between Switzerland and Germany, as a countermeasure against the Currie Agreement. The Swiss bankers in Zurich, Basel, and Bern entertained Puhl and expressed sympathy to his cause. In his letters, Puhl also indicated his conviction that the Swiss central bankers were willing to continue with their services to Germany, and pointed to his exceptionally cordial personal relations with the Swiss authorities.[54] The documents of the U.S. Legation in Bern report that the Swiss claimed that the gold was purchased for diplomatic purposes specifically excluded by the Currie Agreement and that it was not looted gold. This claim was made despite the Allied policy directives since February 1944, to treat all gold coming from Germany as looted.[55]

Orvis A. Schmidt, who was a member of the Currie Mission to Bern and Director of the Foreign Funds Control of the Treasury Department testified before the Kilgore Subcommittee, issuing the following statement:

Even at this late date, the Swiss Government is loath to take the necessary steps to force banks and other cloaking institutions to disclose the owners of assets held in or through Switzerland. This means that German assets held in or through Switzerland will not be identified. Thus, the true picture of German financial and industrial penetration throughout the world will be kept a secret. By the same token, Swiss banks will continue to profit by protecting, through their secrecy laws, Germany's war potential – the hidden assets of its financiers and industrialists.[56]

This statement was widely publicized in the U.S. press, turning the sentiments against Switzerland.

---

53 U.S. Department of State: *U.S. and Allied Efforts To Recover and Restore Gold and Other Assets Stolen or Hidden by Germany During World War II…*, p. 33.

54 See Meier, Heinz K.: *Friendship Under Stress…*, pp. 352–354 for a detailed discussion of the Puhl Affair.

55 U.S. Department of State: *U.S. and Allied Efforts To Recover and Restore Gold and Other Assets Stolen or Hidden by Germany During World War II…*, p. 33.

56 Ibid., p. 33.

The Puhl affair resulted in a strong negative response in the U.S. press and further incensed the American public against the Swiss. The Americans were certain that the Swiss breeched the Currie Agreement. The affair was exploited in later negotiations with the Swiss in Washington.

The Puhl affair offered the Allied negotiators a tactical advantage and valuable evidence with respect to Swiss gold policy during World War II. Puhl was interrogated by the Americans after the war. The Allies were most interested whether the Swiss knew about the provenance of the German gold. The answers provided by Puhl during his interrogation were used by the Americans during the Washington negotiations as their final trump card.[57]

2.4 The Washington Accord

The Paris Conference on Reparations which was held in November and December of 1945 established procedures for the division of German external assets in neutral countries, which were to be used for reparations. The eighteen Allied nations participating in the Conference authorized the U.S., Great Britain, and France to negotiate with the neutrals on their behalf. The gold looted by Germany and transferred to the central banks of the neutral countries was supposed to be submitted to the Inter-Allied Reparations Agency, established at the Conference, and later used for financing reparations. The first $25 million from the liquidation of German external assets in neutral states was to be turned over to the Intergovernmental Committee on Refugees (IGCR) for the support of victims of Nazism.

Moreover, the Allied position was such, that all gold purchased from the Reichsbank by banks in neutral countries was to be considered stolen, unless proven otherwise.

In the beginning of 1946, the U.S. invited the Swiss to Washington to pursue negotiations between the representatives of the Swiss government and the three Allies (U.S., France, and Great Britain) on the disposal of German property in Switzerland. The negotiations began on March 18, 1946.

Since the Swiss rejected Public Law No. 5 of the Allied Control Council and questioned the legal basis for Allied claims to German assets outside of Germany it was clear from the beginning that the negotiations would not be easy.[58]

57 Durrer, Marco: *Die schweizerisch*, pp. 228–230.
58 Meier, Heinz K.: *Friendship Under Stress…*, p. 358.

However, the extent of the divergence of the negotiation positions exceeded the Allied expectations.

When the negotiations commenced, the Allies had a clear advantage in terms of economic arguments which could be used to put pressure on the Swiss: the blacklists were still in force, the Allies had control over a billion Swiss francs frozen in their countries, and Switzerland was not self-sufficient, as it depended upon trade with the Allies, in particular on food and fuel imports, for both its biological and economic survival. The Swiss needed to reconstruct their pre-war export-based economy and to achieve this goal they needed to renegotiate new trade agreements with the U.S. and the Western Allies. Therefore, taking all these factors into consideration, the Allies were most likely in the position to impose upon Switzerland "the most punitive settlement necessary"[59] to obtain the desired outcome of the Washington negotiations. However, due to the split in the ranks of the Allies and the cold war factor, which played an increasingly significant role in shifting the U.S. priorities, the final outcome of the negotiations was far from satisfactory.

The Swiss perceived the Allies, and particularly the U.S., as exercising unjust pressure upon a small neutral state, which acted in consistence with the internationally recognized obligations and rights of a neutral. Contrary to the U.S. convictions, the Allied claims to German assets in Switzerland were illegal in the light of international law and encroached on Swiss national sovereignty.

The Swiss approach hardened, as the rupture between the U.S. and the British delegations became more visible, even before the negotiations commenced. At the end of the war substantial differences in the policy approach of the Americans and the British towards the neutrals existed with respect to the gold issue and the Safehaven program. The Americans were focused on the financial blockade, whereas the British were more oriented towards sustaining a flow in the trade in goods, and they exercised a more lenient approach on the financial front, including the issue of the Reichsbank's transactions using looted gold. The British also rejected the use of economic sanctions if the neutrals would fail to consent to handing over the German assets to the Allied Control Council.[60] As the negotiations progressed, this wedge between the Allies would deepen to the advantage of the Swiss.

59 Steury, Donald P.: "The OSS…"

60 U.S. Department of State: *U.S. and Allied Efforts To Recover and Restore Gold and Other Assets Stolen or Hidden by Germany During World War II…*, pp. 63–64.

2.4.1 The Issue of Looted Gold During Washington Negotiations

The fact that the Germans looted gold on a massive scale to cover their international payments was well known during World War II. The certainty of the Allies on this issue was derived from both intelligence sources and pure mathematical calculation. The Reichsbank was known for its small official gold reserves estimated at around 40 tons and even after taking into account the gold reserves confiscated by the Germans from Austria (88 tons) and Czechoslovakia (30 tons) the total amount could not account for the amounts of gold sold via the Swiss National Bank alone (345 tons).[61]

The Allies issued two warning declarations, one on January 5, 1943, and one on February 22, 1944, alerting all neutral states against accepting looted assets, including looted gold, and reinforcing this admonishment with a threat of reclaiming these assets without the possibility of compensation.

There were other warning signs to Switzerland with respect to the provenance of the German gold. In November 1939, the National Bank of Belgium deposed more than 200 tons of Belgian gold reserves for safekeeping at the Bank of France. The gold was moved by the French to Dakar in French West Africa, but in 1940 the Vichy government succumbed to German pressure and formally gained custody over the Belgian gold, but not its ownership.

The gold was transferred back to Marseilles from Africa[62] and by the end of May 1942 it found its way to the vaults of the Reichsbank in Berlin. In September 1942, this gold was requisitioned by the German government. The Reichsbank proposed a symbolic compensation in Reichsmarks to the Bank of Belgium, but this was refused. The Bank of France declared legal responsibility for the lost Belgian gold. In August 1943, the wartime governor of the Bank of France travelled to Switzerland with the aim to alert the Swiss National Bank and the Bank of International Settlements on the issue of Belgian gold and to warn that if any such gold were to be found in the possession of these institutions, or passed through their hands, the Bank of France would have claims against them for restitution.

Thomas McKittrick, the President of the Bank of International Settlements claimed to be certain that the deliveries of the Reichsbank gold were legitimate,

61 Toniolo, Gianni/Clement, Piet: *Central Bank Cooperation at the Bank for International Settlements, 1930–1973*. Cambridge University Press: Cambridge 2005, p. 249.

62 See Ibid., pp. 249–250, for a suspenseful account of the fate of Belgian gold which was transported back to Europe by means of train, boat, truck, camel and plane from Kayes to Bamako, on the Niger river, then Timbuktu and Gao, crossing the Sahara, then by train to Algiers and on board a plane to Marseilles.

since all the gold from Germany had the marks of the Prussian Mint and therefore could not have been in the possession of the Belgians. The General Manager of the BIS, Roger Auboin expressed his doubts, but to no avail.[63] Meanwhile, as the meetings in Switzerland took place, in Germany, the Belgian gold was delivered to the Prussian Mint, melted down and formed into new bars with the official seal of the Prussian Mint, with false dates from the prewar period ranging from between 1934 and 1939. The Belgian gold was used for German external payments, whereby 109 tons were deposited in the Reichsbank's gold deposit with the Swiss National Bank.[64]

The Swiss accepted German gold until a few weeks before the German surrender, as opposed to a more cautious policy followed by other neutrals.

After the war the Americans took hold of the records of the Reichsbank and the Prussian Mint and obtained evidence that Germany used gold looted from occupied countries, but also from private citizens, including concentration camp victims, to settle its wartime payments. This "victim" gold was melted down together with monetary gold and formed new bars.[65]

In relation to the trade in Belgian gold, a French memorandum of March 15, 1944 pointed to the fact that the Swiss National bank did not apply the most basic precautions in dealing with the Reichsbank, when at the time of the gold transfers it was already common knowledge that Germany had exhausted its gold and silver reserves. The Allies could not have possibly acknowledged the legality of these Reichsbank deliveries and gold transactions and were interested in reaching an agreement with the Swiss with respect to the restitution of the looted gold.[66]

It was obvious to the Allies that Germany had sold more gold than it possessed before the war. However, determining the exact origin and quantities of the Reichsbank's looted gold deposits proved to be quite a challenge. The Allies applied simple mathematics to progress with this issue. The discrepancy between the Reichsbank's own gold holdings and the de facto gold sales was taken as a measure of the looted gold to calculate Allied claims. Based on the accounts of the Reichsbank and the interrogation of Emil Puhl, who was responsible for orchestrating the gold transactions, the Americans estimated the gold imports from Germany to Switzerland in the period from June 1940 until the end of

---

63 Ibid., p. 250.

64 Ibid., p. 251.

65 Ibid., p. 251.

66 Durrer, Marco: *Die schweizerisch*, p. 269.

the war to amount to $391 million.[67] On June 30, 1940, the gold reserves of the Reichsbank totaled at most $232 million. After subtracting the gold looted from Austria and Czechoslovakia – $49 million in total and taking account of the gold purchases from the Soviet Union – $23 million, the true gold reserves of the Reichsbank equaled $206 million. From the difference between $391 million and $206 million a sum of $185 million was calculated as the minimum amount of looted gold acquired by the Swiss in the course of World War II.[68]

The Department of Treasury pointed out that this sum referred only to documented, traceable quantities, and was therefore underestimated to the advantage of the Swiss. The share of looted gold in total Reichsbank gold reserves of $785 million amounted to an estimated 74%. If this rate was to be applied to the gold purchased by the Swiss ($391 million) it would result in a sum of $289 million. The Department of Treasury advised the U.S. negotiators to demand a transfer of $185 million from the Swiss. The claim with respect to $289 million was considered by the Department of Treasury to be reasonable. If the Swiss would challenge these numbers, they would be requested to make the accounts of the Swiss National Bank available for verification.[69]

Alfred Hirs, Member of the Governing Board of the SNB, who represented SNB in Washington, repeatedly emphasized during the negotiations that the Swiss had nothing to do with German looted gold, and according to the information in possession of the SNB two thirds of the Belgian gold were to be found in the U.S. and one third in France. Hirs justified the gold trade of the SNB explaining that the Swiss political neutrality prevented the SNB from refusing to purchase German gold, when at the same time it purchased gold from the Allies.[70] The Swiss delegation claimed, that since 1943 the representatives of the Reichsbank assured the Swiss that the supplies delivered to Switzerland originated from the pre-war period.[71]

67 Ibid., p. 269.

68 Ibid., p. 270.

69 Ibid., p. 270.

70 The gold the Swiss purchased from the Allies was of legitimate provenance, contrary to the German gold.

71 In fact, already in 1941 the authorities at the SNB were well aware that Germany was in possession of looted gold, after 1943 it was clear that the Reichsbank deliveries include gold form occupied countries, but the SN B preferred to continue a policy of "Business as usual". See Independent Commission of Experts Switzerland – Second World War: *Switzerland and Gold Transactions…*, p. 192.

At this point, the allied negotiators referred to the statement made by Puhl during his interrogation, where he admitted that the Reichsbank never provided any explicit guarantees that it was not selling Belgian gold, or gold taken from occupied countries and that the SNB and particularly "the second man after Weber" (which clearly pointed to Hirs) knew that the gold provided to the SNB could have at least partially been of Belgian origin.[72]

Both Puhl's statement and the issue of the Belgian gold were exploited as the key arguments in the negotiations with the Swiss in Washington.[73]

After the first round of negotiations, the head of the Federal Department of Foreign Affairs[74] and of the Swiss delegation to Washington, Walter Stucki, travelled to Bern to discuss the situation with the Swiss government. By this time, it was clear to the Swiss that the issue of German assets in Switzerland was directly connected to the problem of SNB gold transactions and the amount of compensation for these transactions, which the Swiss were prepared to pay, and the Allies were ready to accept.[75]

Stucki came back to Washington on April 10, 1946 with a memorandum which he presented to the Allied delegates. The memorandum was the result of his consultations with the Bundesrat and emphasized again that there was no legal basis for the liquidation of the German assets in Switzerland and that the Swiss National Bank could not be reproached for dealing in German gold. However, Switzerland was ready to make concessions if the Swiss assets in the U.S. would be unblocked. Also, out of international solidarity, Switzerland was prepared to contribute to the reconstruction of Europe. The Bundesrat authorized the Swiss delegation to offer the Allies up to 50% of the proceeds from the

72 Ibid., p. 187.

73 The Washington negotiations were noteworthy in the respect that the U.S. diplomacy could in their course for the first-time resort to intelligence reporting to such an extent. The U.S. was in control of the Reichsbank's archives and the files of the German Foreign Office, as well as the intelligence gathered by field agents as part of the Safehaven reporting. For an analysis of the U.S. intelligence effort in the course of the Safehaven policy implementation see Steury, Donald P.: "The OSS…"

74 The Federal Department of Foreign Affairs "represents Switzerland abroad". It is one of the seven Departments of the Swiss Federal Council and corresponds in its range of tasks to the Ministry of Foreign Affairs in other countries. See Federal Council: "The Federal Department of Foreign Affairs (FDFA)", retrieved 29.09.2016, from https://www.admin.ch/gov/en/start/departments/department-foreign-affairs-fdfa.html.

75 For detailed accounts of the Washington negotiations with respect to the gold issue Durrer, Marco: *Die schweizerisch*, pp. 268–274.

liquidation of German assets and in case of the gold issue, a compensation of up to 250 million Swiss francs ($58 million) for the purpose of financing the reconstruction of Europe.[76]

The Swiss Bundesrat admitted that only the warning of the Allies of February 24, 1944 could be used against Switzerland in the gold issue. The Bundesrat would have claimed it to be a success if the Germans should remain unoffended in Switzerland. Even though Switzerland expected to win a case in front of the International Court of Justice both in relation to the German assets and in relation to the gold issue, the Swiss were weary of the American reaction and of risking the appropriation of the Swiss gold in the U.S., as well as the drawbacks of a potential lawsuit in front of the U.S. courts. Stucki admitted that the Swiss were deceived by Puhl, but nevertheless claimed that their behavior was credulous.[77] Confronted with the statement of the former Reichsbank Vice President, the Swiss questioned the credibility of the information provided by Puhl, on the grounds that the Swiss were not present during his interrogation.[78]

From mid-April the negotiations between the parties took on the form of an exchange of memoranda and letters.

In the exchanged documents the issue of gold was predominant, and the Allies finally stated that there was no point to further exchange memoranda if the Swiss would not make a definitive statement with respect to the looted gold. The Swiss in turn asserted, that the term "looted property" is not determined in any way and were outraged about the allied accusations and pressure exercised upon them.[79] Stucki replied that the Swiss could not possibly respond to claims which were based on facts which came to light only after the war.[80] The Swiss

76 Ibid., p. 275.

77 Ibid., pp. 276–277.

78 U.S. Department of State: *U.S. and Allied Efforts To Recover and Restore Gold and Other Assets Stolen or Hidden by Germany During World War II…*, p. 73.

79 Durrer, Marco: *Die schweizerisch*, p. 278.

80 Interestingly, the information that the gold purchased by the SNB from the Nazis might be looted was included in a letter to the Swiss government, from October 9, 1943. In the letter the SNB Governing Board briefed the Federal Council on its trade with the Reichsbank and pointed to an advice passed by senior U.S. officials to Rudolph Pfenninger the representative of the SNB in New York that the Reichsbank gold might be looted property and that the SNB could not claim to have been acting in good faith. This information, however, did not alert or raise the suspicion of Swiss authorities. See Vogler, Robert: *The Swiss National Bank's gold transactions with the German Reichsbank from 1939 to 1945*. Swiss National Bank, 1984, retrieved 08.01.2017, from http://

compensation offer during this round of negotiations was always limited to 100 million Swiss francs (despite the internally agreed limit of 250 million).

The negotiations came to an impasse. A threat of a breakdown was imminent and did in fact happen on April 23. The Allies demanded $130 million (559 million Swiss francs) compensation and 1/3 of the German assets. The Swiss delegation left the negotiating room.[81] Finally, Stucki decided to present the final offer to the allied side: 250 million Swiss francs – approximately $58 million.[82] On May 8, the Americans relented. The French protested against the solution. They disagreed with the concept, that as a result of the Swiss settlement payment the central banks of the allied countries should relinquish all claims to the gold looted from Belgium and other occupied countries. However, pressured by the U.S. the French reluctantly accepted the compromise.[83]

During the Washington negotiations the U.S. delegation raised the matter of "heirless" claims. These were mainly assets, which belonged to persons who had perished during the war, without leaving any known heirs. The U.S. proposed to use these assets for the relief and resettlement of survivors, or their successors. The Swiss vehemently rejected this proposal since it would constitute an obvious violation of banking secrecy and suggested instead to settle the matter by preparing a diplomatic letter which would include a commitment to a "sympathetic consideration"[84] with respect to the disposition of the heirless assets. Unwilling to jeopardize the arduously achieved prospective conclusion, the U.S. side consented to this proposal.[85] In the letters exchanged between the parties, which later became part of the Washington Accord framework, it was stated that the Swiss government would examine the possibility of placing the proceeds of property of heirless victims of German aggression, which were to be found in Switzerland, at the disposal of the Allies for relief and rehabilitation purposes.[86]

---

www.snb.ch/en/mmr/reference/snb_gold_ww2_vogler/source/snb_gold_ww2_vogler.en.pdf.

81 Durrer, Marco: *Die schweizerisch*, p. 280.

82 Ibid., p. 283.

83 Ibid., p. 285.

84 This term is used by Seymour Rubin, one of the members of the U.S. Delegation during the Washington negotiations in his recollection of the events. See Rubin, Seymour J.: "The Washington Accord Fifty Years Later: Neutrality, Morality, and International Law". American University International Law Review 14, No. 1, 1998, p. 68.

85 Ibid., pp. 68–69.

86 U.S. Department of State: "Report by Mr. Randolph Paul Concerning Allied – Swiss Negotiations on German External Assets in Switzerland. Section V, Final Agreement: Washington, June 3, 1946". In: *Foreign Relations of the United States, 1946, the*

2.4.2 The Provisions of the Washington Accord

Following these arduous negotiations, the final agreement was signed on May 25, 1946. It consisted of an Accord, an Annex, which specified the provisions of the accord, a gentlemen's agreement, and an exchange of letters between the Swiss Delegation and the Allied Delegations.[87] Together, these documents are sometimes referred to more formally as the Washington Accord (or Washington Agreement). The Accord entered into force on June 27, 1946.

The Washington Accord aimed to regulate three major issues: the acquisition of gold by the Swiss National Bank from the German Reichsbank, the status of German assets in Switzerland and the abolition of wartime economic restrictions, which the Allies implemented against Switzerland.

There were four main provisions to the Washington Agreement: first, German assets in Switzerland were to be identified and liquidated by the Swiss, second, the liquidation proceeds were to be equally divided between the Allies and the Swiss, whereby the Allied share was to be turned over to the Inter-Allied Reparations Agency for the rehabilitation of Europe, third, Switzerland agreed to contribute \$58.1 million in gold as compensation for the gold looted from occupied countries by Germany and sold via Swiss banks, this gold was to be placed in a gold pool, as established by the Paris Reparations Agreement, and distributed among the countries from which gold was looted, fourth, the Allies agreed to cease blacklisting Swiss companies and the U.S. committed to releasing Swiss assets blocked in the United States. An annex to the Agreement provided that the Allies were allowed to immediately draw up to \$12 million from their share of the liquidated assets, which would be used for the rehabilitation and resettlement of non-repatriable victims of Nazi Germany, this in fact referred predominantly to stateless Jews.[88]

In the course of the negotiations, the heads of the Allies' delegation demanded an amount of \$130 million, the equivalent of 560 million Swiss francs, as a

British Commonwealth, Western and Central Europe, Volume V. U.S. Government Printing Office: Washington, D.C. 1969. Office of the Historian Website, retrieved 17.12.2016, from https://history.state.gov/historicaldocuments/frus1946v05/d140.

87 Ibid.

88 U.S. Congress, House of Representatives: *The Eizenstat Report and Related Issues Concerning United States and Allied Efforts to Restore Gold and Other Assets Looted by Nazis During World War II: Hearing Before the Committee on Banking and Financial Services*, 105th Congress, 1st Session, 25.06.1997, U.S. Government Printing Office: Washington, D.C. 1997, p. 82.

minimal compensation for the looted gold and two thirds of the funds acquired through the liquidation of the German assets. The Swiss delegation reiterated with an offer for SFr 250 million in gold (equivalent to $58 million) and half of the proceeds from the liquidation of German assets[89] and this Swiss proposal was finally accepted.

As regards the German assets, the Swiss Compensation Office was assigned the task of liquidating German property in Switzerland. The Germans whose property was liquidated were entitled to compensation in German currency. A Joint Commission composed of Allied representatives was to participate in the liquidation procedure. The liquidated assets were to be divided between Switzerland and the Allies, with each party receiving 50% of the proceeds. The U.S. committed to unblock Swiss assets in the U.S. and the Allies would discontinue blacklisting of Swiss entities.

The agreement was a partial success for the Swiss negotiators with respect to banking secrecy laws. On the one hand, the Swiss proposal to make a complete census of German assets located in Switzerland or in the hands of Swiss companies and subsequently to expropriate them anonymously was rejected.[90] The Swiss banks were instead obliged to disclose the names of the German asset holders and to communicate them to the Allies, and thereby to violate Swiss banking secrecy. On the other hand, however, Switzerland managed to secure that a Swiss-controlled organ, the Swiss Compensation Office, should carry out the liquidation of German property. Additionally, a provision of the Agreement pertaining to the release of Swiss assets held and frozen in the U.S. made no mention of an obligatory disclosure of the names of the asset holders, thereby fulfilling the secrecy provisions in line with the Swiss banking law and custom. This was an issue of major importance for the Swiss negotiating party.[91]

The signing of the Washington Accord marked the beginning of the post war period for the Swiss, since with this settlement the U.S. – Allied economic warfare against Switzerland finally came to an end.[92]

The Washington Agreement was perceived in the U.S. press as being too easy on both the Germans and the Swiss, since too much German property was allowed to remain under Swiss control.[93] In Switzerland, the Accord, which had

89 Meier, Heinz K.: *Friendship Under Stress…*, p. 360.
90 Guex, Sébastien: "The Origins…", p. 263.
91 Ibid., p. 264.
92 Durrer, Marco: *Die schweizerisch*, p. 287.
93 Ibid., p. 289.

to be approved by the Parliament, was broadly criticized for being too large a concession. Finally, following a vehement public and parliamentarian debate the agreement was ratified by the Swiss National Council on June 26, 1946.[94]

2.4.3 Fulfillment of the Washington Accord

Two days after the signing of the Accord the U.S. lifted the freezing order on Swiss public assets. This facilitated the acceptance of the treaty in the Swiss parliamentary process.[95] The unfreezing of private assets was a more complicated issue, it was executed only gradually, and led to further conflicts between the U.S. and Switzerland.

The Americans distinguished between operating (industrial) and non-operating (financial) corporations. In the case of Swiss holding companies with German equity participation, which invested their money in the U.S., their assets could be unfrozen only if the German share was identified and transferred to a U.S. blocked account. This procedure prevented the German shares to be liquidated in line with the Washington Agreement, which ascertained that half of German assets liquidated in Switzerland would fall under Swiss discretion. In addition, in case of holding companies the German share could not exceed 5% and in case of financial companies 25%. Leading Swiss companies such as Aluminum, Bally or Nestlé were classified as non-operating companies. Such sanctions were not part of the Washington Agreement and the custodial conflict over sequestered assets embittered the U.S.-Swiss relations in the 1950s.[96] A prominent example of this conflict over unfreezing of private assets blocked in the U.S. was the Interhandel Affair. General Aniline and Film, the American subsidiary of Interhandel, which was seized by the Department of Treasury fell under these special measures. The Interhandel Affair, which strained U.S.-Swiss relations well into the post-war period will be discussed in detail.

The Washington Agreement specified that the Swiss contribute to the allied gold pool 250 million Swiss francs ($58.1 million) in gold. In 1946, the Swiss Legation informed the U.S. State Department that it was prepared to pay 50,807 kilograms of gold to settle its obligation, however this amount was 800 kilograms

---

94 Meier, Heinz K.: *Friendship Under Stress…*, pp. 365–366.

95 See Castelmur, Linus von: *Schweizerisch – Allierte Finanzbeziehungen im Übergang vom Zweiten Weltkrieg zum Kalten Krieg. Die Deutschen Guthaben in der Schweiz zwischen Zwangsliquidierung und Freigabe 1945–1952.* Chronos: Zürich 1992, p. 123 for a discussion of this issue.

96 Durrer, Marco: *Die schweizerisch*, pp. 303–304.

short of the required weight in gold, which would equal to $1 million short of the agreed amount of $58,1 million. The Swiss devalued the Swiss franc to 4,920 per fine kilo of gold instead of employing the value used for transactions in the exchanges in London and New York. The Swiss suggested an arbitration of the gold value of the Swiss franc and refused to employ the official rate of exchange set by the markets in the major financial centers.[97]

In 1947, Switzerland finally deposited the lump sum of 250 million Swiss francs in gold to the Allied Reparations Fund, without recognizing any legal basis for the Allied claims, and declaring instead its willingness to contribute its share to the reconstruction of Europe, thereby circumventing and further refuting the validity of the concept of looted gold.[98]

The U.S. government unfroze the assets of the Swiss Government and the Swiss National Bank already in May 1946, in the same month that the Agreement was reached. The wartime economic sanctions against Switzerland were lifted completely by 1948. However, the provisions concerning the liquidation of German assets were never carried out. According to the Washington Agreement, the German owners were to be compensated for their assets, although in the course of negotiations the Allied side demanded a liquidation of these assets without any compensation. The German assets were to be sold in Swiss francs, and the German owners compensated in German currency. Unfortunately, the rate of exchange for this conversion had not been determined by the Washington negotiations, and the dispute over this issue delayed the fulfillment of the settlement by a few years.

The Swiss refused to begin liquidating German assets without prior establishment of a "fair" Reichsmark-Swiss franc exchange rate, which would ensure that the Germans facing expropriation in Switzerland would be adequately indemnified. The Allies, on the other hand, perceived the issue as a purely formal requirement and during the negotiations referred to the decision of the Allied Control Council in Berlin to establish the procedures for the compensation of the Germans.

Following the ratification of the Accord in parliament, the Swiss demanded to fix a fair exchange rate prior to commencing the liquidation procedure, whereas the Allies called for prompt action and suggested determining the exchange rate

---

97 U.S. Department of State: *U.S. and Allied Efforts To Recover and Restore Gold and Other Assets Stolen or Hidden by Germany During World War II...*, p. 98.

98 Meier, Heinz K.: *Friendship Under Stress...*, p. 361.

retroactively.[99] As the process of liquidation of German assets in Switzerland lagged on, the U.S. pointed out that the establishment of an exchange rate was not a prerequisite set forth in the Washington Accord or during the preceding negotiations. The Swiss argued that they could not act like the Poles or the Czechs and nationalize assets without establishing a prior indemnification. The U.S., in response, proposed to set an exchange rate equal to that which was used in the German-Swiss clearing during the war, and the rate at which German property was acquired in Switzerland: 173 Swiss francs to 100 Reichsmarks. This rate of exchange was four times lower in terms of Reichsmarks than the parity proposed by the Swiss: 100 Reichsmarks equal to 43 Swiss francs.

The U.S., annoyed by the delay, suggested to issue an inter-allied diplomatic note stating the common position on the exchange rate issue, but the French refused to join this effort and expressed support for the Swiss position on both the exchange rate and the need to establish it before the liquidation process would begin. The breach in allied unity on the exchange rate issue further delayed the fulfillment of the Agreement and the Allies realized that they in fact had a limited impact on the Swiss, since the assets in question were deposited in Swiss banks and were under the sole discretion of the Swiss authorities.[100] The Allied Control Council in Berlin refused the preferential treatment of German creditors in Switzerland in terms of the indemnification process, pointing to legal, economic and political problems. The payment of such hefty sums would strain the German budget and could lead to inflationary pressure. In addition, the Soviet side insisted on settling the issue of German reparations, before deciding on the compensation of German external assets. At this point the provisions of the Washington Accord contradicted the allied policy with respect to Germany.[101]

In May of 1947, the U.S. prompted the Swiss to begin liquidating German assets independently of the issue of the exchange rate, threatening with a negative press campaign against Switzerland, but the Swiss were left unimpressed, pointing out in their answer that the Agreement was signed with three parties, the U.S., the U.K. and France and not merely with the United States. The French stood side by side with the Swiss on the exchange rate issue, which would have to be settled, before any other steps were undertaken. The French supported the concept of implementing the clearing exchange rate of 100 RM = 173 SFr for the

99 See Castelmur, Linus von: *Schweizerisch…*, pp. 161–166 for a detailed analysis of this issue.

100 Ibid., pp. 165–166.

101 Ibid., pp. 169–171.

purpose of indemnification of German asset owners. The other two allied parties to the Washington Agreement finally accepted the French proposal and a diplomatic note was issued to the Swiss, proclaiming this Swiss-German clearing rate as the provisional rate for the indemnification, until a market rate of exchange would be established in Germany.

The joint allied proposal was refused by the Swiss on the ground that an exchange rate could not be unilaterally fixed. After further debate, the British and the French were finally willing to accept the Swiss proposal of the Truppenkurs/Militärkurs of 100RM = 43 SFr. However, in the meantime the U.S. lost its faith in the feasibility of the Accord and a reorientation of the U.S. policy was about to take its course.[102]

In 1947 and 1948, the U.S. proposed a renegotiation of the Agreement with the Swiss, threatening with a withdrawal of the U.S. from the obligations of the Paris Reparations Agreement. The liquidation of German assets in Switzerland was supposed to be left to the sole discretion of the Swiss and in return for the complete withdrawal of the Allies from the process the U.S. demanded the 50% share, that is 250 million Swiss francs. This unilateral U.S. proposal was rejected by Great Britain and France, which were both convinced that any attempt at renegotiating the Agreement would lead to further delays and excuses on the part of the Swiss.[103]

The liquidation of German property in Switzerland in line with the Washington Accord pertained to all German assets, including Jewish property. This would mean that also survivors of Nazi death camps would lose access to their assets. As has been mentioned, during the Washington negotiations the U.S. secured an informal "gentlemen's agreement" that such assets would be an exception and these assets would be released by the Swiss. However, despite repeated U.S. enquiries, the Swiss Compensation Office denied requests for exemption on the grounds that the owners were persecutees.[104]

The Washington Accord provided that the Allies could draw up to 50 million Swiss francs against the Swiss share of the money obtained from the liquidation of German property for the rehabilitation and resettlement of non-repatriable victims of Nazi Germany, mainly Jewish refugees. The Swiss delayed making the

---

102 For a detailed analysis of the exchange rate debate see Castelmur, Linus von: *Schweizerisch...*, pp. 172–180.

103 U.S. Department of State: *U.S. and Allied Efforts To Recover and Restore Gold and Other Assets Stolen or Hidden by Germany During World War II...*, pp. 95–98.

104 Ibid., pp. 102–103.

funds available and finally, pressured by the U.S., made an advance payment of 20 million Swiss francs in 1948. The Swiss justified their refusal in providing the funds by quoting the delay in the liquidation of German assets and the unresolved custodial conflicts with the American authorities. Only in 1953 did the Swiss advance another due amount – 13 million Swiss francs, as part of their final overall settlement. In total, the Swiss contributed 33 million Swiss francs to the cause. But in the modified Allied – Swiss agreement signed in 1952 the Swiss lump sum payment of 121.5 million Swiss francs ($28.3 million USD) to the Allies as compensation for the German assets was reduced by the sum of the 1948 advance of 20 million Swiss francs ($4.7 million USD).[105]

Since 1947, the Swiss brought up the "intercustodial" conflict with the U.S. as an impediment for liquidating German assets in Switzerland. The conflict concerned the Swiss demand to release assets blocked in the U.S. and considered as Nazi property during the war, which the Swiss claimed as their own.

As the fulfillment of the Accord was continuously delayed, in 1948, at the initiative of the U.S. the Allies met in Paris to discuss their position with respect to Switzerland. As a result of this meeting the Allies presented the Swiss with a strongly worded note, urging them to fulfill their obligations under the Washington Accord, including the request for an advanced payment of 100 million Swiss francs for reparations and 20 million Swiss francs for the refugee fund. The Swiss replied to this by asking the Allies whether they were able to guarantee the compensation provisions of the agreement and proposed to submit the issue of the liquidation of German assets to the court of arbitration.[106]

This cat and mouse game went on for another couple of years.

The U.S. proposed an Allied – Swiss conference to discuss all the outstanding issues of the Agreement. The conference was held in 1949 but failed to produce results.[107] The Allies insisted that the assets belonging to creditors from the soviet occupation zone would have to be liquidated along with other German assets in Switzerland. However, the Swiss maintained that since the Allies could not guarantee that the Germans in the Eastern occupation zone would be adequately indemnified, these assets would have to continue to be blocked.[108] Another issue which emerged during the conference was the intercustodial question, namely

105 Ibid., pp. 99–101.

106 See Castelmur, Linus von: *Schweizerisch…*, pp. 189–201 for detailed analysis.

107 U.S. Department of State: *U.S. and Allied Efforts To Recover and Restore Gold and Other Assets Stolen or Hidden by Germany During World War II…*, pp. 106–107.

108 Castelmur, Linus von: *Schweizerisch…*, p. 221.

the issue of the liquidation of German property in other countries, which was raised by the Swiss and overshadowed the issue of the exchange rate. As part of the Safehaven policy the Allied countries engaged in the blocking and seizure of German external assets which, by the provisions of the Paris Agreement on Reparations of January 14, 1946, they were entitled to dispose of and charge against their reparation share.[109] As regards assets such as property, shares and other tangible assets which belonged directly and unambiguously to Germans in Germany, no doubts existed. However, in case of complex holding structures, where the German ownership was concealed or involved third country structures, the answer to the question which country was responsible for the liquidation of these assets was much less straightforward. The issue of finding a solution to this intercustodial conflict was now elevated by the Swiss to a precondition of proceeding with the liquidation of the German assets. The Allies insisted that this ought to be solved within the scope of bilateral negotiations and this procedure in turn led to further delays.

The parties met again in Bern in June 1950. In the preliminary talks, the Swiss explicitly linked their willingness to consent to any agreement on the outstanding issues to a settlement with the U.S. on the intercustodial conflict. The U.S. delegation left Bern before the conference resumed, convinced that the Swiss side had no intention to actually implement the Washington Agreement.[110]

The Swiss repeatedly insisted on the release by the U.S. Office of Alien Property Custodian $15 to $50 million worth of assets, claiming that the companies which owned these assets were no longer controlled by Germany, or never actually had been. The U.S. opposed this request stating that German assets in the U.S. were never covered by the provisions of the Agreement.[111]

The U.S. contemplated withdrawing from the Agreement but finally proposed a resumption of Allied – Swiss discussions. The conference resumed in March 1951. During the negotiations a consensus was reached on a number of issues, including the Reichsmark-Swiss franc exchange rate for the liquidation of German property in Switzerland. The Swiss confirmed their unwillingness to grant exemption from liquidation to persecutees.[112]

---

109 See Article 6 of the "Agreement on Reparation from Germany, on the Establishment of an Inter-Allied Reparation Agency and on the Restitution of Monetary Gold" opened for signature at Paris, 14.01.1946, United Nations Treaty Series, No. 8105.

110 U.S. Department of State: *U.S. and Allied Efforts To Recover and Restore Gold and Other Assets Stolen or Hidden by Germany During World War II…*, p. 109.

111 Ibid., p. 118.

112 Ibid., pp. 111–114.

The Swiss were determined to reach a settlement on the German wartime debts on the bilateral clearing account, which amounted to 1.2 billion Swiss francs ($275 million) and were guaranteed by the blocked German assets in Switzerland. In February 1952, the Allies finally agreed to direct German-Swiss negotiations, in pursuit of reaching a final conclusion on the fulfillment of the Washington Agreement.

During the Washington negotiations the most important priority for the Allies was to liquidate German assets and make the proceeds obtained from the liquidation of those assets available for reparations. The provisions of the Agreement pertaining to the compensation of the German owners in their own currency were only a concession made towards the Swiss and the Allies failed to clearly specify the precise procedure to be followed in this respect, both during the negotiations, and in the text of the treaty. The Swiss in turn adhered to a precise and legalistic implementation of the Agreement. The reputation of the Swiss financial center could be called into question if the rule of law pertaining to the protection of private property would be violated. Therefore the issue of indemnification of German owners became the main hindrance in the fulfilment of the Agreement and superseded the economic interest of Switzerland resulting from the participation in the liquidation proceeds, 50% of which accrued to Switzerland in line with the Agreement.[113] By 1948, the Swiss came up with a new argument to delay the implementation of the Washington Agreement and used the leverage of the fulfillment of its provisions to exert pressure on the U.S. to free Swiss assets blocked in the U.S. by the 1941 freezing order. As the cold war antagonisms developed, the Swiss refused to liquidate assets belonging to residents of East Germany on the grounds, that their owners could not be adequately compensated. The scope of application of the treaty was thus narrowed down to West Germany. And time was on the side of the Swiss. By prolonging the liquidation of German assets, the Swiss were able to take advantage of a new political constellation, which gradually emerged after the war.

In the beginning of the 1950s, the increasing importance of the economic rehabilitation of Germany in the face of the Cold War contributed to moderating the approach of the U.S. government towards the issue of German assets in Switzerland and the fulfillment of the Washington Agreement. The European Recovery Program devised by the U.S. included West Germany and stood in direct opposition to the concept of liquidation of foreign German assets. With the advancement of the Cold War Switzerland was being increasingly perceived as

113 Castelmur, Linus von: *Schweizerisch...*, p. 399 and p. 408.

an ally, due to its maintenance of free democratic institutions in Europe and its determination to defend its territory against any potential aggression. In this respect, the small neutral Alpine country contributed to hindering the expansion of Soviet influence in Western Europe.

In a State Department policy paper on Switzerland, of August 1950, the Swiss contribution to the European economic recovery was emphasized and the Washington Agreement in turn was criticized for causing "difficulties" in the U.S. relations with Switzerland "disproportionate to the intrinsic importance of the matter."[114] In 1951, a U.S. National Security Council Staff Study further emphasized the changing attitude towards Switzerland: "By virtue of its geographic position Switzerland is of strategic importance to the defense of Western Europe and therefore of security interest to the United States."[115] The Study pointed to the military strength of Switzerland and advocated closer Swiss military cooperation with the Allies. The reversal of U.S. policy objectives, increasingly shaped by the Cold War, resulted in a more lenient approach with respect to the Swiss implementation of the Treaty's provisions towards the end of the 1940s and in the beginning of the 1950s, and facilitated the Swiss pursuit of a complete revision of the Washington Agreement.

Eventually, the Washington Agreement was replaced by three separate agreements: two signed on August 26, 1952 between Switzerland and Germany and one signed two days later between Switzerland and the Allies. The first two treaties regulated the financing of the redemption sum paid out to the Allies and the Swiss claims against Germany. By means of the third treaty Switzerland agreed to pay the Allies a lump sum of 121.5 million Swiss francs, instead of the sum which would be collected from the liquidation of the German assets. From this amount the 20 million Swiss francs advance payment to the International Refugee Organization was subtracted. The lump sum paid to the Allies was in

---

114 U.S. Department of State: "Policy Statement Prepared in the Department of State, Washington, August 17, 1950: Switzerland". In: *Foreign Relations of the United States, 1950, Western Europe, Volume III*. U.S. Government Printing Office: Washington, D.C. 1977. Office of the Historian Website, retrieved 17.12.2016, from https://history.state.gov/historicaldocuments/frus1950v03/d694.

115 U.S. Department of State: "National Security Council Staff Study: The Position of the United States With Respect to Switzerland: Washington, November 20, 1951". In: *Foreign Relations of the United States, 1951, Europe: Political and Economic Developments, Volume IV, Part 1*. U.S. Government Printing Office: Washington, D.C. 1985. Office of the Historian Website, retrieved 17.12.2016, from https://history.state.gov/historicaldocuments/frus1951v04p1/d414.

turn to be reimbursed to the Swiss by the German Federal Republic via a loan taken out with a Swiss banking consortium. The Allies accepted this solution.

Switzerland renounced its claim to the share in the liquidation funds, since the new settlement also comprehensively tackled the issue of Swiss claims against Germany – the Swiss were to receive 650 million Swiss francs from the German Federal Republic as a repayment of Germany's debts. The money was to be used for providing support to Swiss war victims. The German owners of assets in Switzerland, which exceeded the value of 10,000 Swiss francs were able to retrieve their property upon paying one-third of its value to the government of West Germany, thereby creating a fund for the compensation of the reimbursement payment by the German government. For assets valued at less than 10,000 Swiss francs and assets, which belonged to those who suffered persecution from Germany, a compensation payment by German owners was not required. East Germany did not participate in these agreements.[116]

The government of West Germany in Bonn voiced its gratefulness to the Swiss for their determined pursuit of a fair solution. In the end the Swiss managed to defend the principles of private ownership of property[117] and safeguard banking secrecy with respect to German assets in Switzerland.

The distinctiveness of the Allied Safehaven policy and the Washington Agreement was due to the fact that the reparation claims were exercised with respect not only towards the defeated belligerents but also third parties – the neutral states. The Americans perceived the close economic relationship between the Axis countries and the neutrals and the Swiss-German bank transactions as undermining the allied war effort and the allied concept of peace. The Allies criticized the neutrals for not supporting the struggle to destroy the war potential of the belligerents and for profiting from purchases of German looted gold. After the war the neutrals were therefore expected to contribute to the financial pool and to make up for their dubious behavior. However, despite the diverse positions of the Allies and the Swiss, for the most part of the negotiations the arguments provided by both sides were not determined by the question of moral principles or even legal considerations, but rather the discussion turned into a quarrel over the amount of the compensation for looted gold.

---

116 See Meier, Heinz K.: *Friendship Under Stress…*, p. 369 and U.S. Department of State: *U.S. and Allied Efforts To Recover and Restore Gold and Other Assets Stolen or Hidden by Germany During World War II…*, pp. 119–120.

117 Meier, Heinz K.: *Friendship Under Stress…*, p. 370.

At the moment of its signing in 1946, the Washington Agreement was the best possible outcome, which could have been achieved. Its failure lay in its implementation, or rather lack thereof.

From the legal point of view, the parties to the agreement, in anticipation of potential problems in its execution, attempted to resolve at least the procedural conflicts. Inherent in the 1946 document was a complicated system of arbitration, which derived from the anticipation that numerous disagreements could arise.[118] However, the aim to settle disputes finally and promptly was compromised by simultaneously providing an elaborate system of obligatory appeals.[119] Notwithstanding the legal nuances, every agreement international or not, must reflect the true willingness of the contracting parties to fulfill its provisions and this was not the case with this treaty.

Would a more effective monitoring and supervision of the implementation of the Washington Agreement have sufficed in the absence of good will? A complete and exhaustive census of German assets was never provided by the Swiss because the Swiss institutions and Swiss public were reluctant to implement the Agreement. In the absence of contractual mechanisms for its enforcement, sufficient pressure exercised by the Allies could have induced the Swiss to abide by its provisions. But with time the U.S, policy diverted strongly from its wartime standpoint. The adoption of the Marshall Plan reflected the U.S. aim to rebuild, not to eliminate German economic and industrial power.[120]

2.4.4 U.S.-Swiss Sentiments in the Aftermath of the Washington Accord

During the Washington negotiations, there was friction within the U.S. party between those judging Swiss conduct in the light of moral criteria and those supporting a broader strategy, which took into consideration long-term interstate relations. This latter approach gradually took over, as the perspective of the cold war became imminent.

---

118 King, Nat B.: "An Innovation in international Arbitral Tribunals -- The Swiss – Allied Accord". *The American Journal of International Law* 46, No. 3, July 1952, p. 481.

119 Ibid., p. 465.

120 For an analysis of the Washington Agreement along these lines see Rubin, Seymour J.: "The Washington Accord Fifty Years Later...," pp. 71–73.

The U.S. delegation perceived the Washington Agreement as an acceptable compromise, as regards the financial settlement. The Agreement also facilitated the U.S. pursuit of further negotiations with the remaining neutral states.[121]

However, the outcome of the negotiations was criticized in the U.S. by certain political circles, with Senator Harley Kilgore being one of the most prominent representatives of a tough stance of the U.S. policy with respect to the Swiss. The Senator expressed his disapproval in a protest letter to President Truman, sent on May 24, 1946 where he pointed out that Switzerland ought to have been made responsible for all of the looted gold accepted from the Nazis, the entire estimated sum of $300 million, and not merely a fifth of it. Kilgore urged the President to break the negotiations with the Swiss and bring the issue before the United Nations. Kilgore voiced his protest to no avail. The settlement as stipulated in the Washington Agreement was fully endorsed by U.S. President Truman.[122]

The reaction in the U.S. press was relatively moderate, compared to that of the press in Switzerland, where the treaty was analyzed and discussed with utmost attention.

The Swiss offered the U.S. a goodwill payment and persistently refused to acknowledge that the purchased gold was war looted. The Swiss press perceived the American stance on the issue of looted gold and German assets in Switzerland as an unfair exploitation of U.S. political strength and dominance and reported the events as a case of David versus Goliath. The Allied aim to confiscate and liquidate German assets was simply illegal since only their owners could dispose of them. The sanctity of private property was under threat from the Great Powers but Switzerland stood firm guard against any infringements of both personal rights and Swiss sovereignty.[123] The Swiss press pointed to the fact, that although the Washington Agreement violated foreign property rights and imposed a heavy economic burden upon Switzerland and amounted to a great legal injustice, it was nevertheless a necessary sacrifice, which had to be made in order to restore good political and economic relations with the Allies.[124]

121 Castelmur, Linus von: *Schweizerisch...*, p. 121.

122 U.S. Department of State: *U.S. and Allied Efforts To Recover and Restore Gold and Other Assets Stolen or Hidden by Germany During World War II...*, pp. 83–84 and Castelmur, Linus von: *Schweizerisch...*, pp. 121–122.

123 U.S. Department of State: *U.S. and Allied Efforts To Recover and Restore Gold and Other Assets Stolen or Hidden by Germany During World War II...*, p. 77.

124 For a detailed discussion of the reaction of the Swiss press to the Washington Agreement see Castelmur, Linus von: *Schweizerisch...*, pp. 104–107.

In a speech delivered by the chief Swiss negotiator, Walter Stucki, in Basel in November 1946, he accused the Allies of violating the principles embodied in the Atlantic Charter and claimed that the pressure that the U.S. exercised upon Switzerland was worse than the solicitations of Herman Göring in 1935. Stucki, who never once surrendered any moral ground during the negotiations pointed out, that Switzerland found itself in "dangerous political isolation" and in a world lacking "material and moral foundations."[125] In the light of this political situation, the country could not completely reject the Allied demands and was forced to succumb to the heavy external pressure, despite the fact, that the outcome of the negotiations, especially the contribution of 250 million Swiss francs was severely criticized in Switzerland.[126] During the Washington negotiations Stucki vigorously denied any moral or legal obligation on the part of Switzerland to return the gold purchased by the Swiss National Bank from the Germans. The Swiss contribution was to be only an act of good will.[127] His approach reflected the general sentiment in Switzerland, where the Washington Agreement was perceived as an infringement of the universal human rights to property and privacy.[128]

Moreover, the Washington Agreement was publicly criticized as a diplomatic defeat in Switzerland, a bitter bow to a superior power, since the U.S. took the lead in the tough Allied policy towards the Swiss.[129] The ratification of the Agreement was "one of the unhappiest episodes in U.S.-Swiss relations."[130]

---

125 U.S. Department of State: *U.S. and Allied Efforts To Recover and Restore Gold and Other Assets Stolen or Hidden by Germany During World War II...*, p. 87.

126 Ibid., p. 87.

127 Meier, Heinz K.: *Friendship Under Stress...*, p. 360.

128 In the 1990s, the Swiss double standards with respect to what they considered a violation of private property rights came to light when the details of a secret agreement signed in 1949 with communist Poland became known. The Swiss government traced the heirless accounts of deceased Polish citizens (most of them of Jewish decent) in Swiss financial institutions, the assets were then used to settle Swiss claims against the Swiss property confiscated in the process of the nationalization of assets in communist Poland. In this case banking secrecy did not seem to play any role and it did not hinder the Swiss authorities in any way from locating these assets and releasing them to settle any possible Swiss claims. See Korman, Edward R.: "Rewriting the Holocaust History of Swiss Banks: A Growing Scandal". In: Bazyler, Michael J./Alford Roger P. (eds.): *Holocaust Restitution. Perspectives on the Litigation and Its Legacy*. New York University Press: New York et al. 2006, pp. 115–134.

129 Meier, Heinz K.: *Friendship Under Stress...*, pp. 366–367.

130 Ibid., p. 366.

2.5 The Evaluation of Swiss Conduct During World War II in the Context of International Law: Legalism versus Morality

After 50 years from its conclusion, the Washington Agreement became the subject of intense scrutiny and was reevaluated in the 1990s, when the U.S.-Swiss conflict over Holocaust assets and dormant accounts of Jewish victims erupted. This conflict also led to an assessment of the Swiss policy with respect to Germany during World War II. The arguments in this discussion are briefly examined below.

The Allies often invoked moral arguments in their criticism of the Swiss relations with Germany during the war. However, it is worth noting that the Swiss conduct during this turbulent period is defended by Swiss and American scholars alike, using the neutrality argument.

The neutrality of Switzerland had a special foundation in international law – it was due to an international consensus that Switzerland should remain neutral and this principle was established in the form of an international declaration of the Congress of Vienna of November 20, 1815. Switzerland was recognized as "permanently neutral". Therefore, the neutrality of Switzerland was not a unilaterally assumed concept, but instead has been guaranteed by the major powers. Switzerland as a recognized neutral state was obliged to perform certain services for all the belligerents and in return was allowed to trade with them upon fulfilling certain requirements. Trade with the warring nations was generally permitted under the traditional concept of neutrality. The Hague Convention only specified that if any limitations on trade are introduced, they should not discriminate between sides and that the government is not allowed to trade with the warring parties. From a purely legal perspective the fact that the Swiss traded with the Nazis was therefore fully defendable.[131] From the perspective of the survival of the Swiss nation, it could also be regarded as inevitable, since for the most part of the war Switzerland was surrendered on all sides by the Axis powers. A mountainous country, it was not self-sufficient before the war, with half of its food supply coming from exports. The trade with Germany was therefore as indispensable to the survival of the Swiss, as Switzerland was indispensable to the German war effort. Moreover, Switzerland also traded with the Allies, admittedly to a lesser extent.

---

131 For this argument see Vagts, Detlev F.: "Switzerland, International Law and World War II". *The American Journal of International Law* 91, No. 3, July 1997, p. 469.

With the fall of France and the German advancement in the West Switzerland found itself at the disposal of Germany and faced with, if not complete annexation, then with what amounted to an imminent "economic Anschluss."[132] The trade concessions made by the Swiss and the gold transactions with the Reichsbank in particular contributed to preventing economic warfare against Switzerland in 1943.

As regards the financial dealings of the Swiss Government and Swiss banks with the German government and individuals, there was nothing inconsistent with either international law or the status of neutrality in these transactions per se. Doubts could be raised with respect to the legality of Swiss trade in gold, looted from countries occupied by Germany in the course of the war.

Article 53 of the Hague Convention follows the "to the victor belong the spoils" principle by stating that "An army of occupation can only take possession of cash, funds, and realizable securities which are strictly the property of the State."[133] Article 46 of the Convention stipulates: "Family, honor and rights, the lives of persons, and private property, as well as religious conventions and practice, must be respected. Private property cannot be confiscated."[134] In the light of Article 53 of the Hague Convention, the Swiss behavior could be excusable. However, considering the provenance of the German gold, Article 46 could raise reasonable doubts as to the legitimacy of German – Swiss gold trade and there is also the possibility of Swiss conduct falling under Article 55,[135] whereby taking the wealth of an occupied country and depriving it permanently of its resources would violate this provision. The Swiss state responsibility would be in such a case derivative of the German, and subject to Switzerland proving that it had

132 The term "L'Anschluss économique" which the Swiss managed to avoid by trading economic neutrality for state sovereignty is used by Daniel Bourgeois in Bourgeois, Daniel: *Le Troisième Reich et la Suisse 1933–1941*. Éditions de la Baconnière: Neuchatel 1974. See pp. 173–182 for a discussion of this issue.

133 See Article 53 of the "Convention (IV) Respecting the Laws and Customs of War on Land and its Annex: Regulations Concerning the Laws and Customs of War on Land" signed at The Hague, 18.10.1907, 36 Stat. 2277, Treaty Series 539.

134 See Article 46 of Ibid.

135 See Article 55 of the Hague Convention states: "The occupying State shall be regarded only as administrator and usufructuary of public buildings, real estate, forests, and agricultural estates belonging to the hostile State, and situated in the occupied country. It must safeguard the capital of these properties, and administer them in accordance with the rules of usufruct". See "Convention (IV) Respecting the Laws and Customs of War on Land and its Annex."

acted in good faith, without the knowledge of the precise origins of the gold.[136] Notwithstanding any potential doubts as regards the violations of international law with respect to the German – Swiss gold transactions which could arise, and were in fact voiced by the U.S. in the course of the debate over the role of Swiss banks in blocking the release of Holocaust assets in the 1990s, these issues were conclusively settled by the Washington Accord of 1946. And despite the sharp U.S. criticism of the Washington Accord in the 1990s, and attempts to undermine it, no legal basis exists to question its validity.[137]

Following this line of argument, it is clear that Switzerland could maintain its independence only by making significant concessions to Germany and the criticism it received for its wartime conduct is undeserved, especially since once the Allies gained higher ground, the Swiss had to succumb to their pressures accordingly.[138] The Swiss conduct during World War II was compatible with the rules of international law, whereas the issues of humanity and morality are a completely separate consideration.[139]

An opposing view is held by Gerhard L. Weinberg, who chooses to ignore the "special" status of Switzerland and points to the moral considerations as being decisive in evaluating the Swiss conduct during World War II.

Swiss neutrality during World War II was merely tolerated and exploited by the Nazis due to the prolonged war effort in the West.[140] Had the war with the West been won, the Germans would have invaded Switzerland and partitioned

---

136 The Swiss authorities obtained legal assessments from three leading experts in international law, all confirming the Swiss position that under the Hague Convention, the allies had no legal claim to German assets in Switzerland. See Fleury, Antione/Möller, Horst/Schwarz, Hans-Peter (eds.): *Die Schweiz und Deutschland 1945–1961.* Oldenbourg Verlag: München 2004, pp. 125–126. The issue was however more complicated, since the Allies could argue that the looted gold had been private property. See Vagts, Detlev F.: "Switzerland, International Law…", p. 473.

137 For an analysis of this issue see Ibid., pp. 466–475.

138 Meier, Heinz K.: *Friendship Under Stress…*, p. 292.

139 This argument is emphasized by Detlev F. Vagts also in relation to the Swiss policy with respect to refugees. Neutrals have a moral obligation to furnish shelter for refugees fleeing war and persecution. However, the Swiss authorities applied a tough stance on admitting refugees from war-torn Europe, in particular by defining refugee status as based solely on political criteria and not racial ones. The Swiss turned away thousands of Jews, and in doing so sentenced them to a certain death. As morally reprehensible as this may be, such conduct did not violate international law per se. See Vagts, Detlev F.: "Switzerland, International Law…," pp. 471–472.

140 An invasion of Switzerland was planned already in June 1940.

it with Italy within the operation Tannenbaum, in total and unconditional violation of Swiss neutrality. However, since this step was postponed, Switzerland was useful to Germany and served Hitler's purposes with its transport network, by providing certain manufactured goods and finally, as the author puts it, by "laundering stolen gold and other valuables." Weinberg criticizes Switzerland for taking the position that looting is legal and confers a legal title, meaning that such looted assets belong to the looters. He points out that had Switzerland been invaded, following their own logic, the Swiss could hardly invoke any legal objections to the "re-looting" of their assets by the Germans.[141] The fact is that the Allies and countries of occupied Europe, in whose interest the Allies acted, suffered huge loss of life, impoverishment, humiliation and military casualties, whereas "Switzerland emerged in 1945 as one of the wealthiest countries in the world with burgeoning trade and gold reserves far surpassing its totals for 1938."[142] This stark contrast in the economic and physical wellbeing, and the fact that the Swiss acted as the principal bankers and financial brokers to the Germans during World War II, rendered the Allied cause to recover and restore gold stolen by Germany and use it together with other German assets deposited in Switzerland for the reconstruction of postwar Europe, as well as for the relief of the non-repatriable victims of Nazism, predominantly Jews, a higher moral legitimization than that, which could be awarded to the juridical considerations of the Swiss.

The argument that during the war the Allies sold more gold to the Swiss National Bank than the Germans was also put forward in defense of the Swiss conduct. The U.S. alone sold 2.242 million Swiss francs worth of gold to the SNB. However, the majority of the U.S. gold sales were executed from mid-1944, that is only when the defeat of the Nazi power became imminent and as opposed to gold purchases from Germany, the Gold acquired form the Allies was exclusively legal. The gold transactions between Switzerland, the U.S. and Great Britain were part of international capital movements and served to finance Swiss exports, and the gold so acquired was used by the Allies to fulfill humanitarian duties and to pay for the Allied war effort.[143]

---

141 See Weinberg, Gerhard L.: "German Plans and Policies Regarding Neutral Nations in World War II with Special Reference to Switzerland". *German Studies Review* 22, No. 1, February 1999, pp. 99–103.

142 U.S. Department of State: *U.S. and Allied Efforts To Recover and Restore Gold and Other Assets Stolen or Hidden by Germany During World War II…*, p. 62.

143 Independent Commission of Experts Switzerland – Second World War: *Switzerland and Gold Transactions…*, p. 193.

Swiss historian, Antoine Fleury takes the view that the various economic measures undertaken by the U.S. and its Allies exacerbated the overall position in which Switzerland found itself, surrounded by Axis countries and dependent upon them for its survival, both political and physical. In this broader geopolitical context, the U.S. policy which was aimed at cutting all economic ties between Switzerland and Germany in fact contributed to making the small non self-sufficient Alpine country even more contingent on its powerful belligerent neighbor.[144] The "economic trump card"[145] which the Swiss could play with respect to Germany, namely the industrial and financial cooperation with the Nazis, in fact enabled Switzerland to remain independent and not request Allied military support. Fleury goes as far as to say that: "In truth of fact, Switzerland's greatest merit and its most important contribution to the victory over the Axis lies in its not having been occupied and in not having obliged the Allies to invest manpower and resources in the liberation of this Alpine country had it been taken over by the Axis like all of the other states in Central and Eastern Europe, with the subsequent burden of feeding it and reconstructing it."[146] Indeed, in the light of these somewhat distorted considerations, the wartime conduct of neutral Switzerland, including its dealings with Nazi Germany, could indeed be considered a morally justified behavior, which in fact eased the war effort of the Allies.

2.6 The Final Act: The Interhandel Case

One last far-reaching outcome of the Washington Accord and the World War II policy of the U.S. with respect to Switzerland was the Interhandel case.

---

144 See "Statement by Professor Antoine Fleury" in "U.S. Department of State, U.S. and Allied Wartime and Postwar Relations and Negotiations With Argentina, Portugal, Spain, Sweden, and Turkey on Looted Gold and German External Assets and U.S. Concerns About the Fate of the Wartime Ustasha Treasury". Supplement to Preliminary Study on U.S. and Allied Efforts To Recover and Restore Gold and Other Assets Stolen or Hidden by Germany During World War II. Coordinated by Eizenstat, Stuart E., prepared by Slany, William. U.S. Government Printing Office: Washington, D.C. 1998, p. 251. In his statement, the Swiss historian Atoine Fleury provides various arguments to justify and defend the Swiss conduct during World War II. Fleury goes as far as to claim that the U.S, by targeting Switzerland with its freezing order "treated Switzerland as an enemy state in complete disregard for the 1907 Hague Convention on the rights and obligations of neutral powers in the case of war".

145 Ibid., p. 252.

146 See Ibid., p. 252.

At the onset of World War II, the U.S. government sequestered an American firm General Aniline & Film Co, the second largest U.S. manufacturer of photographic equipment and third largest manufacturer of dye-stuffs. The company was owned by I. G. Chemie, which owned 90% of General Aniline shares. I.G. Chemie of Basel was a Swiss holding company and the Americans suspected that it had ties to a powerful German chemical conglomerate, I.G. Farben. In response to this step, the Swiss Federal Council pursued a diplomatic intervention in support of I.G. Chemie. This intervention was used as a pretext by the Treasury Department to press for the introduction of exchange controls over all Swiss assets in the United States. In fact, the Treasury Department favored the concept of general measures of exchange controls and pressed for the acceptance of this solution, but was thwarted by the Department of State, which feared that such measures would have had a profound impact on U.S. foreign relations.

Following the Swiss incident an Executive Order 8785 of June 14, 1941 was issued, declaring all assets of continental European countries frozen. In all likelihood the Swiss incident was not decisive in the introduction of the Order, or the inclusion of Switzerland in it, however it did provide additional arguments for the Treasury Department in its debate with the Department of State.[147]

The Interhandel case is most certainly suspenseful,[148] but above all it is instructive in the sense that it presents a mechanism of machinations which exploited the Swiss secrecy provisions in many ways, and in doing so strained U.S.-Swiss relations for many years after World War II. For this latter reason it will be discussed here in some detail.

The history of Interhandel begins in Germany before World War I, where two men – a German, Hermann Schmitz and a Swiss citizen, Eduard Greutert, worked for a German company Metallgesellschaft AG. Greutert returned to Switzerland in 1920 and set up a private bank in Basel – Greutert & Cie. The 1920s was a period when German firms began increasingly using the structures

147 Meier, Heinz K.: *Friendship Under Stress…*, p. 278.

148 Already in 1944, the U.S. President Franklin D. Roosevelt said that "the history of the use of the I.G. Farben trust by the Nazis reads like a detective story". This is a quote from a letter of September 6, 1944, from President Franklin D. Roosevelt to the Secretary of State, Cordell Hull, in Roosevelt, Franklin D.: *The Public Papers and Addresses of Franklin D. Roosevelt, Compiled with Special Material and Explanatory Notes by Samuel I. Rosenman: 1944–1945 Volume: Victory and the Threshold of Peace.* Harper & Brothers Publishers: New York 1950, pp. 255–259. The Interhandel history continued for another twenty years, and through the claims of I.G. Farben with respect to the Swiss bank UBS continues to this day.

of Swiss corporations, among other reasons to circumvent the negative sentiments against Germany and to cover up their foreign operations and their foreign ownership of companies. Greutert & Cie[149] was established as such a cover up operation for Metallgesellschaft AG, but after a couple of years Greutert came into contact with Schmitz, who at the time was running a large German dyestuff firm, BASF – Badische Anilin und Soda Fabrik.[150] As a result of this meeting Gerutert & Cie expanded to provide services for Schmitz and BASF.

In 1925, six of the largest German chemical and dye companies merged[151] to create a powerful chemical conglomerate: Interessen-Gemeinschaft Farbenindustrie Aktiengesellschaft or IG Farben as it came to be better known. By 1929 the German giant was producing almost all German chemical products, pharmaceuticals, rayons, and synthetics. As a result of takeovers both in Germany and abroad, by 1939 IG Farben became the largest company in Europe and the largest chemical concern in the world, with over 200 000 employees.[152] Hermann Schmitz was responsible for the exterior department of the chemical giant and, as was the case with BASF, he ran the business operations of IG Farben through Greutert. Subsequently, IG Farben acquired the Metallgesellschaft stake in the Greutert bank.

Despite becoming one of Nazi officials, Schmitz was governed by a distrust of the Nazi economic policy and preferred to channel his foreign operations through Switzerland. This was fueled by the unfavorable public image of the Hitler regime abroad. The financial structure of IG Farben in Basel included a dozen corporations and over sixty accounts. The corporations and consortia which Schmitz created were owned by each other and intertwined in a structure which was even awarded its own term: the Greutert-Sturzenegger Circle, from the names of the two owners.[153] Companies were formed and dissolved, assets were moved between them, loans and credits were extended, all within the cover provided by Swiss banking secrecy. The structure served to conceal IG Farben ownership of numerous companies all over the world.[154] These foreign entities

---

149 The bank exists and continues to do business until this day under the name Baumann & Cie.

150 Today BASF is the largest chemicals manufacturer in the world.

151 The six companies were: BASF, Bayer, Hoechst, Agfa, Chemische Fabrik Griesheim-Elektron, Chemische Fabrik Weiler ter Meer.

152 IG Farben exists until today, since 1952 as a company in liquidation.

153 In this circle, only three companies had individual stockholders, 11 in total.

154 Parta-Bayer (France), Parta-Chehamij – Mapro (Dutch with operations in the U.K., the Netherlands, Belgium and Sweden), Romanil and Budanil (both Hungarian), Defa (Netherlands), Athanil (Greece), Norsk Hydro (Norway), Trafford Chemical

of IG Farben were given access to German patents and licenses for their industrial production.

The holdings of IG Farben in the U.S. included the Bayer Company of New York, General Aniline Works, Agfa Ansco Corporation and the Winthrop Chemical Company. In 1928, Schmitz grouped them into one holding company – for this purpose a new entity was created in Switzerland: The Internationale Gesellschaft für Chemische Unternehmungen AG or, as commonly used, IG Chemie.

The purpose of the creation of IG Chemie was the subject of various theories. The Americans claimed that the only role this company had was to hold the interest of IG Farben companies in the United States. This assertion was widely advocated by the U.S. and prevalent in American publications.[155]

The Swiss, on the other hand, claimed that the foundation of the company was not an isolated case but rather reflected a trend which was present in the Swiss economy on a larger scale in the late 1920s, whereby holding and investment companies were incorporated in Switzerland by foreign interests to execute control of their international operations and to consolidate their participation in foreign entities.[156] In fact the establishment of IG Chemie was driven by a legitimate business interest and the connection to IG Farben was not concealed but rather highlighted. The incorporation prospect of IG Chemie explicitly provided that all interests of IG Chemie in other companies could be bought back at book value by IG Farben at any time.[157] There was also a guarantee of dividend, which was publicly announced: the shareholders of IG Chemie were entitled to a dividend at least as high as that, which was paid on shares of IG Farben, and could exchange their shares for the shares of IG Farben. These contractual provisions were established to make the incorporation of IG Chemie attractive to potential investors, as asserted in an extensive study of the Interhandel case conducted on behalf of the independent Commission of Experts Switzerland – Second World War (ICE).[158] The connection of IG Chemie to IG Farben was not concealed, on the contrary, it was essential for the credibility of the venture, which was aimed at raising capital for IG Farben. The American claim, that IG Chemie was

---

Company (UK), even the Winnica Chemical Plant in Poland was the property of IG Farben, as well as many others. See Fehrenbach, T.R.: *The Gnomes…*, p. 245.

155 See for example Ibid., pp. 246–247.

156 König, Mario: *Interhandel. Die schweizerische Holding der IG Farben und ihre Metamorphosen – eine Affäre um Eigentum und Interessen (1910–1999).* The Chronos Verlag: Zürich 2001, p. 33.

157 Ibid., pp. 34–35.

158 Ibid., p. 36.

incorporated for the purpose of camouflaging the IG Farben interest in the company is therefore without merit, according to the ICE study, and was a result of the U.S. war propaganda.[159]

On the other hand, the ICE study admits that IG Chemie was a stock owning company which did not produce anything and its sole purpose of existence was to hold securities on behalf of IG Farben, thereby bringing under control the internationally scattered interests of the German chemical group. This control was not easily comprehensible.[160] The company never employed more than a few dozen employees and nevertheless controlled enormous financial assets.[161]

Hermann Schmitz assumed the chairmanship of the Board of Directors of IG Chemie. The voting power of the company was always owned by members of the board, which were also IG Farben employees, or by the executives of the Greutert Bank. Following its establishment, IG Chemie was run through the Greutert – Sturzenegger Circle structure. In 1929, in Delaware yet another company was set up, called American IG Chemical Corporation, this name was later changed to General Aniline and Film (GAF). The stocks of IG Farben's U.S. entities: General Aniline Works and Agfa Ansco were then transferred to GAF. The stocks of GAF changed hands in the following years. At one point IG Chemie claimed 89% of ownership in GAF. In 1928, the stocks of Winthrop were sold by IG Farben to Greutert and then in 1929 by Greutert to GAF. As a result of these operations GAF emerged as a holding company for IG Farben's U.S. corporations. The whole purpose of these transactions, according to the U.S. side, was to conceal the true ownership of these companies and prevent the seizure of IG Farben assets in the United States.[162]

IG Chemie sheltered IG Farben's international interests including the group's U.S. factories which accounted for 88% of the IG Chemie portfolio in 1940. These U.S. holdings were in turn pooled together in a financial holding – General Aniline & Film Corporation (GAF).[163] The relationship between the IG Farben group and the IG Chemie holding was not bound by a capital ownership but instead was governed by an exceptionally complicated contractual structure and a web of convoluted companies, to secure it from external access.

159 Ibid., p. 34.
160 Ibid., p. 36.
161 Ibid., p. 14.
162 See Fehrenbach, T.R.: *The Gnomes…*, pp. 249–251.
163 König, Mario: *Interhandel…*, p. 14.

In June 1940, the Swiss and German press announced the unconditional cancellation of the contractual relationship between IG Farben and IG Chemie. [164] This move was presumably made to protect the assets of IG Chemie from seizure by the American authorities. The ICE study holds, in line with the Swiss argumentation, that the association contract was terminated unconditionally and finally, that there is no proof that the situation was a cloak for what was in fact a German possession. The U.S. side on the other hand perceived the Swiss ownership as a mere trusteeship agreement which was supposed to conceal the true German interest. The termination of the legal ties of IG Chemie to IG Farben was never recognized by the United States. The U.S. factories belonging to IG Chemie were perceived as a front for German interests in the U.S. and seized as enemy assets during World War II. Despite the attempts by IG Farben to disguise the connection of GAF to the German chemical giant, 93.5% of GAF shares were seized by the U.S. and the U.S. government-maintained control of GAF for 20 years.

The ICE study asserted that thousands of Swiss shareholders were denied access to their own property, whereas the U.S. side pursued its own goals using legal arbitrariness, without sufficient proof and in "continuous violation of Swiss sovereignty."[165]

In December 1945, IG Chemie changed its name to Internationale Gesellschaft für Handels- und Industriebeteiligungen AG, Basel, known in abbreviated form as Interhandel.

In 1945–1946, the Swiss Compensation Office conducted two audits of Interhandel and found no evidence of a covert agreement between IG Chemie and IG Farben after 1940.

In 1948, Interhandel sued the United States for the restitution of property which was considered by the U.S. as Nazi-controlled and seized by the Alien Property Custodian during World War II. The American side requested records of the Swiss bank, Sturzenegger, to verify whether Interhandel was the actual owner of the GAF shares and whether Interhandel together with the Sturzenegger bank supported a conspiracy to disguise the German ownership of the assets. When the bank Sturzenegger & Co, successor to the Greutert & Cie since 1940, was asked to provide records pertaining to the case, it vehemently refused, shielding behind Swiss banking secrecy laws. Hans Sturzenegger was summoned to testify before a U.S. court and he did, for five months, buy without providing any conclusive facts. Finally, the Swiss government stepped in and seized the records of

164 Ibid., p. 90.
165 Ibid., p. 18.

the bank to prevent them from being passed on to the U.S. authorities and used as evidence in the case.[166]

In the 1950s, the Interhandel affair was the subject of a heated public and media debate in both countries. The Swiss press followed the conflict with interest but also outrage at the approach of the Americans. The negative, anti-American press campaign lasted for years and was accompanied by titles such as: "The Americans, a gang of criminals or a civilized nation?"[167]

The legal battle dragged on for 15 years. The Swiss even brought the case to the International Court of Justice at the Hague in 1957, but the Court dismissed the case on the grounds that it was still pending inside the U.S. legal system.

The case was finally settled in February 1963 with the mediation of U.S. Attorney General Robert F. Kennedy.[168] The assets of the company were to be sold and the price divided among the parties. The Swiss grudgingly accepted a division on a 50-50 basis, and the fact that they were to cover all tax expenditures. Before the sale of GAF, the Swiss bank Schweizerische Bankgesellschaft (SBG) increased its stake in Interhandel, which it begun to acquire in the 1950s.

The public sale of GAF, which took place in March 1965, yielded $341 million. The U.S. Government received $207 million (60.7%) out of this sum[169] and Interhandel received $122 million (39.3%), at the time this amounted to 500 million Swiss francs. In the following year, the Swiss bank SBG (now UBS) merged with Interhandel and the massive influx of capital elevated SBG to become Switzerland's leading financial institution.[170]

---

166 Ibid., pp. 188–189. See also Faith, Nicolas: *Safety in Numbers...*, p. 161.

167 König, Mario: *Interhandel...*, pp. 184–185.

168 Nicolas Faith provides a most interesting account of the Interhandel case in his book, including the details of the Kennedy deal. Following the appointment of the Kennedy administration, the Swiss managed to secure the support of Stanisław Radziwiłł, a Polish aristocrat who was at the time married to Lee Bouvier, Jacqueline Kennedy's sister. As a result, the Kennedys took an interest in the GAF-Interhandel case. The confidants of the powerful family were put on the GAF payroll. After the case was settled, President Kennedy defended the deal with the Swiss by stating that he doubted that a better arrangement was feasible even if the U.S. would have continued the litigation for another ten years. Faith, Nicolas: *Safety in Numbers...*, pp. 170–174.

169 Out of this amount $189.2 million was paid into the U.S. War Claims Fund, set up to settle war claims of American citizens against Germany and other former enemy states.

170 König, Mario: *Interhandel...*, pp. 229–230.

Since 1983, the bank UBS, as successor to Interhandel, is involved in a legal dispute with IG Farben in liquidation,[171] which demands a share of the GAF proceeds on the grounds that Interhandel was still linked to IG Farben via a trusteeship relation. This claim was made based on the fact that the Swiss blocked all files pertaining to the case in the Swiss Federal Archive, in particular the so-called Rees Report, which was the outcome of a Swiss investigation of Interhandel in 1946, conducted to prove to the Allies that Interhandel was in fact a Swiss company. The Swiss always referred to the report in their dispute with the U.S. as containing proof that there was no link between IG Chemie and IG Farben. The ICE study found that the report did not contain any explicitly incriminating evidence, but it did not contain any conclusive proof either. In fact, the report expressed doubt about the sincere intentions of the representatives of Interhandel, and for this reason the access to its contents was restricted.[172]

All the Swiss files pertaining to this case are restricted from access in the Swiss Federal Archives to this day.

2.7 Conclusions

The U.S. policy during World War II with respect to Switzerland was firm and uncompromising. U.S. authorities condemned the Swiss trade with Germany and the fact that Switzerland did not revoke the right of transit passage for Axis traffic via its Alpine passes. But the issues which mainly contributed to the deterioration of U.S.-Swiss relations during this period was the Swiss gold trade with the Nazis and the lack of Swiss support for the Safehaven Program.

---

171 The IG Farben conglomerate was essential in supporting the military effort of the Nazi regime. During the war it profited from employing slave labor and among others was responsible for the establishment of the Monowitz Auschwitz III concentration camp which provided slave labor for the IG Farben Buna factory. IG Farben was also responsible for the production and distribution of Zyklon B used to murder people in Nazi extermination camps. In 1951, the group was split into the original founding entities and put into liquidation. However, it continued to exist to pay its debts and settle its wartime claims which so far has not been done. The directors of IG Farben were tried in one of the twelve Nuremberg Trials, the so-called IG Farben Trial. Hermann Schmitz, who was IG Farben's chairman was sentenced to 4 years in prison. He was released in 1950 and was appointed a member of the supervisory board of Deutsche Bank in Berlin and honorary chairman of the supervisory board of Rheinische Stahlwerke AG.

172 König, Mario: *Interhandel…*, pp. 257–258 and p. 376.

The Swiss banks participated in trade with the German Reichsbank, which used the Swiss francs that it obtained in exchange for its gold to pay for the imports of raw materials essential for the German war effort. Switzerland was the most important recipient of German gold and received $444.1 million in gold from the Reichsbank during the war. The Allies had issued repeated warnings that the gold traded by the Reichsbank had to be looted gold, however, the Swiss refused to acknowledge this. The issue of Swiss participation in trade in gold with the German Reichsbank became one of the key areas of conflict with the U.S. during the war and the main stumbling block in the Washington negotiations with the Allies.

However, there were other conflicting areas. As World War II erupted on the European continent, the U.S. introduced measures of economic warfare aimed at preventing Nazi Germany from using the resources of occupied countries to finance its war effort. By the U.S. Executive Order of June 14, 1941, the assets of numerous European countries were frozen, including those belonging to Switzerland. The U.S. Treasury Department feared the potential infiltration of the Swiss banking system by the Nazis and the abuse of Swiss banking secrecy by German companies and individuals and ordered an investigation into the activities of Swiss banks in the United States. As a result of this investigation Swiss financial institutions were condemned for undertaking steps to circumvent the U.S. freezing order and criticized for their policy of maintaining collective accounts and defending customer anonymity.

In addition to freezing Swiss assets, the U.S. introduced the blacklisting of Swiss persons and companies which had business dealings with the Axis countries.

Since 1943, the neutral states were repeatedly warned by the Allies that after the war they will be made accountable for their gold and capital transactions with the Axis powers.

On February 22, 1944, the U.S. Treasury Secretary Morgenthau issued a warning in which the looting of gold by the Nazis was explicitly condemned, as well as the policy of gold trade with the Germans by the neutrals. The U.S. also explicitly stated that it would not recognize the transfer of ownership rights to looted gold acquired in world market. The Gold Declaration, as it was called, initiated a hardline approach of the Allies, as led by the U.S., on the gold issue towards the neutrals, and especially Switzerland.

In response to the U.S. government's fears of a revival of German aggression resulting from German economic capacity, recovered from capital and resources hidden in neutral countries, the U.S. Foreign Economic Administration devised the Safehaven Program. Its main aim was to track down German assets in neutral countries and prevent them from being re-used by the Nazis. The German assets found and reclaimed were to be used for the economic rehabilitation of war-torn Europe.

On July 22, 1944, during the United Nations Monetary and Financial Conference at Bretton Woods, in response to the U.S. efforts, Resolution Number VI was adopted, which called for action by the neutral countries to prevent the disposition or transfer of assets or gold, which belonged to occupied countries or their citizens as well as the concealment of such assets. The Resolution therefore encompassed the basic goals of the U.S. Safehaven Program.

The U.S. pressured Switzerland to implement the Safehaven principles as outlined in the Bretton Woods resolution No. VI, and in 1945 sent a diplomatic mission to Switzerland, to negotiate an agreement which was signed in March of that year. Although the Currie Agreement, as it was known, secured U.S. interests on paper, it was never fulfilled in its scope pertaining to the Safehaven goals. The Swiss failed to provide a complete census of German assets.

At the initiative of the U.S. a draft of a vesting decree, was proposed during the Potsdam Conference which lasted from July 16 to August 1, 1945. During the conference Stalin relinquished all Soviet claims to gold found by the Allies in Germany. In August 1945, the U.S. government requested the right of ownership or control of all German assets in Switzerland. The authority over all enemy assets was to be held by the Allied Control Council as the de facto government of Germany. The Swiss Federal Council declined this request, which according to the Council had no legal foundations.

On October 30, 1945, the Allies passed a Law No. 5, which placed German assets in neutral states under the control and disposition of the Allied Control Council, however, the Swiss contested the international legal effectiveness of this decree and the Allied claim to German external assets.

The Swiss Federal Council persistently refused to recognize the rights of ownership or control of the Allies over German property in Switzerland. To resolve this impasse, the U.S. government invited the Swiss to Washington to negotiate a settlement on the disputable issues.

The Washington negotiations were confrontational, lasted for months, and terminated in signing an Accord that brought satisfaction to neither side.

In the course of the Washington negotiations the Swiss started from an inferior bargaining position and yet managed to secure an agreement, which in fact reflected their own proposal.

Since Germany did not possess sufficient gold reserves to finance its purchases, it resorted to using gold looted from occupied countries and their citizens, including the victims of the Holocaust. This fact could have been easily determined, according to the Allies, since the Reichsbank's gold transactions by far exceeded the pre-war gold reserves of Germany. However, during the Washington negotiations the Swiss persistently refused to acknowledge that part of the gold the SNB purchased from the Reichsbank was in fact looted and provided their own estimates of the legitimate pre-war reserves of Germany. Unfortunately for the Swiss, the Allies had proof that at least part of the gold looted from Belgium was transferred by Germany to Switzerland.

During the Washington negotiations the Swiss emphasized their traditional neutrality, which, as they pointed out, had permitted trade useful to the Allies, as well as to the Germans, and emphasized the fact that the Swiss Central Bank had purchased more gold from the Allies, than it had from the Germans. The Swiss government had conformed to international law, including the Hague Convention, and as a neutral Switzerland was in the position to pursue economic relations with Germany. The Swiss delegation persistently insisted that the SNB acted in good faith in accepting gold from Germany.

The Swiss refused to make a firm commitment with respect to heirless claims, namely the assets belonging to persons, who had placed their holdings in Swiss banks, and later perished in the war without leaving any known heirs. The U.S. wanted to use these assets for the relief and resettlement of Jewish survivors. The Swiss declaration that the Swiss Government would examine the matter of putting the proceeds of property of heirless victims of German aggression at the disposal of the Allies for relief and rehabilitation purposes never materialized. A careful census of heirless property and the allocation of the proceeds to organizations supporting the designated cause would have prevented the future conflict over this issue, which erupted in the 1990s.

In the negotiations Switzerland confronted three great powers which were equipped with a superior moral justification for their negotiating position. The funds were to be used to finance war reparations for the economic damages suffered from German aggression and occupation. Moreover, the Allied position stood for the right to recover stolen property, in particular if it was accepted by the Swiss in bad faith. Although the Allies had all the trump cards in their hands – Swiss assets remained blocked in the U.S., the blacklists were still in force and Switzerland was dependent on trade agreements with the Allies, the Swiss negotiators still managed to secure an agreement which fulfilled their own bargaining position. Although at the time of its ratification the Agreement was perceived as a failure in Switzerland, it was in fact a remarkable feat of Swiss diplomacy.

Switzerland never recognized any legal basis for the Allied claims and refused to assume moral responsibility in regard to its wartime conduct. The Accord was perceived by the Swiss as their goodwill contribution to the reconstruction of Europe, as well as a necessary gesture to secure good political and economic relations with the Allies. The outcome of the Washington negotiations was met with bitter resentment in Switzerland. The U.S. was perceived as a superior power, which imposed a punitive agreement upon a sovereign nation, whose only fault was that it acted in line with the principles of its traditional neutrality.

The issue of the fulfillment of the Accord and in particular the disposition of German assets in Switzerland dominated the relations between the U.S. and Switzerland well into the post-war period. Another source of conflict resulted from the custodial issues over Swiss assets, which were frozen by the U.S. government during the war. The U.S. refused to unblock the assets of certain Swiss private companies in cases where doubts existed in relation to the true ownership of these assets.

One such case discussed in this chapter in detail refers to the U.S. assets of Interhandel, a Swiss company based in Basel. These assets were blocked in the U.S. under the suspicion of Interhandel being a front for German operations. The legal battle engaged the governments of the two countries and lasted for 18 years after the war before the case was finally resolved in 1963 by the Kennedy administration. Swiss banking secrecy played a leading role in fueling this conflict, since it prevented the Swiss side from releasing to the U.S. the documents, which would have provided conclusive evidence on the true ownership of Interhandel.

Despite continuous pressure on the Swiss to fulfill the provisions of the Washington Agreement Switzerland managed to hold out for long enough for a new political constellation to appear on the world stage. By the late 1940s, the U.S. was interested in rebuilding and not eliminating German economic and industrial power. Morgenthau's hardline policy with respect to Germany was replaced by a plan for the reconstruction of Europe, devised by George Marshall, which was aimed at preventing the spread of communism and encompassed West Germany. In the beginning of the 1950s, as the Cold War progressed, the security issue which was to be safeguarded by eliminating the postwar threat of Nazi resurgence with the aid of German external assets was replaced by the threat of the Soviet Union. The U.S. was more interested in fostering the economic rehabilitation of Germany and securing the support of its western Allies, including Switzerland, than it was in enforcing the provisions of the Accord.

The main failure of the Washington Accord was to be found in the lack of monitoring and supervision mechanisms, as well as the insufficient willingness to implement its provisions on the part of Swiss banks and authorities.

The Swiss commitment to identify, liquidate, and turn over the proceeds of German holdings in Switzerland was never fulfilled. The Swiss raised the issue of the exchange rate to be applied for the compensation of the German owners and the issue of Swiss private assets which remained blocked in the U.S. under suspicion of being actual German property as the reasons which prevented them from making a complete census of German assets.

In 1952, the Washington Accord was revised and replaced by three separate agreements, whereby the Swiss managed to secure the integrity of private property and banking secrecy with respect to German assets.

In the course of World War II, the Swiss were condemned in the U.S. for aiding Germany's war economy and Swiss neutrality was widely criticized in U.S. press.[173] Swiss banking secrecy was perceived with suspicion in the U.S. during the whole period of World War II, and resented in its aftermath, when the issue of the liquidation of German assets dragged on and the custodial conflict intensified.

In the following chapter, a dispute which emerged in the 1990s as a direct consequence of the atrocities of World War II, as well as of the Swiss conduct during this period, is examined. In the 1990s, the Swiss banks were finally made accountable for their wartime dealings and forced to pay for them handsomely.

Although the resolution of the Interhandel case marked a closure in the wartime conflict of the U.S. with Switzerland, a new set of problems connected directly with Swiss banking secrecy disrupted the relations between the two countries in the 1960s and 1970s.

173 Meier, Heinz K.: *Friendship Under Stress…*, pp. 330–331.

Chapter 3. The Conflict Over Holocaust-Related Claims in the 1990s

indifference is the epitome of evil[1]

This chapter deals with a complex, ambiguous and sensitive issue of the responsibility for the involvement of Swiss banks in the collaboration with the Nazi regime as well as their refusal to return Jewish assets in the post war period. Both the issue of plundered gold discussed extensively in Chapter 2 and the issue of dormant and heirless accounts came under intense scrutiny 50 years after the end of World War II, in the mid-1990s.

Unfortunately, both the Washington Accord and the agreements signed in 1952 failed to settle all wartime disputes between Switzerland and the United States. The way the Swiss authorities handled the implementation of the provisions of the Accord and the subsequent insufficient effort of the Swiss to clarify and deal with the controversies of the country's wartime economic conduct, especially with respect to the financial sector, had overwhelming consequences for

1 The full quote: "Indifference, to me, is the epitome of evil" is by Elie Wiesel. Quotes along similar lines include: "the banality of evil" and "the bureaucracy of evil". Most people are not evil in the "traditional" sense and the enormity of the dimension of Holocaust would not have been possible without the "innocent" bystanders or the efficient bureaucratic collaborators. This interpretation is at the core of the famous concept of Hannah Arendt's "banality of evil" first used as a subtitle for her book which contained articles-reports from the trial of Adolf Eichmann. Although much criticized (see for example Rosenbaum, Ron: "Eichmann and the Banality of Evil". *The Observer*, 23.08.1999, retrieved 23.05.2018, from http://observer.com/1999/08/eichmann-and-the-banality-of-the-banality-of-evil/, who discusses briefly all concepts of evil used by Hannah Arendt) this seems to be a good philosophical starting point for an analysis provided in this chapter. The question of how far we extend the responsibility of the indifferent societies and politicians remains to be answered. In the broadest sense, the whole world was responsible for the Holocaust and still is for the atrocities of today. This chapter deals with the issue of responsibility of Switzerland for its conduct during World War II and thereafter, and among other issues examines the conflict which resulted from the divergent perception of the moral value of neutrality by the two countries. The Swiss conduct during the war was not monstrous or demonic within the "absolute" or "radical" evil concepts (also devised by Hannah Arendt) rather it was interpreted by the U.S. as being self-serving, bureaucratic and indifferent.

the dispute of Switzerland with the United States in the 1990s and – as a result of this dispute – for the international image of Switzerland. The unsettled issues resulting from Switzerland's wartime policy and the moral ambiguity of Swiss neutrality during World War II opened the door to Holocaust-related claims which exploded in a legal, political, and economic conflict with the United States of unprecedented scale. Again, the concept of banking secrecy is fundamental to the understanding of this controversy.

The preliminary initiative in this conflict was taken by Jewish organizations, subsequently supported by the U.S. Government. The campaign set in motion by Edgar Bronfman, the President of the World Jewish Congress, was backed by powerful politicians within the U.S. Senate and the Clinton administration.

Why did the issue of Holocaust-related claims resurface with such strength after over 50 years? Most authors point to the end of the Cold War as the triggering mechanism. During the period of the Cold War, the ideological division between the East and the West suppressed any potential controversies over ethical issues. Neutral Switzerland was by implication a member of the Western camp. Despite the fact that the Western decision-makers were well aware of Switzerland's wartime conduct, for political reasons they preferred to ignore the issue.[2]

In the debate concerning Holocaust-related claims, two different matters have been raised: the first is the issue of the so-called heirless accounts, that is the accounts belonging to war victims which were not claimed by their heirs, or dormant accounts, that is ones to which access was denied to the victims or their heirs by the bankers. These assets were therefore left at the disposal of Swiss banks. The second issue concerns 'victim gold,' which was stolen from Holocaust victims by the Nazis during World War II. The Nazi gold controversy challenged the Swiss national mythology with respect to its role during World War II. However, the confrontation which put these issues on the Swiss political agenda was not raised from within, but rather instigated from the outside, by the World Jewish Congress, the U.S. Senate, and the U.S. Government.

In the mid-1990s, the allegations that the Swiss benefited both from World War II and the Holocaust reemerged with renewed force and were boldly stated in media campaigns where stories of victims' experience were retold and used to defame Swiss banks. The American public was especially supportive and sensitive to the plight of the victims of the Holocaust. This, coupled with the fact

---

2 Cowell, Alan: "Switzerland's Wartime Blood Money". *Foreign Policy*, No. 107, Summer 1997, p. 140.

that the Swiss banks sought means to expand their presence on the U.S. market, provided both survivors and Jewish organizations with a window of opportunity.

Following the eruption of the dormant accounts and heirless assets scandal in the 1990s, Swiss banks were accused of having used banking secrecy to conceal such assets and create a "smoke screen of secrecy"[3] around this problem. The issue of Jewish assets in Switzerland was often associated and mentioned together with a number of Swiss wartime misconducts such as Swiss refugee policy, including changes in Swiss law aimed at prohibiting asylum for religious as opposed to political reasons, which led to denying refuge to Jews during the war, or inventing the idea of stamping Jewish passports with the letter "J", which signified religious affiliation, and finally the turning back of Jewish refugees at the Swiss-German border.[4]

Initiated by the World Jewish Congress, the movement for Holocaust-era restitution in the mid-1990s soon mobilized all three branches of the U.S. government to aid its cause: the U.S. courts responded to class action suits filed on behalf of the victims and their heirs, the U.S. Congress held hearings and authorized historical studies, and the Clinton administration turned to the State Department to conduct an executive response.

This chapter examines the issues surrounding this U.S.-Swiss conflict in detail. The first section provides the background to the subject matter. It begins with an overview of Holocaust compensation efforts before the conflict erupted in 1996, which allows to better understand the problems the Jewish heirs were facing in their pursuit of a just indemnification for the assets which were stolen from them and puts the amounts in question into perspective. The role of Jewish organizations in this process is also discussed. The legal questions surrounding the problem of heirless assets are analyzed briefly in this section, as well as the role which the Holocaust assumed in the American public life. Finally, the attempts to settle the issue of dormant accounts and heirless assets before the 1990s are examined.

In the following section of this chapter, the development of the conflict is researched, including the involvement of the U.S. Senate Committee on Banking, Housing and Urban Affairs, the Swiss initial response to the conflict, and the formation of the independent commissions: the Volcker Commission and the

---

3 Bilenker, Stephanie A.: "In Re Holocaust Victims' Assets Litigation: Do the U.S. Courts Have Jurisdiction Over the Lawsuits Filed by Holocaust Survivors Against the Swiss Banks?". *Maryland Journal of International Law* 21, No. 2, 1997, p. 140.

4 Ibid., p. 255.

Bergier Commission. The class action suits filed against Swiss banks are discussed in detail. The controversial report prepared by the U.S. Department of State which was met with indignation in Switzerland is analyzed as well as the Swiss reaction to its publication. The Meili affair and the diplomatic gaffes made by top Swiss officials are examples of unnecessary mistakes made by the Swiss in addressing the emerging problem and discussed in this chapter. The issue of Holocaust Victims' gold is thoroughly examined since it was exploited during the conflict to provide justification for the increased demands of Jewish organizations.

The U.S. exercised not only diplomatic pressure upon Switzerland during the negotiations, but also employed severe economic sanctions, which are closely examined in this chapter, as the main source of U.S. bargaining power. The Holocaust litigation with respect to Swiss banks had important distinctive features as well as profound consequences for future compensation initiatives and resulted in an unprecedented legal and historical legacy. These developments are examined here and followed by an analysis of the discussion on the moral ambiguity and legitimacy of the Holocaust litigation. Finally, the role of Switzerland in the context of the issues raised by the conflict is evaluated, whereby the different perceptions of the Swiss conduct, as a silent bystander, willing accomplice or righteous neutral, are examined.

3.1 Cold War Era Efforts to Resolve the Issue of Holocaust-Related Claims

3.1.1 Overview of Holocaust Compensation Efforts Before 1996

An overview of restitution and compensation efforts, as well as the difficulties facing Jews throughout this process in the post war period before the 1990s is provided in this section. To facilitate the understanding of further analysis it is also important to put the overall amounts of lost and unrestored Jewish assets into perspective. This historical context will shed some light on the scale of the problem and at least partially explain the determination with which Jewish organizations pursued their cause with respect to Swiss financial institutions.

The renewed demands for the restitution of Jewish assets and more generally for Holocaust compensation, which were made in the 1990s, also raised awkward moral and material questions: how much compensation is appropriate if at all, considering that the loss of life and suffering encountered by Holocaust victims is priceless. For the victims of Nazi crimes, restitution represented the acknowledgment of their hardship and suffering, whereas for the perpetrators it was a settlement of claims. The term "Holocaust compensation" refers to a broad category of payments arising from the material claims which result from World War II persecution of Jewish people, and includes indemnification, reparations and restitution.[5]

During the Holocaust, Jewish assets were confiscated and misappropriated by the German Nazi regime in Germany and in the occupied countries. The confiscation of Jewish property was an integral part of Nazi policy from the very beginning of the party's ascendance to power. The Holocaust was "on the grandest scale in history, a form of robbery combined with murder, with a network of victims, murderers, fences, and profiteers extending across a whole continent. Nazi gold has become a metaphor for stolen valuables of every kind – stocks and shares, bonds, rights of property, art, antiques, and jewelry."[6]

Throughout World War II and shortly thereafter, the issue of the restitution of Jewish assets figured prominently on the international agenda, as reflected in numerous explicit international agreements and declarations on this subject. Unfortunately, to the present day less than 20% of the value of stolen Jewish assets has been restored. Although it is impossible to calculate the exact amount of Jewish property stolen during the Holocaust, it is nevertheless possible to provide an estimate of its value.[7] Using late 1930s prices, the value of Jewish assets as estimated by historians equaled roughly $10–$15 billion. Accounting for

5 Although the terms restitution and compensation are used interchangeably, restitution in the context of Holocaust assets is understood as "the return or recovery of identifiable assets, including machinery, real estate, business enterprises, and cultural properties that are restored to the original owners – nations, communities, institutions or individuals." Restitution is not to be confused with other terms connected with Holocaust compensation, which is a broader term, and also encompasses indemnification (compensation for specific personal losses or damages, typically paid out in the form of one-time settlements or monthly pensions) and reparations (payments from one nation to another for inflicted damages). For detailed definitions see Henry, Marilyn: "Fifty Years of Holocaust Compensation". In: Singer, David/Grossman, Lawrence (eds.): *The American Jewish Yearbook*. American Jewish Committee: New York 2002, pp. 3–84 and pp. 4–5.

6 Ruth, Arne: "Postwar Europe: The Capriciousness of Universal Values". *Daedalus* 126, no. 3, Summer 1997, p. 270.

7 The approach includes estimating the share of wealth belonging to the Jewish population for each country in Nazi-occupied Europe, tax records, country estimates published at the time and the asset declarations forced upon the Jews by the Nazis. See Zabludoff, Sidney: "Restitution of Holocaust-Era Assets: Promises and Reality". *Jewish Political Studies Review* 19, No. 1/2, Spring 2007, pp. 3–14 and p. 4.

inflation allows to further estimate the present value of these assets by applying the annual increases in the U.S. Consumer Price Index in today's prices. The present value of these assets for 2005 was calculated to be in the range of between $143 billion and $215 billion.[8]

Not more than 15% of Jewish assets confiscated during the period from 1934 to 1945 were returned to their rightful owners, their heirs, or Jewish organizations. The value of unrestored assets amounted to $120–$180 billion expressed in 2005 prices.

The first attempt to resolve the issue of compensation payments in a comprehensive way was initiated by Israel in the early 1950s with respect to West Germany. Representatives of 23 Jewish organizations met in 1951 in New York at a Conference on Jewish Material Claims Against Germany (Claims Conference).[9] Some Jewish representatives opposed negotiations with Germany, claiming that such talks were immoral and that it was impossible to request "blood money" from the persecutors of Jews.[10] Others responded that there was nothing moral in discharging Germany from paying for the committed crimes. The Claims Conference requested heirless and unclaimed Jewish assets to be transferred to Jewish organizations which cared for Holocaust survivors. The issue of individual claims against Germany was finally settled by the Luxembourg Agreements of September 10, 1952.[11]

---

8 These numbers do not take into consideration earnings from financial holdings or the increase in the valuation of real estate, it is also based on gross values in that it does not consider loans and mortgages. See Ibid., p. 4.

9 The Conference on Jewish Material Claims Against Germany (known as the Claims Conference) was created to pursue the material claims of the Jewish people and to represent them in Holocaust restitution and compensation negotiations as well as for the purpose of the implementation of agreements and the distribution of proceeds of settlements. See Heilig, Karen: "From the Luxembourg Agreement to Today: Representing a People". *Berkeley Journal of International Law* 20, No. 1, 2002, p. 176.

10 Henry, Marilyn: "Fifty Years of Holocaust...," p. 29.

11 Under this settlement West Germany paid Israel DM 3 billion in goods and services over a period of more than 10 years, provided under the so-called Protocol II DM 450 million to the Claims Conference to aid Jewish refugees in recognition of uncompensated Jewish losses and under the so-called Protocol I West Germany was obliged to enact laws that would compensate Nazi victims directly for indemnification and restitution claims arising from Nazi persecution. There was no ceiling on the number of payments in this latter case or the number of claimants, who had only to fulfill the eligibility criteria. In total Germany has paid around $89 billion in compensation for Nazi crimes since 1952. See Rising, David: "Germany Increases Reparations for

There was no legal precedent to the Luxembourg Agreements since an international law which would regulate individual financial reparations does not exist. It was the first such broad agreement between a sovereign state, the Federal Republic of Germany and voluntary Jewish organizations. Moreover, compensation was paid not only to individuals but to a state, which did not exist at the time, when the crimes, for which it was compensated were committed.[12] The Claims Conference paved the way for subsequent Holocaust compensation initiatives. The experience drawn from the Claims Conference influenced the distribution of settlement proceeds resulting from the Swiss Banks Settlement. The Special Master appointed by the judge within the settlement process in 1999 stressed the significance of the Claims Conference in Holocaust compensation, pointing to the fact that every significant indemnification and restitution program is directly attributable to the Claims Conference initiative.[13]

The low priority of Holocaust restitution in later years was a result of a shift in policy interests of the former Allies. The Cold War became the overriding political objective for the U.S. government. The Western European countries concentrated on economic recovery, and the communist regimes abandoned the question of restitution of private assets altogether as they were instead preoccupied with their own process of nationalization of assets. The new state of Israel was focused on its own survival. Issues such as the Holocaust and even more so the Swiss conduct during World War II were of secondary importance. The problem of dealing with the property of the millions of Jews who perished during the war was given little if any attention at all. On the local level, governments felt no obligation to deal with the consequences of the Holocaust, given the few remaining Jewish residents and the fact that many non-Jews saw themselves as the new rightful owners of looted Jewish property. In addition, many governments and businesses were covering up their collaboration with the Nazi regime, including in the neutral countries, and would rather retain Jewish assets then return them to their rightful owners.[14]

The movement for Holocaust-era restitution and compensation resurfaced with renewed intensity in the 1990s, prompted by the fall of the Iron Curtain and with new information made available to the public, following the opening

---

Holocaust Survivors". *The Times of Israel*, 16.11.2012, retrieved 20.10.2017, from http://www.timesofisrael.com/germany-increases-reparations-for-holocaust-survivors/.

12 Heilig, Karen: "From the Luxembourg Agreement…," p. 180.

13 Ibid., p. 177.

14 Zabludoff, Sidney: "Restitution of Holocaust-Era Assets…," p. 8.

of archives after the collapse of the communist regime in Russia and Eastern Europe. The efforts for the restitution and compensation of Holocaust victims in the post-communist states advanced, including the pursuit of compensation both from East and West Germany to victims of Nazi persecution in the East. In 1992, the World Jewish Restitution Organization was established to handle the return of Jewish property in post-communist Eastern Europe.[15]

The U.S. government followed this trend by opening its own archives. Jewish organizations were highly effective in mobilizing top U.S. politicians in support of their cause and aggressive class action suits were filed.

The initial restitution movement in the 1990s evolved beyond looted gold and Swiss dormant accounts to include looted art, unpaid insurance policies, and the compensation for wartime suffering of slave and forced laborers in Germany, Austria, and France. The settlements concluded as part of the 1990s restitution movement amounted together to over $8 billion.[16]

3.1.2 Legal Impediments

There were many impediments to the process of restitution after World War II[17] with the main one being the fact that most Jewish owners as well as their close heirs had perished in the Holocaust. The remaining heirs, even if they were alive, had no knowledge of the assets nor did they possess the documentation necessary to prove the legal title to their inheritance.

When the conflict over dormant accounts and heirless assets erupted, Switzerland had no escheat laws in place.[18] This meant that if the deposits were

---

15 Ibid., p. 6.

16 This figure is widely quoted in literature, see for example Bazyler, Michael J.: "The Holocaust Restitution Movement in Comparative Perspective". *Berkeley Journal of International Law*, No. 1, 2002, p. 12.

17 For an extensive list of the factors which inhibited the process of restitution see Zabludoff, Sidney: "Restitution of Holocaust-Era Assets…," p. 7.

18 An escheat law is a law, whereby "dormant accounts and other assets escheat (or are transferred to) the government after a statutorily defined period so that the owners are protected by locating them and restoring to them their property, as well as to give the state, rather than the holders of the unclaimed property, the benefit of its use". For this definition see Bradfield, Michael/Sak, Pamela: "Swiss Law on the Treatment of Dormant Accounts: A Comparison with European and U.S. Law". In: *Current Developments in Monetary and Financial Law.* Volume 2. International Monetary Fund: Washington, D.C. 2003, pp. 773–797 and p. 774. Such a regulation protects the rights of the original owners of the property, a mechanism is provided for finding the rightful owners

unclaimed, they remained with the bank forever. In contrast to the Swiss lack of regulations, in the United States "it is a recognized principle that states, as sovereigns, may take custody or assume title to abandoned property."[19] Most jurisdictions in the world do have some form of escheat laws providing for the transfer of bank accounts to the state after a certain period of time. The fact that the Swiss legal system has no escheat laws, and therefore the banks were able to keep the assets in dormant bank accounts, was one of the issues raised in defense of the Swiss banks in the dormant accounts debate.

Another legal issue was the lack of a statute of limitations on dormant bank deposits. The ten-year limitation period for claims, as specified by Swiss law, starts to run when an obligation becomes due, but since Swiss banks maintained dormant accounts indefinitely, the limitation period never started to run. This meant that a customer's claims on dormant accounts was not subject to a statute of limitations[20] and even after a substantial amount of time the rightful owners could attempt to claim the funds if they possessed sufficient proof of their claim.

In accordance with the Swiss principle of direct and immediate succession, the heirs become immediately entitled to all rights over the estate of the deceased and by the same principle they are entitled to all assets of the deceased deposited in a bank.[21] However, in order to prevent any potential fraud, the heirs are required to furnish the bank with three obligatory documents: a death certificate, the name of the depositor's bank, and a bank account number. The fulfillment of these requirements was not possible in the case of Holocaust victims for obvious reasons – concentration camps simply did not issue such certificates. Often the bank account information was also missing. The main obstruction for Holocaust survivors and their heirs to retrieving their money was therefore a lack of sufficient documentation as requested by Swiss banks and as a result, many claimants were rejected.[22]

---

and the government benefits from holding the property until it is claimed rather than allowing the banks or other institutions to profit from holding it.

19 See Report of the Independent Committee of Eminent Persons: "Swiss Law on the Treatment of Dormant Accounts: A Comparison to European and U.S. Law", Annex 9 to the Independent Committee of Eminent Persons: *Report on Dormant Accounts…*, p. 128.

20 Ganz, Jodi Berlin: "Heirs Without Assets and Assets Without Heirs: Recovering and Reclaiming Dormant Swiss Bank Accounts". *Fordham International Law Journal* 20, No. 4, 1996, p. 1322.

21 Mueller, Kurt: "The Swiss Banking Secret…," p. 364.

22 Meier, Henri B./Marthinsen, John E./Gantenbein, Pascal A.: *Swiss Finance…*, 139.

3.1.3 The Role of the Holocaust in the United States

The U.S. Senate and the U.S. Executive readily embraced the Jewish cause, almost immediately after it was raised by the Jewish organizations and did so with full commitment. Just like the Swiss have played the "neutrality" trump card in justifying their approach towards Germany during World War II, the Americans have played their "Holocaust" trump card in the conflict with Swiss banks. To facilitate the understanding of the U.S. approach it seems therefore worthwhile to point out the importance of the Holocaust in American public life.[23]

In all likelihood, the Holocaust plays a more significant role in the U.S. society as compared to Europe.[24] Since the 1970s, the Holocaust became a symbol of Jewish identity and oppression. A prominent U.S. historian, Peter Novick called it "virtually the only common denominator of American Jewish identity in the late twentieth century" and "a central symbol of Jewishness" and the American Jewish collective memory.[25] But the Holocaust has a deep symbolic meaning not only for Jewish Americans. The Holocaust is centered in the American life and collective memory of the American society, and this despite the fact that it took place thousands of miles away from the U.S. and the U.S. did not participate in it in any way and last but not least, only an estimated 1.7% to 2.6% of the American population is Jewish. The "Holocaust consciousness" evolved in the U.S. through the influence of the Jewish elites on American culture at large.[26] The Holocaust carries universal lessons which apply to all, or at least it has become a moral

23 For a multi-dimensional and deeply interesting discussion of the Holocaust "phenomenon" in the United States see Novick, Peter: *The Holocaust in American Life*. Mariner Books: Boston 2000.

24 Wikipedia lists 59 Holocaust memorials and museums in the United States (in 26 U.S. states there is at least one such institution) including two online ones, compared to 11 in Israel, 7 in Poland (five of them being on former concentration camp sites), and only 2 in Germany (this list excludes memorials to commemorate victims of the Nazi regime, but not ones specifically dedicated to the Jewish Holocaust). The U.S. capital is home to the United States Holocaust Memorial Museum, whereas not one single federally funded museum dedicated to slavery exists in the United States. See for example Amsden, David: "Building the First Slavery Museum in America". *New York Times*, 26.02.2015, retrieved 30.09.2017, from http://www.nytimes.com/2015/03/01/magazine/building-the-first-slave-museum-in-america.html and "List of Holocaust memorials and museums". Wikipedia, retrieved 04.02.2018, from https://en.wikipedia.org/wiki/List_of_Holocaust_memorials_and_museums.

25 Novick, Peter: *The Holocaust…*, p. 7.

26 Ibid., p. 12.

reference point. It has been used "for the purpose of national self- congratulation: the 'Americanization' of the Holocaust has involved using it to demonstrate the difference between the Old World and the New and to celebrate, by showing its negation, the American way of life."[27] This moral higher ground of the U.S. with respect to Switzerland in the context of providing justice to the Holocaust victims was often emphasized in the media reports and academic papers which dealt with the conflict discussed in this chapter.

3.1.4 Efforts to Settle the Dormant Accounts and Heirless Assets Issue Before the 1990s Conflict

Immediately after the war the Allies were primarily concerned with the burden of providing financial aid to refugees, especially so called "non-repatriable refugees" which were mainly stateless Jews. Under the 1945 Paris Reparations Agreement a total of $25 million was to be allocated to such persons. This amount was to be covered by reclaiming German assets in neutral states. During the conference two other sources of funds were designated for the same purpose of refugee assistance – German nonmonetary gold and heirless property found in neutral countries. During the Washington negotiations in 1946 Switzerland, at the request of the U.S., committed itself to taking the necessary measures to make available for aid purposes any heirless assets belonging to victims of acts of violence perpetrated by Germany. This commitment, however, remained largely unfulfilled.[28]

The Swiss Bankers Association, concerned with the possibility that banking secrecy might be lifted to allow for external inquiries, warned the government against complying with the Allied request to identify looted property and to introduce legislation which would enable restitution. This was in line with the prevailing popular presumption that the policy of reparations was aimed at the economic weakening of Switzerland.[29]

---

27 Ibid., p. 13.

28 Independent Commission of Experts Switzerland – Second World War: *Switzerland, National…*, pp. 444–445.

29 For this argument see Ludi, Regula: "'Why Switzerland?' Remarks on a Neutral's Role in the Nazi Program of Robbery and Allied Postwar Restitution Policy". In: Dean, Martin/Goschler,Constantin/Ther, Phillip (eds.): *Robbery and Restitution. The Conflict over Jewish Property in Europe*. Berghan Books: New York et al. 2008, pp. 182–210 and p. 195.

In December 1945 and February 1946, the Swiss nevertheless passed their own restitution legislation – the Decrees on Looted Assets (Raubgutbeschlüsse). Unfortunately, there was a short deadline for the submission of claims, which expired at the end of 1947 and there was no international publication of information regarding the Decrees. Both their territorial and time range were limited and encompassed only property transactions in occupied countries during the war, this excluded expropriation within the pre-war period and the pre-war territory of the Third Reich.[30]

Since the end of World War II, in response to numerous requests from Jewish organizations there were several attempts by the Swiss government to introduce legislation which would regulate the issue of dormant assets. The first initiative to secure a legal settlement of the issue of heirless Jewish assets was undertaken already in 1947 by the Swiss Federation of Jewish Communities, later joined by the Israeli government.[31] In 1947, Swiss legislators drafted a federal decree which required the registration of assets dormant since May 9, 1945, but it was never enacted. In 1952, the Swiss government again proposed to resolve this issue by introducing appropriate legislation. For the following ten years discussions about the legal measures necessary to regulate the dormant accounts problem continued between the Swiss Federal Justice Department, the Department of Foreign Affairs and the SBA with the involvement of Jewish organizations.[32] However, these efforts were impeded by Swiss banking secrecy regulations. The Swiss Jewish community lobbied for a change of these regulations to facilitate the identification process, but without success.[33] The Swiss Bankers Association and its members persistently resisted all such initiatives, downplaying the amounts in question.[34] In 1947, upon the request of the Swiss Bankers Association, banks voluntarily reported balances worth a mere total of SFr 487,000. In 1959, because of a follow-up investigation, this figure increased but it remained well below SFr 1 million.[35]

---

30 Ibid., p. 196.

31 Sagalowitz, Benjamin: "Switzerland". *The American Jewish Year Book* 65, 1964, p. 234.

32 Independent Committee of Eminent Persons: *Report on Dormant Accounts…*, p. 134.

33 Blau, Gisela: "Switzerland". *The American Jewish Yearbook* 98, 1998, p. 296.

34 See Report of the Independent Committee of Eminent Persons, "Swiss Law on the Treatment of Dormant Accounts: A Comparison to European and U.S. Law", Annex 9 to the Independent Committee of Eminent Persons: *Report on Dormant Accounts…*, p. 134 and Independent Commission of Experts Switzerland – Second World War: *Switzerland, National…*, pp. 445–446.

35 Meier, Henri B./Marthinsen, John E./Gantenbein, Pascal A.: *Swiss Finance…*, p. 139.

Following the nationalization of private property in Eastern Europe the Swiss were interested in protecting external Swiss investments. In 1949, an agreement with communist Poland was concluded and came into force in May 1950. Pursuant to this agreement, the Swiss government promised to transfer the proceeds from the Polish heirless assets in Switzerland to the Polish government, obtaining in exchange a global compensation payment for Swiss assets nationalized by the communists in Poland. Presumably, the bulk of the Polish heirless assets belonged to Polish Holocaust victims or survivors, who in fear of sanctions by the communist government, did not claim their assets in Switzerland. The Swiss-Polish agreement was clearly a violation of victims' and their heirs' property rights, and of Swiss banking secrecy, moreover it ignored the claims of Jewish organizations and the Allied policy of introducing restitution legislation whereby heirless assets were designated for the rehabilitation of survivors and assigned to Jewish successor organizations. It was with this principle in mind that the U.S. military government in Germany refused to hand over Polish assets on German territory to the Polish government. In the light of the Swiss-Polish agreement it was suddenly possible for the banks to conduct an internal investigation to provide a list of dormant accounts and Swiss banking secrecy in this case was not an obstacle in any way.

In 1950, the Swiss Bankers Association reported dormant accounts of Polish nationals worth SFr 598,000. However, in the 1960s only SFr 15,498 were transferred to Poland, this sum increased only following the implementation of the Registration Decree in 1962. An agreement similar to the Swiss-Polish one was signed with Hungary in 1950.[36]

In March 1954, the Israeli government intervened with the Swiss government on behalf of two Jewish organizations.[37] The Jewish demands were followed by a global newspaper propaganda campaign. As the Swiss banks were not compelled to any reporting in this respect, there was no exact estimate of the amount of money held in dormant or unclaimed accounts. The Israeli government referred to a figure of $30 million, which corresponded to the rough assumption of the total amount of unclaimed assets in Swiss banks. The Swiss reaction was prompt. The Swiss government insisted that every effort had been made to locate Jewish

---

36 Independent Commission of Experts Switzerland – Second World War: *Switzerland, National...*, pp. 450–451.

37 "The State of Israel: International Relations". In: Oron, Yitzhak (ed.): *Middle East Record.* Volume Two. Israel Program for Scientific Translations: Jerusalem, Israel 1961, p. 317.

heirs in the years 1945–46 with millions of dollars repatriated at the time. The Swiss Bankers Association dismissed the claim of the Israeli government that it had the authority to act on behalf of the Jewish victims of World War II. The big banks issued a coordinated response in May, 1954, whereby they decided not to provide any information on transactions dating back more than ten years "under any circumstances."[38] The problem of determining the actual size of Jewish assets in Switzerland remained unsolved since no outside agency or government department could have been assigned the authority to examine Swiss banks. This would have violated both Swiss banking practice and banking secrecy law.

Finally, in 1962 a Federal resolution, the Registration Decree, was passed by the Swiss Federal Council, upon which Swiss financial institutions were required to report all dormant accounts belonging to foreign or stateless persons. The assets on these accounts were later to be transferred to their rightful owners, successors, or to a special fund.[39] The new law set a ten-year period (September 1963 – September 1973) for Swiss banks to determine whether they had any dormant accounts belonging to Holocaust victims and to track down their owners. The banks were to report property held for foreign citizens and stateless persons, with respect to whom it was known or presumed that they were victims of racial, religious, or political persecution, on accounts dormant since May 1945. An office called the Claims Registry was created for the purpose of such reporting in the Justice Division of the Federal Department of Justice and Police in Bern. Theoretically, the compliance with the law was legally binding but since no outside examination was introduced, the determination of the accounts was left to the discretion of the banks. By 1974, the Swiss received and processed 7000 claims but only 961 were identified with a total sum of 9.5 million Swiss francs (then about $2 million). However, most of the applications were rejected on the grounds of insufficient information and only about 132 claims were approved, for a total of 1.6 million Swiss francs, 151 accounts were identified as belonging to owners from eastern bloc countries and their return was not pursued further,

38 Independent Commission of Experts Switzerland – Second World War: *Switzerland, National…*, p. 446.

39 The Bergier Commission attributes the sudden change in the Swiss approach to the publicity created by the Adolf Eichmann trial which had begun in Jerusalem in 1961 and which drew attention to the atrocities of the Holocaust. The Swiss could no longer ignore the claims of survivors, heirs and Jewish organizations. See Ibid., p. 452. See also Hug, Peter: "Unclaimed Assets of Nazi Victims in Switzerland: What People Knew and what else They Ought to Know". In: Kreis, Georg (ed.): *Switzerland and the Second World War*. Frank Cass Publishers: London 2000, pp. 81–102.

228 identified Jewish owners could not be located. As a result of this survey, almost 2 million Swiss francs were placed in a fund and distributed among the Swiss Federation of Jewish Communities[40] (60% of this amount) and the remaining balance was allocated to the Swiss Refuge Aid Society.[41]

The internal audit conducted by Swiss banks was lacking both in supervision and an enforcement mechanism, as many scholars and analysts have pointed out in the 1990s. As a result, the Swiss financial institutions did not have any incentive to thoroughly report dormant accounts.[42] Only federal intervention and supervision of banks would have enabled to credibly identify dormant accounts in Swiss banks, but at the time this was not a viable solution, which Swiss banks would have accepted.

As the Bergier Commission ascertained: "Throughout the post-war period the banks relied on a combination of discreetly playing down the problem and erecting barriers to investigation: time and again they would bring banking secrecy into play in order to legitimize their reluctance to provide information while at the same time charging high search fees for conducting investigations."[43] The Swiss banks were determined to thwart any legislation which would unblock victims' assets and succeeded in containing the government on this issue.[44]

The banks had a clear economic interest in obstructing any legislation which would effectively enforce the releasing of heirless assets since they could continue charging bank fees on dormant accounts and unclaimed safe-deposit boxes, and in case of interest-bearing assets banks could reap commission earnings. Interest was usually not paid on dormant accounts and bank charges accumulated over the long term. Before finally closing an account, banks were inclined to charge fees and expenses upon the account to the point of wiping out any balances it contained. When an account was reduced in such a way to a minimum amount,

---

40 German – Schweizerischer Israelitischer Gemeindebund (SIG).

41 For these figures see Blau, Gisela: "Switzerland," p. 296.

42 For example, see Bilenker, Stephanie A.: "In Re Holocaust...," p. 256, Blau, Gisela: "Switzerland," p. 296, and the Report of the Independent Committee of Eminent Persons, "Swiss Law on the Treatment of Dormant Accounts: A Comparison to European and U.S. Law", Annex 9 to Independent Committee of Eminent Persons: *Report on Dormant Accounts...*, p. 135, and Weber, Rolf H.: "Holocaust-Related Claims and Liability of Swiss Banks – Political and Legal Implications". *The International Lawyer* 36, No. 4, Winter 2002, p. 1221.

43 Independent Commission of Experts Switzerland – Second World War: *Switzerland, National...*, p. 446.

44 Ibid., p. 445.

it was cashed in by the bank. Banks also transferred unclaimed balances to their general reserves. More often, however, they were transferred to collective accounts and smaller dormant accounts were closed. When the ten-year archiving limit expired, banks could destroy all personal records pertaining to these accounts, and they often did. There was no loss to be incurred from safeguarding dormant accounts and unclaimed assets, on the contrary, there were only gains to be made for the financial institutions.[45]

No further attempts were made on the part of Swiss authorities or banks to resolve the issue of dormant accounts until 1995, when, in reaction to publications appearing in Israeli press from 1994 onwards and referring to dormant accounts, the Swiss Bankers Association (SBA) issued its Guidelines on the Treatment of Dormant Accounts, Custody Accounts, and Safe-Deposit Boxes held in Swiss Banks. The new regulation entered into force on January 1, 1996. The Swiss banking ombudsman was put in charge of processing the claims of victims and their heirs. As a result of this regulation, in February 1996 an additional 776 heirless accounts were identified, with assets of 38.7 million Swiss francs.[46] But this initiative came too late; the issue of dormant accounts in Switzerland had already aroused the interest of Jewish organizations, the World Jewish Congress, and the World Jewish Restitution Organization both led by Edgar Bronfman, a prominent Jewish activist and businessman,[47] who turned for support to Alfonse D'Amato, a republican senator and chairman of the United States Senate Committee on Banking, Housing and Urban Affairs. The Senator eagerly endorsed the campaign of Jewish organizations and brought the case before the Senate Committee. The restitution effort targeted at Swiss banks was now well on its course.

3.2 The Development of the Conflict

3.2.1 The Initial Stage: Involvement of Jewish Organizations and the U.S. Congress

The issue of dormant accounts was revisited in Switzerland in December 1994 when following foreign press reports on the existence of such accounts in Swiss banks Otto Piller, member of the Council of States, the upper house of the Swiss

45 Ibid., pp. 446–449.

46 Weber, Rolf H.: "Holocaust-Related Claims...," p. 1215.

47 Edgar Bronfman was the President of both organizations at the time of the conflict with Swiss banks.

Federal Assembly, enquired by means of the ordinary question about the status of unclaimed assets in Swiss banks.[1] This was followed by an ordinary question submitted by Jean Ziegler in March 1995 regarding assets of Holocaust victims deposited in Swiss banks. Ziegler demanded an explanation concerning the amounts of funds belonging to Jewish victims of Nazi genocide which remained dormant in Swiss banks. The Federal Council in a reply to Ziegler repeated the same arguments it used in the reply to the Piller request, namely that the banks performed their contractual duty in safekeeping dormant assets and the Council is not in the position to reveal the amounts in question as it is not clear whether such assets are still in the possession of Swiss banks.[2] Two weeks later a parliamentary interpellation was filed by Verena Grendelmeier, who enquired again about the unclaimed assets of victims of National-Socialist persecution and demanded the clarification of their status, including the partial lifting of banking secrecy in relation to this issue.[3] The initiative was withdrawn following the initiative of the National Council's Legal Affairs Committee, which took over the enquiry. Subsequently, the Piller-Plattner motion in June 1995 put forth the proposal of the creation of a central office where unclaimed assets would be reported and which would clarify the ownership of such assets and support Nazi victims

1 See Federal Assembly: "Motion Piller-Plattner: Herrenlose Vermögen auf Schweizer Banken: Eingereicht am 12.06.1995", *Amtliches Bulletin der Bundesversammlung*, 20.12.1995, Federal Department of Foreign Affairs, retrieved 17.04.2017, from https://www.eda.admin.ch/content/dam/parl-vor/2nd-world-war/1990-1999/herrenlose-vermoegen-auf-schweizer-banken.pdf and Federal Assembly: "Einfache Anfrage: Herrenlose Vermögenswerte: Eingereicht von: Otto Piller", 06.12.1994, retrieved 17.04.2017, from https://www.parlament.ch/afs/data/d/gesch/1994/d_gesch_19941147.htm. "An ordinary question, in the same way as an interpellation, enables members to request information on important events or matters relating to foreign or domestic policy affecting the Confederation. However, contrary to interpellations, ordinary questions are not put before the Federal Council, but are answered in writing by the Federal Council". See Federal Council: "Switzerland's..."

2 Federal Assembly: "Einfache Anfrage: Ziegler Jean: Vermögenswerte von Holocaust Opfern", 07.03.1995, Federal Department of Foreign Affairs, retrieved 17.04.2017, from https://www.eda.admin.ch/content/dam/parl-vor/2nd-world-war/1990-1999/vermoegenswerte-von-holocaust-opfern-bei-schweizer-banken.pdf.

3 Federal Assembly: "Parlamentarische Initiative: Herrenlose Vermögen von Opfern Nationalistischer Verfolgungen: Eingereicht von Verena Grendelmeier", Dossier 95.407, 24.03.1995, retrieved 28.04.2018, from https://www.parlament.ch/de/ratsbetrieb/suche-curia-vista/geschaeft?AffairId=19950407.

in their search for dormant accounts in Swiss banks, as well as distribute the assets for which no heirs have been found.[4]

In the beginning of 1995, the Federal Banking Commission ordered Swiss banks to look for accounts dormant for more than 10 years.

In 1995, in a speech to the Swiss Federal Assembly, commemorating the 50th anniversary of the end of World War II, the Swiss President Kaspar Villiger apologized for his nation's failure to protect the victims of Nazi persecution and for turning away Jewish refugees at the boarders.[5]

One month later an article in the Wall Street Journal described the struggle faced by Holocaust victims' heirs to gain access to Swiss bank accounts and mentioned a plan put forth by the Swiss Bankers Association to establish a centralized independent entity to handle claims for Holocaust era accounts.[6]

In September 1995, the World Jewish Restitution Organization (WJRO) released a letter from Israeli Prime Minister Yitzhak Rabin to WJRO president Edgar Bronfman, urging him to address the issue of Jewish dormant accounts in Switzerland.[7]

Shortly thereafter, a meeting took place between the representatives of the World Jewish Congress, Edgar Bronfman and Israel Singer, and the Swiss Bankers Association to discuss the appropriate procedure for processing claims to dormant accounts and for handling unclaimed accounts. The president of the

---

4 Federal Assembly: "Motion: Herrenlose Vermögen auf Schweizer Banken: Eingereicht von Otto Piller", 12.06.1995, retrieved 17.04.2017, from https://www.parlament.ch/de/ratsbetrieb/suche-curia-vista/geschaeft?AffairId=19953257.

5 "There is no doubt in my mind, that with our policy with respect to persecuted Jews we have burdened ourselves with guilt [...] we have made the wrong choice acting upon narrowly understood national interest. The Federal Council deeply regrets this and apologizes for this, knowing that this failure is in the end inexcusable." (Own translation from German). See Villiger, Kaspar: "Gedanken zum Kriegsende vor 50 Jahren, Sondersession", speech by Kaspar Villiger, President of the Swiss Confederation, 07.05.1995, retrieved 27.02.2017, from https://www.admin.ch/cp/d/1995May9.165750.4088@idz.bfi.admin.ch.html.

6 Gumbel, Peter: "Secret Legacies: Heirs of Nazis' Victims Challenge Swiss Banks On Wartime Deposits – Do Vaults Still Hold Jewelry or Cash in Accounts Dating to the Holocaust? – Pressure for Full Disclosure". *Wall Street Journal*, 21.06.1995, p. A1.

7 World Jewish Restitution Organization: *Framework for Allocation Plan of Funds Received in Global Settlement with the Swiss Banks & Others. Proposal to the Court.* Swiss Banks Settlement: In re Holocaust Victim Assets Litigation Official Website, October 1999, retrieved 28.05.2017, from http://www.swissbankclaims.com/DOCUMENTS_NEW/WJRO.pdf.

Swiss Federation of Jewish Communities asked the Commission and the Swiss Bankers Association to extend the search to include accounts dormant for longer than 50 years. The World Jewish Congress joined the request and finally the parties agreed for the search to include accounts opened between 1933 and May 8, 1945.[8] The Central Contact Office, which was established in January 1996 in response to pressure from Jewish organizations, was run by the Swiss ombudsman and was to process all individual inquiries.[9] In the period between 1996 and 1997, the office of the Swiss Banking Ombudsman received 2500 applications from claimants. The Swiss ombudsman uncovered 10 million Swiss francs out of a claimed 17 million by June 1997.[10]

At this stage the Jewish representatives demanded an external audit of Swiss banks as the basis for compensation, whereas the SBA offered a lump sum settlement.[11] Their respective positions would be reversed in the course of the development of the conflict.

The World Jewish Congress estimated the unclaimed assets to be in the range from tens of millions of dollars to billions of dollars. However, when in February 1996 the SBA proclaimed the results of an internal survey which found 775 dormant accounts in Swiss banks valued at $38.7 million,[12] the World Jewish Congress perceived this amount to be unsatisfactory and described the investigative process as one-sided and lacking transparency.[13]

The president of the World Jewish Congress, Edgar M. Bronfman, claimed that the search was insufficient, and turned for formal support to Alfonse D'Amato, a U.S. Senator and chairman of the Senate Committee on Banking, Housing and Urban Affairs, which supervises the activities of foreign banks in the United States.[14] The WJC was convinced that the only way to induce Swiss banks to open

8 Blau, Gisela: "Switzerland," p. 297.

9 Lamont, Kathryn H.: "Banking Secrecy Lifted: The Swiss Act to Counter Attacks Launched as a Result of Their Banks' Actions During World War II and Thereafter". *Penn State International Law Review* 16, No. 1, p. 239.

10 Blau, Gisela: "Switzerland," p. 297.

11 Eizenstat expressed his view, that if at the initial stage of the conflict the Swiss would have agreed to an independent audit, the whole affair would not have developed to the extent that it did. See Eizenstat, Stuart E.: *Imperfect Justice…*, p. 59.

12 Federal Assembly: "Chronology: Switzerland and the Second World War", retrieved 27.02.2017, from https://www.parlament.ch/centers/documents/en/do-ch-wk2-chronologie-e.pdf.

13 Henry, Marilyn: "Fifty Years of Holocaust Compensation…," pp. 3–84 and p. 29.

14 Stuart Eizenstat asserts in his memoir that Senator D'Amato agreed to take up the dormant accounts problem since if handled adequately, the Swiss banks controversy

their files to an external audit and to assign the control over heirless assets to the WJC for the benefit of Holocaust survivors was through the pressure of a public campaign.[15] Equipped with this additional political leverage the WJC targeted Swiss financial institutions in an unprecedented public relations battle for what many victims as well as the U.S. public opinion perceived as a fight for justice, but what the Swiss saw as yet another American violation of Swiss sovereignty.

In April 1996, the Senate Committee began the first of over a dozen congressional hearings on the fate of Jewish Holocaust era accounts and the difficulties encountered by Holocaust survivors in reclaiming their assets. With the purpose of reinforcing claims for Jewish dormant accounts Senator D'Amato and the World Jewish Congress began releasing to the press documents from the files of the U.S. Safehaven operation.[16] The effect surpassed all expectations as it led to a broad review of the relations of Switzerland with Nazi Germany and fueled a negative media campaign all over the world.

During the hearings conducted by Senator Alfonse D'Amato the agreement concluded on June 25, 1949 between Switzerland and the Polish communist regime was also brought to light. This agreement allowed the Polish state to acquire in Switzerland the assets of deceased Polish citizens without heirs; the balance of the Polish heirless accounts and the proceeds from the liquidation of other financial assets, such as insurance policies, could then be used to pay for Swiss claims against Poland, resulting from the nationalization of Swiss property. When the U.S. obtained information about the agreement from press reports, the State Department urged the U.S. Legation in Bern to transmit a note to the Swiss expressing U.S. concern. The note was sent in December 1949 and pointed to the inconsistency of the Swiss-Polish agreement with the declarations previously made by Swiss officials regarding the disposition of heirless assets found in Switzerland. The U.S. transmitted a second note in March 1950; however, the Swiss diplomatic response rejected the U.S. arguments and evasively suggested that more information was needed on the assets for any further commitments.[17]

---

would have provided a career boost for the senator, making it a winning issue for his 1998 reelection campaign. See Eizenstat, Stuart E.: *Imperfect Justice…*, p. 61.

15 Eizenstat, Stuart E.: *Imperfect Justice…*, p. 63.

16 Upon their release the documents were labelled "newly declassified", however many of these sources were not new at all, some were in fact released two decades before, but without attracting any interest. See Henry, Marilyn: "Fifty Years of Holocaust Compensation…," p. 30.

17 U.S. Department of State: *U.S. and Allied Efforts To Recover and Restore Gold and Other Assets Stolen or Hidden by Germany During World War II…*, p. 200.

Revelations about this agreement, although known in the U.S. already in 1949, resurfaced and further fueled international outrage as it became obvious that the firm adherence to banking secrecy by Swiss banks was not absolute, but rather a question of selective choice.[18]

The D'Amato hearings were broadcast live on Swiss television and took over front page headlines in Swiss newspapers.

3.2.2 Independent Committee of Eminent Persons-Volcker Commission

Confronted with mounting public pressure and negative press the SBA finally agreed to set up a special body designated to investigate the status of Holocaust assets in Swiss banks.

On May 2, 1996, a Memorandum of Understanding was signed between the World Jewish Congress, the World Jewish Restitution Organization (WJRO) and the Swiss Bankers Association, which established the Independent Committee of Eminent Persons (ICEP).[19] Paul Volcker, former chairman of the U.S. Board of Governors of the Federal Reserve was appointed as the head of the Committee.[20] The Volcker Commission,[21] as it came to be known, conducted the largest bank audit in the history of world finance. The investigation of all Swiss banks which operated during World War II commenced in January 1998.[22] The Commission appointed independent accounting firms[23] which were granted unprecedented

---

18 The Polish democratic government distanced itself from the agreement and condemned the undertakings of the Communist regime in this respect as unethical.

19 "Memorandum of Understanding between The World Jewish Restitution Organization and the World Jewish Congress representing also the Jewish Agency and Allied Organizations and the Swiss Bankers Association". New York 02.05.1996, *Swiss Banks Settlement: In re Holocaust Victim Assets Litigation,* retrieved 28.05.2017, from http://www.swissbankclaims.com/Documents/DOC_1_memo_of.pdf.

20 The choice of Volcker as chairman was a compromise between Swiss and Jewish interests. He was American, the son of German immigrants, he served as chairman of the U.S. Federal Reserve Board of Governors under presidents Carter and Reagan. Since 1988, he was also a member of the board of Nestlé, a Swiss corporate giant. See Eizenstat, Stuart E.: *Imperfect Justice*..., pp. 69–70.

21 The Independent Committee of Eminent Persons consisted of three members and two alternates appointed by the SBA, and three members and two alternates appointed by WJRO.

22 Blau, Gisela: "Switzerland," p. 297.

23 The auditing firms were the biggest names in the world of finance: Arthur Andersen, Coopers & Lybrand, Deloitte & Touche, KPMG, and Price Waterhouse.

access to internal bank information in line with the provision of the Memorandum of Understanding, which stated that: "The SBA will assure the auditors unfettered access to all relevant files in banking institutions regarding dormant accounts and other assets and financial instruments deposited before, during and immediately after the Second World War."[24]

The investigative task which the Volcker Commission undertook was a challenging one. There were numerous difficulties in identifying dormant accounts. Some accounts were opened as numbered accounts and the true names of the owners were all too well concealed. Some owners used intermediaries since it was illegal in many European countries to deposit money into foreign bank accounts. Banks have merged, closed, and moved deposits to other countries.[25]

The Volcker Commission in the course of its investigation evaluated 4.1 million accounts (out of an estimated total of 6.8 million accounts which have existed in the prewar and postwar period) which were either open or opened between 1933 and May 1945 and had been inactive for a period of more than 10 years and audited records of 254 Swiss banks existing in 1945. The cost of this three-year audit, which employed up to 650 forensic accountants amounted to 300 million Swiss francs and was fully covered by Swiss banks. This cost was perceived by the banks as disproportionate to the estimated and the actual amounts found in the dormant accounts.[26] The Volcker Commission finally concluded its findings in December 1999: the total number of accounts with a probable or possible relationship to Holocaust victims amounted to 53,886. The Commission estimated the current value of these accounts amounts to be between 643 million USD and 1.36 billion USD and urged Swiss banks to publish the names of 25,187 account holders as defined in the top three categories of the conducted study.[27] Out of these 53,886 accounts with a probable or possible relationship to victims of Nazi persecution, a total of 38,980 had been closed by the banks, and out of this number 36,258 accounts had been closed without explanation in surviving records, 2,305 had been closed as the balance was transferred to profits or had

---

24 "Memorandum of Understanding between The World Jewish Restitution Organization..."

25 For an analysis of these problems connected with the work of the commission see Independent Committee of Eminent Persons: *Report on Dormant Accounts...*, p. 2, p. 6, and p. 12.

26 Ibid., p. 4.

27 Ibid., p. 20.

been eaten up by fees and 417 accounts were transferred to Germany by means of coercion of the account owner by the Nazi authorities.[28]

The Report emphasized that the identification of accounts as having a probable or possible relationship to victims of Nazi persecution warrants a claims resolution process with respect to these accounts, to determine whether the owner of the account was in fact a victim. The Report explicitly stated that "The inclusion of an account in this group is not necessarily conclusive evidence that any one account is in fact that of a victim of Nazi persecution, or that such accounts have been withheld, deliberately or otherwise, from Holocaust victims."[29]

However, the Report also stated that there exists "confirmed evidence of questionable and deceitful actions by some individual banks in the handling of accounts of victims, including withholding of information from Holocaust victims or their heirs about their accounts, inappropriate closing of accounts, failure to keep adequate records, many cases of insensitivity to the efforts of victims or heirs of victims to claim dormant or closed accounts, and a general lack of diligence – even active resistance – in response to earlier private and official inquiries about dormant accounts."[30] The Report also found evidence of mitigating factors, such as the "many cases in which banks actively sought out missing account holders or their heirs, including Holocaust victims, and paid the account balances of dormant accounts to the proper parties."[31] In most cases the banks treated foreign and domestic customers with respect to dormant accounts in a similar way.

On the other hand there were documented cases when the banks did not provide information to claimants and resumed an indifferent approach towards them, out of "fear of embarrassment and litigation arising out of transfers of victims' accounts to Nazi authorities after these victims had been coerced into signing transfer papers."[32] The participation of Swiss banks in these so called forced transfers was condemned by the Jewish representatives and used as an important argument in the negotiations of the settlement.

28 Ibid., p. 10.
29 Ibid., p. 10.
30 Ibid., p. 13.
31 Ibid., p. 14.
32 Ibid., p. 15.

3.2.3 Class Action Suits

By mid-1996 it seemed that the Swiss bank controversy was put under control: the Swiss were cooperating and accommodated the U.S. requests. In response to the demands of the WJC and the U.S. government the Volcker Committee conducted an independent audit of Swiss bank accounts. However, this situation changed in October 1996 with the filing of class-action lawsuits.

The class action device which was employed in the Swiss bank litigation, namely Rule Twenty Three of the Federal Rules of Civil Procedure, is a mechanism unique to the U.S. legal system, and has served as a powerful litigation tool. Class actions are "representative suits on behalf of similarly suited persons,"[33] whereby claims are pooled together and filed as a single suit by a representative plaintiff, who satisfies the requirements of the class action and has individual standing to bring a claim on behalf of other class members, who do not need to prove their individual standing.[34] A proposed class must satisfy a number of prerequisites[35] for an action to be certified by the court as a class action:[36] numerosity (the class should be so numerous that it is impracticable for each member to appear individually before a court), commonality (there are common legal or factual issues to the class), typicality (the claims of the representatives are typical of the claims of the class), and finally the adequacy of representation (the representatives protect the interests of other class members fairly and adequately).[37]

The construct of class action suits is often employed to raise politically sensitive issues in cases of discrimination of civil rights or other social concerns. Even minor misdemeanors can be elevated to enormous damage claims using the vehicle of class actions. The attorney's fees are dependent upon the result of the legal process, this is why they are called contingency fees. They are expressed

---

33 Ganz, Jodi Berlin: "Heirs Without Assets...," p. 1344.

34 "Standing is the ability of a party to bring a lawsuit in court based upon their stake in the outcome. A party seeking to demonstrate standing must be able to show the court sufficient connection to and harm from the law or action challenged". Otherwise, the court will dismiss the case due to a lack of standing. See "Standing Law and Legal Definition". US Legal, retrieved 22.03.2017, from https://definitions.uslegal.com/s/standing/.

35 Rule 23 – Class Actions, Federal Rules of Civil Procedure, retrieved 25.09.2017, from https://www.federalrulesofcivilprocedure.org/frcp/title-iv-parties/rule-23-class-actions/.

36 Ibid.

37 Ganz, Jodi Berlin: "Heirs Without Assets...," pp. 1345–1346.

as a percentage of the total payoff, and these sums are very high in case of winning the suit. Due to these high potential payoffs, the lawyers are determined to pursue lengthy battles in and out of court and this is why in case of litigation involving Swiss banks the lawyers did not limit the lawsuits to individual dormant accounts, but instead included claims for damages resulting from the Swiss banks accepting deposits of German looted assets and deposits from German companies, which employed slave labor. By extending the scope of the lawsuits beyond dormant accounts the potential stakes were elevated to multimillion-dollar payoffs. As Stuart Eizenstat firmly stated in his memoirs: "The lawyers hijacked the Swiss bank dispute,"[38] since they "were not in it to find the historical truth. Most were in it for the money."[39] The lawyers representing the lawsuits were not unanimous, in fact they soon organized into two competing sets: Fagan-Swift and Hausfeld-Weiss.[40]

It is important to emphasize here that at this stage the lawsuits involved only private individuals suing private companies.

The first lawsuit was filed in the U.S. District Court for the Eastern District of New York. Friedman and four other named plaintiffs sued Union Bank of Switzerland, Swiss Bank Corporation, and Credit Suisse, the three largest Swiss banks, alleging in the complaint that Swiss banks have withheld Jewish assets deposited by Holocaust victims prior to, or during World War II, accepted looted Nazi assets and laundered them, accepted profits from the Nazi regime by exploiting slave labor[41] and participated in a conspiracy to conceal and prevent the recovery of these assets. The plaintiffs sought $20 billion in damages and a full accounting of the deposits belonging to survivors and their families.

In the second lawsuit, which followed weeks later, Gizella Weisshaus and three other named plaintiffs alleged that the defendant banks concealed and converted

---

38 Eizenstat, Stuart E.: *Imperfect Justice…*, p. 75.

39 Ibid., p. 77.

40 Ibid., p. 84.

41 Slave labor in the context of Holocaust litigation meant labor "performed in settings in which the lifespan of the laborer was measured in months", whereas forced labor meant "labor performed for minimal or no pay and under force, but by those for whom the traditional economics of slavery still applied". As opposed to slave labor, forced labor was employed with the intention that the victims would survive and continue to perform labor for their captors. See Weiss, Melvyn I.: "A Litigator's Postscript to the Swiss Banks and Holocaust Litigation Settlements". In: Bazyler, Michael J./Alford, Roger P. (eds.): *Holocaust Restitution. Perspectives on the Litigation and Its Legacy*. New York University Press: New York et al. 2006, p. 113.

assets deposited in Swiss accounts prior to 1946 and profited from looting of personal property by the Nazis.

In both cases, the defendant banks were to disclose all looted assets and accounts dormant since 1946. The Friedman lawsuit also requested the banks to release all profits from slave labor, which were reaped from the work of concentration camp workers and deposited in Swiss bank accounts.

The third lawsuit was filed in January 1997 by the World Council of Orthodox Jewish Communities, Inc. which represented predominantly the interests of the orthodox Satmar Hasidic Jews.

There were three types of claims shared by all three lawsuits against Swiss banks: 1) the "dormant accounts" claims pertaining to the failure of the banks to return the funds deposited in Swiss banks by their Jewish clients, 2) the "looted assets" claims referring to the banks making profits from assets looted by the Nazis from Jews and deposited in these banks, 3) the "slave labor" claims which referred to the banks profiting from money which was earned as a result of employing slave labor by German and Swiss companies and deposited in Swiss banks.[42]

All three suits were consolidated for discovery purposes in April 1997 as "In Re Holocaust Victim Assets Litigation".

The Swiss banks filed several motions to dismiss the class action lawsuits in May 1997.[43] The banks attempted to dismiss the suits on legal grounds (non-justiciability, international comity, failure to state a claim, lack of subject matter jurisdiction), but the judge never ruled on these motions.

Numerous doubts were expressed with respect to the class action suits, such as the statute of limitations, since the transactions that the lawsuits referred to took place over fifty years before the cases were brought before court. However, the plaintiffs argued that the defendant banks could not raise the statute of limitations due to the ongoing activities of the banks to conceal their common scheme to prevent access to, and knowledge of, the dormant assets. Furthermore, the plaintiffs and the plaintiff class had not acted without due care or without essential diligence since they remained without access to vital information in order to pursue their claims.[44]

The legal base for bringing the case before the U.S. courts as the appropriate jurisdiction was threefold:

---

42 Bazyler, Michael J.: "The Holocaust…", p. 14.
43 Bilenker, Stephanie A.: "In Re Holocaust…," p. 253.
44 Ibid., p. 275 and p. 277.

28 U.S. Code § 1332 – Diversity of citizenship; amount in controversy; costs:

(a) The district courts shall have original jurisdiction of all civil actions where the matter in controversy exceeds the sum or value of $75,000, exclusive of interest and costs, and is between—[...]
(2)
citizens of a State and citizens or subjects of a foreign state.[45]

Plaintiffs in the first two suits rested subject matter jurisdiction over defendants on diversity under this provision.

28 U.S. Code § 1331 – Federal question:

The district courts shall have original jurisdiction of all civil actions arising under the Constitution, laws, or treaties of the United States.[46]

28 U.S. Code § 1350 – Alien's Action for Tort (Alien Tort Claims Act):

The district courts shall have original jurisdiction of any civil action by an alien for a tort only, committed in violation of the law of nations or a treaty of the United States.[47]

Plaintiffs in the Friedman case-based jurisdiction for additional claims of international human rights and treaty violations upon these two last provisions: § 1331 and § 1350. Whereas § 1331 requires an action to arise under the laws or a treaty of the United States, § 1350 requires only a violation of the law of nations in order to warrant jurisdiction of U.S. district courts. In particular the Friedman complaint points out, that by conspiring with the Nazis and profiting from the Nazi regime's looting and exploiting of slave labor the Swiss banks violated various international treaties, customary international laws and fundamental human rights laws which prohibit genocide, war crimes, crimes against humanity, slavery, slave and forced labor, and so forth. The court would have had to find that such indirect involvement violated a treaty to which the United States was a party. This was unlikely, however, since international treaties usually do not provide a right to sue with respect to private individuals. As regards the issue of violation of customary international law, courts have mixed rulings on whether violations of international law or the law of nations provides a private right of action. Certain court rulings have asserted that the enforcement of international law is left to the individual states and because international law is not a source of a private right of action, a plaintiff's claims related to human rights

45 28 U.S. Code § 1332 – Diversity of citizenship; amount in controversy; costs.
46 28 U.S. Code § 1331 – Federal question.
47 28 U.S. Code § 1350 – Alien's action for tort.

violations cannot arise under federal common law. Under this interpretation § 1331 cannot justify jurisdiction over such claims. If the court was to confirm jurisdiction under § 1331 or § 1332, it would have had to be proven that the Swiss banks looted and concealed Jewish assets and that these activities in turn supported the Nazis in committing human rights violations.[48] Upon the Alien Tort Claims Act federal courts have the jurisdiction to decide whether plaintiffs who are not citizens of the United States can maintain a private course of action. This provision has been successfully applied to civil suits alleging a violation of international law and federal courts have found subject matter jurisdiction over such claims.[49]

Similar considerations as to whether the three class action suits would hold up in court were raised in a 1996 paper by Jodi Berlin Ganz. The suits faced "serious certification challenges"[50] and the international nature of the cases called into question "the overall appropriateness of resolving international claims in U.S. courts."[51] Interestingly, the author concluded the analysis of the fulfillment of certification requirements by stating that "the Court will likely choose to rule consistently with its earlier rationale and dismiss the claims in favor of a more appropriate tribunal."[52]

Legal rulings on the merits of the asserted claims were never issued in the course of the legal proceedings. Nevertheless, the banks finally agreed to an unprecedented final settlement of $1.25 billion.

Why then, taking all these factors into consideration, did the Swiss banks decide to settle? A victory in court might have had only a limited value over the long term, since it could generate intense political and economic pressure in the context of claims asserted by the victims, which conclusively could have been more threatening to the banks, than a lawsuit. The mechanism of pressure on the Swiss banks is discussed further in the text. The banks, however, never assumed any legal responsibility, claiming that the settlement reflected only moral responsibility.

While the Swiss bank litigation process was under way, the World Jewish Congress attempted to settle all claims with the banks by pursuing an alternative to the litigation procedure. The scheme of the WJC failed to impede the litigation,

48 Bilenker, Stephanie A.: "In Re Holocaust…," pp. 267–269.
49 For an analysis of these cases see Ibid., pp. 270–273.
50 Ganz, Jodi Berlin: "Heirs Without Assets…," p. 1366.
51 Ibid., p. 1366.
52 Ibid., p. 1368.

nevertheless the WJC intervened in the litigation process and claimed a right to recovery of "heirless claims". In fact, the WJC was seeking a recovery for the organization to fund its goals. Had this strategy succeeded, instead of full funds being assigned to victims with real claims, a significant portion of funds would have gone to the WJC.[53]

The transnational Holocaust restitution lawsuits which were brought before U.S. federal courts in the 1990s were a successful example of the use of civil litigation and private law doctrines in international judicial procedure.

Over the long run, the lawsuits imposed additional continuous pressure on the Swiss banks to reach an agreement with the World Jewish Congress. They forced Swiss authorities to reexamine Swiss dealings with the Nazis and the questionable conduct of the Swiss during World War II, as well as exposed and won international publicity for the unfair postwar treatment of Holocaust survivors and the heirs of Holocaust victims. The gravity of the crisis which followed led to the involvement of the Swiss government and elevated the case to diplomatic levels.[54]

The immediate effect of the lawsuits was to induce the Swiss banks to undertake measures to appease claimants and preserve their image. On February 5, 1997, the three Swiss banks: Union Bank of Switzerland, Swiss Bank Corporation, and Credit Suisse announced that they would open a fund for Holocaust survivors. The Swiss government also reacted to the international criticism of Switzerland's role during World War II, which accompanied the lawsuits, by proposing the creation of a humanitarian fund with assets worth $4.7 billion.[55]

The Swiss government, which up to the mid-1990s supported the stance that the issue of dormant accounts was a private business of the banks, finally took to action. In October 1996, a task force was established within the Swiss Foreign Affairs Ministry with the aim to investigate the controversy over Holocaust assets.[56] Thomas Borer, a Swiss diplomat, headed the task force and struggled with the burden of coordinating the response of the Swiss government to the developing crisis. Even though the Swiss government refused to take part in the class-action negotiations or the settlement process, prompted by the fear of the settlement

53 Swift, Robert A.: "Holocaust Litigation and Human Rights Jurisprudence". In: Bazyler, Michael J./Alford, Roger P. (eds.): *Holocaust Restitution: Perspectives on the Litigation and Its Legacy*. New York University Press: New York et al. 2006, p. 54.

54 Henry, Marilyn: "Fifty Years of Holocaust Compensation…," p. 32.

55 Bilenker, Stephanie A.: "In Re Holocaust…," p. 253.

56 Blau, Gisela: "Switzerland," p. 299.

being submitted to a public referendum, the Swiss responded to the mounting crisis by enacting a legislation which would examine the Swiss wartime history in every possible detail.

3.2.4 The Bergier Commission

The Memorandum of Understanding, which created the Volcker Commission promised to engage the Swiss government in investigating the issue of looted assets in Swiss banks.[57] However, it was the Swiss Parliament which passed legislation to create a special commission of historians, which was entrusted with fulfilling this task. As counteraction to the U.S. Senate investigations, the Swiss Parliament, by a Federal Decree of December 16, 1996[58] established an Independent Committee of Experts under the chairmanship of Swiss professor and renown historian Jean François Bergier.[59] The aim of the Bergier Commission, as it was called, was to pursue within a period of 5 years from its creation a comprehensive examination of Switzerland's wartime conduct with focus on financial dealings with the Nazis, including gold and currency transactions and Holocaust victims' assets. A legal basis for the investigation was provided by the Decree, which temporarily lifted banking secrecy in order to avoid a potential violation of the law by Swiss banks.[60] The Bergier Commission's investigation

57 "(5) The parties of the agreement will cooperate to assure that the Swiss government will deal with the question of looted assets in Swiss banks or other institutions which were not reported or returned under the relevant laws during the years before, during and immediately after the Second World War". See "Memorandum of Understanding between The World Jewish Restitution Organization…"

58 Federal Assembly: "Federal Decree Concerning the Historical and Legal Investigation of the Fate of Assets Which Reached Switzerland as a Result of National Socialist Rule of December 13, 1960." In: Independent Committee of Eminent Persons: *Report on Dormant Accounts of Victims of Nazi Persecution in Swiss Banks*. Stämpfli Verlag AG: *Bern* 1999, Appendix F: Report of the Independent Committee of Eminent Persons, retrieved 14.04.2018, from http://www.swissbankclaims.com/Documents/DOC_4_bergier_.pdf, pp. A-21–A-28.

59 Other members of the Commission included among others Sybil Milton form the U.S. Holocaust Memorial Museum in Washington, Harold James of Princeton University, Władysław Bartoszewski, prominent Polish historian and Auschwitz survivor and Saul Friedlander, the Israeli historian and Holocaust survivor. Swiss historian Dr. Jacques Picard was the research director.

60 See Article 5: Obligation to Grant Access to Records "2. The obligation to grant access to the records takes precedence over any legal or contractual secrecy obligations" of

was not limited to the financial aspects of Swiss conduct during the war, instead extending to issues such as the involvement of Swiss companies in employing forced labor, Swiss refugee policy, foreign trade policy, trade in looted goods and art, as well as overall cooperation with Germany, including the involvement in German covert operations and transit policy.[61] The Bergier Commission produced numerous reports on all these issues, providing a vast array of knowledge on the subject.

The prolific findings of the Bergier Commission in many aspects questioned the Swiss self-representation as a neutral safe-haven which resisted Nazi oppression, presenting in certain cases a harsh assessment of Swiss policy, as with respect to refugees, or trade in gold.

As the Bergier Commission pointed out, as a result of the ten-year limitation period on archiving records and the common bank practice of closing small unclaimed accounts, they often disappeared rendering the findings of the Independent Committee of Eminent Persons incomplete.[62]

Certain conclusions made by the Bergier Commission supported the claims made by Jewish organizations, however, they were published already after the settlement with the Swiss banks was reached, and therefore played no part in influencing the final outcome of the negotiations.[63]

While the establishment of the Bergier Commission was perceived as a step in the right direction, this positive impact was soon countered by Swiss diplomatic lapses and misconduct of one of Switzerland's largest banks. The Meili affair, examined below, called the credibility of Swiss banks into question and created a major public relations disaster, further fueling the conflict.

---

the Federal Assembly: "Federal Decree Concerning the Historical and Legal Investigation..." pp. A-21–A-28.

61 Independent Commission of Experts Switzerland – Second World War, retrieved 02.02.2017, from https://www.uek.ch/en/.

62 Independent Commission of Experts Switzerland – Second World War: *Switzerland, National...*, p. 446.

63 An evaluation of the Bergier Commission's work and findings is provided in an interesting article by a member of the Commission, Junz, Helen B.: "Confronting Holocaust History: The Bergier Commission's Research on Switzerland's Past". Jerusalem Center for Public Affairs, 01.05.2003, retrieved 15.06.2017, from http://www.jcpa.org/phas/phas-8.htm.

3.2.5 The Meili Affair

Christoph Meili was a security guard at the Zürich headquarters of the Union Bank of Switzerland. On January 8, 1997, during his afternoon shift he entered the bank's shredding room and found metal bins with ledgers inside. One contained document dating from 1864 until 1970 for three banks: UBS, the Swiss National Bank and the Eidgenössische bank, which was taken over by UBS in 1945. He also found books of the German Reichsbank, which listed stock and real estate holdings from the period during World War II. Other entries involved the names of German companies such as Bayrische Sodawerke, Degussa and Degesch, which was partly owned by Degussa (the company had a controlling stake in Degesch). Degussa, a chemicals company processed the gold dental fillings removed from concentration camp prisoners, Degesch was a company which made Zyklon B, the gas used to exterminate prisoners of Nazi concentration camps. The books also listed entries for real estate transactions in Berlin during the period from 1933–1945. On attached notes there was information on the prices in Reichsmarks and annotations that these were forced sales of property.[64]

Of course, Meili most probably did not know of all the above-mentioned details about the German companies, however Meili knew about the Decree, introduced only three weeks before his finding, which explicitly prohibited the destruction of all bank documents from the Nazi era.[65] Following the introduction of the legislation, Swiss banks, including UBS issued strict internal regulations forbidding the destruction of any internal documents.

Meili took some sixty pages and three ledgers with him. The documents taken by Meili included a handwritten record of loans from the 1920s and account records from the 1930s until the 1970s, identifying properties in the possession of the Eidgenössische Bank and later of UBS.[66]

Meili tried to pass the documents to an appropriate entity, beginning with a Zurich newspaper, then the Israeli Embassy, the Israeli Cultural Center in Zürich, where finally he was put in contact with a journalist for Jewish press in Zurich, whom he gave some of the documents.[67]

---

64 Eizenstat, Stuart E.: *Imperfect Justice...*, pp. 94–95.

65 This legislation was introduced together with the legislation creating the Bergier Commission. See Article 4 of the Federal Assembly: "Federal Decree Concerning the Historical and Legal Investigation..."

66 Blau, Gisela: "Switzerland," p. 302.

67 Eizenstat, Stuart E.: *Imperfect Justice...*, p. 95.

As news of the discovery spread, Meili became an international media personality. Senator D'Amato tried to convince him to appear before his Committee. However, in Switzerland Meili was temporarily suspended by the security company which employed him, immediately after it became known that he took with him the documents from the bank. Subsequently, his employment was terminated. The chairman of UBS, Robert Studer, attacked Meili on Swiss Television claiming that his actions were a purposeful act, aimed at discrediting the bank. Meili received threats and hate mail, and finally decided to leave Switzerland with his family and seek refuge in the United States.

In May 1997, he testified before the U.S. Congress. Senator D'Amato intervened on Meili's behalf and Meili was the only Swiss national ever to be granted political asylum in the U.S., which was executed via a private bill signed by President Clinton.[68]

In July 1997, Senator D'Amato threatened to revoke or suspend the banking license of United Bank of Switzerland which would effectively ban it from doing business in the U.S., if Switzerland continued its policy towards Mr. Meili. The republican Senator demanded an apology to Mr. Meili from the Swiss government and an end to the criminal investigation against him, as well as a Swiss enquiry into the behavior of the bank, to explain the destruction of the documents. UBS refused to disclose the contents of the documents until July, when it finally stated that some of them were related to the forced sale of Jewish property in Berlin by the Nazis.[69]

The Swiss legal system needed nine months to decide whether or not to accuse Meili of breaching banking secrecy, before the case was finally suspended. The persons responsible for the unlawful destruction of documents in the UBS archive were never held accountable.[70]

Owing to the Meili affair Switzerland was once again in the headlines. The press depicted Switzerland as a wrongdoer, a country which profited from looted and victim's gold, which sold arms to the Nazis, turned over Jewish refugees to

---

68 See Schapiro, Jane: *Inside a Class Action: The Holocaust and the Swiss Banks*. University of Wisconsin Press/Terrace Books: Madison, Wisconsin 2003, p. 131 and "Christoph Meili Returns – as Hero or Villain?". *Swissinfo*, 09.04.2009, retrieved 20.10.2017, from https://www.swissinfo.ch/eng/christoph-meili-returns---as-hero-or-villain-/7330344.

69 Sanger, David E.: "D'Amato Threatens Action Against Swiss Banks in Shredding Case". *New York Times*, 31.07.1997, retrieved 20.05.2018, from http://www.nytimes.com/1997/07/31/world/d-amato-threatens-action-against-swiss-bank-in-shredding-case.html.

70 Blau, Gisela: "Switzerland," p. 302.

the Gestapo and dealt with the Reichsbank.[71] Although all these claims with respect to Swiss wartime dealings were in fact true to some extent, the context in which they were divulged did not support the Swiss cause, instead adding to the already strained U.S.-Swiss relations.

As Stuart Eizenstat aptly pointed out, the Meili affair "did more than anything to turn the Swiss banks into international pariahs by linking their dubious behavior during and after the war to the discovery of a seemingly unapologetic attempt to cover it up."[72]

3.2.6 Diplomatic Blunders and the Holocaust Fund

The World Jewish Congress urged the creation of a fund of $250 million to accommodate the claims of elderly Jews waiting for the outcome of the investigations.

Swiss President, Jean-Pascal Delamuraz on January 1, 1997, his last day in office, called the proposal "extortion" and "blackmail"[73] and rejected it on the grounds that it would constitute an admission of guilt by the Swiss. He also claimed that the way this issue was handled reflected the desire to "destabilize and compromise Switzerland."[74] The Swiss banks and politicians, according to the President, perceived the publicity attacks as aimed at weakening the Swiss financial center and its increasingly global role.[75] Delamuraz bluntly stated that in view of the attacks on Switzerland he had to ask himself whether Auschwitz was in fact in Switzerland rather than in Poland.[76]

Shortly after the derogatory remarks made by President Delamuraz, on January 28, 1997 the Swiss Ambassador to the U.S., Carlo Jagmetti resigned after a leaked diplomatic cable was made public, in which he stated that the conflict with the U.S. "is a war which Switzerland must conduct on the foreign and

71 Ibid., p. 303.

72 Eizenstat, Stuart E.: *Imperfect Justice…*, p. 94.

73 "Swiss President Says Pleas for a Holocaust Fund Are 'Blackmail'". *Reuters*, 01.01.1997, retrieved 30.03.2018, from http://www.nytimes.com/1997/01/01/world/swiss-president-says-pleas-for-a-holocaust-fund-are-blackmail.html.

74 Ibid.

75 Ibid. Delamuraz promptly apologized for his comments. See "Former Swiss President Apologizes". *Chicago Tribune*, 15.01.1997, retrieved 04.04.2018, from http://articles.chicagotribune.com/1997-01-15/news/9701160323_1_world-jewish-congress-nazi-victims-swiss-government.

76 The spokesman for Delamuraz demanded the withdrawal of this statement, but only one paper complied with the request. See Blau, Gisela: "Switzerland," p. 304.

domestic front, and must win."[77] He referred to the Jewish groups as "opponents" who "cannot be trusted."[78] The Clinton Administration responded promptly, denouncing the remarks.

Following the derogatory statements made by Jean-Pascal Delamuraz on January 1, 1997, the City and the State of New York threatened to apply sanctions with respect to Swiss banks operating in the United States. The Meili affair which erupted in the beginning of January also added to the tensions.

The big three Swiss banks reacted to the rapidly growing crisis and on February 5, 1997 agreed to set up a humanitarian fund for needy Holocaust victims, with assets worth 100 million Swiss francs ($70 million). Other Swiss banks, insurance companies and businesses subsequently contributed to the fund. Finally, the Swiss National Bank's contribution of 100 million Swiss francs[79] raised the total amount in the fund to $200 million. The fund was managed predominantly by the World Jewish Restitution Organization.[80] The purpose of the fund was not to assist in the restitution of specific claims, but rather it was a humanitarian gesture towards all Holocaust victims, purposefully set up to demonstrate that the Swiss nation cared about their fate.[81] While the Swiss financial sector was attempting to pursue damage control, at the same time anti-American sentiment was growing in Switzerland in response to the D'Amato hearings. The Swiss public resented to have its wartime behavior scrutinized by a foreign power.

The Swiss banks agreed to set up the fund, however they argued that two issues were still to be determined: the exact amounts in the dormant accounts, as well as how much of these assets actually belonged to Holocaust victims. There was a number of solutions available to Swiss banks as they faced negative press and pressure from the U.S. litigation, such as returning the money to dormant account owners in cases where there was a reasonable match to the owner or heir, providing compensation in cases where the banks could not find any money, or providing a lump sum of funds to Jewish organizations to be redistributed among

---

77 Sanger, David E.: "Swiss Envoy to U.S. Resigns After His Report on Holocaust Dispute is Disclosed". *New York Times*, 28.01.1997, retrieved 14.03.2018, from http://www.nytimes.com/1997/01/28/world/swiss-envoy-to-us-resigns-after-his-report-on-holocaust-dispute-is-disclosed.html.

78 Ibid.

79 It was debated, whether the large contribution of the SNB should not be put to a parliamentary vote, but finally the SNB was left to make its own decision, out of fear that the proposal would be rejected. See Blau, Gisela: "Switzerland," p. 299.

80 Ibid., p. 299.

81 Ibid., p. 300.

claimants. The problem was that the amount which the banks were willing to distribute to the claimants was much lower than the figures estimated by the Jewish organizations to be still deposited in dormant accounts. The World Jewish Congress purported that the Jewish money remaining dormant in Swiss accounts amounted to between $3 billion and $7 billion.[82]

In March 1997, the Swiss President, Arnold Koller, proposed to create a 7 billion Swiss francs ($4.7 billion) solidarity fund from the reevaluation of the gold reserves of the Swiss National Bank. The concept included drawing several hundred million Swiss francs from the solidarity fund annually and donating it to support victims of natural disasters, genocide, and oppression around the world, including Holocaust survivors.[83] Christoph Blocher, Swiss right-wing leader strongly opposed the proposal and threatened to call a national referendum. Moreover, Blocher was determined to campaign for a referendum on any settlement with foreign Holocaust claimants, which would involve the Swiss government. Submitting a settlement to a popular vote would likely mean its rejection by the Swiss public. Presumably this factor prevented the Swiss government from participating in the negotiations and the banks were left to themselves.[84]

3.2.7 The Eizenstat Report and the Involvement of the U.S. Government

In 1996, the Senate Committee on Banking, Housing and Urban Affairs, which held hearings on Holocaust related claims, requested executive branch agencies to produce historical records on Nazi assets. In September 1996, the State Department authorized its Historian's Office to respond to this request for documents by conducting a comprehensive study of the diplomacy surrounding the issue of Nazi gold. Around the same period of time President Clinton delegated U.S. diplomat and Undersecretary of Commerce, Stuart Eizenstat, to coordinate a government-wide interagency study of both the problem of the gold still remaining with the Tripartite Gold Commission, and the issue of German looted gold.[85] As a result, two reports were published, in 1997 and 1998. The first report

---

82 Bilenker, Stephanie A.: "In Re Holocaust...," p. 259.

83 Federal Chancellery: "Schweizerische Stiftung für Solidarität", Press Release, Federal Council, 05.03.1997, retrieved 27.02.2017, from https://www.admin.ch/cp/d/1997Mar5.125025.7407@idz.bfi.admin.ch.html.

84 Eizenstat, Stuart E.: *Imperfect Justice...*, p. 60.

85 The relevant U.S. government agencies participating in the study eagerly cooperated with Eizenstat. However, on several occasions, he was compelled to intervene to ensure sufficient resources for the project and make sure that the relevant documents were

took Switzerland's wartime economic dealings with Nazi Germany into focus, the second report analyzed the policy of the other neutrals during World War II, including Argentina, Portugal, Spain, Sweden, and Turkey. This was the beginning of six years of U.S. government's participation in investigations, negotiations, and litigation of Holocaust-era claims.

The involvement of the U.S. State Department in the Swiss bank controversy was prompted by Edgar Bronfman, the President of the World Jewish Congress. Already in the first half of 1996 Bronfman managed to secure the support of U.S. President, Bill Clinton for the Jewish cause.[86] In September 1996, Edgar Bronfman, in a letter to President Clinton, informed him about the findings of the World Jewish Congress in relation to the gold issue. American documents confirmed that Nazi Germany transferred $500 million worth of gold to Switzerland (in 1945 dollars), whereas the Washington negotiations managed to secure only $58.1 million in gold from the Swiss. Moreover, there still remained 6 tons of gold under the jurisdiction of the Tripartite Gold Commission, which was never distributed. Two of the remaining 6 tons were still in the vaults of the Federal Reserve Bank of New York. Bronfman suggested that the 6 remaining tons of gold should be assigned for the benefit of Holocaust survivors.[87] In response to this request, the U.S. President assigned the role of investigating allied and neutral nations' dealings with Germany and the handling of Nazi assets to Stuart Eizenstat.

In October 1996, Eizenstat established the interagency working group which comprised historians and officials from the following government institutions and agencies: U.S. State Department, U.S. Treasury Department, U.S. Holocaust Memorial Museum, Justice Department's Office of Special Investigations, CIA, U.S. Army Center for Military History, National Security Agency and the Federal Reserve Bank of New York.

---

declassified. See Slany, William Z.: "The State Department, Nazi Gold, and the Search for Holocaust Assets". In: Bazyler, Michael J./Alford, Roger P. (eds.): *Holocaust Restitution: Perspectives on the Litigation and Its Legacy*. New York University Press: New York et al. 2006, p. 34.

86 President Clinton officially expressed his firm support for the cause of the WJC in a letter to Edgar Bronfman, of 2 May, 1996. See "Clinton Backs Efforts to Track Bank Accounts of Nazi Victims". Jewish Telegraphic Agency, 05.05.1996, retrieved 23.05.2018, from http://www.jta.org/1996/05/05/archive/clinton-backs-efforts-to-track-bank-accounts-of-nazi-victims.

87 Eizenstat, Stuart E.: *Imperfect Justice…*, p. 90.

The interagency historical study conducted by State Department historians led by William Slaney produced a preliminary report, published in May 1997 under the title: "U.S. and Allied Efforts to Recover and Restore Gold and Other Assets Stolen or Hidden by Germany during World War II."[88] The report came to be better known, from the name of its coordinator, as the Eizenstat Report.

In his testimony before the Senate Banking, Housing and Urban Affairs Committee Eizenstat stated: "Our mandate from the President in preparing this report was to focus on the fate of Nazi gold and other assets during and after World War II. Because Switzerland was the principal banker and financial broker for Nazi Germany, it figures prominently in our report."[89]

The major conclusions of the report stipulated that: 1) Nazi Germany looted more than $700 million worth of gold from both occupied countries and private individuals, 2) the German gold reserves during World War II included gold of

---

88 U.S. Department of State: *U.S. and Allied Efforts To Recover and Restore Gold and Other Assets Stolen or Hidden by Germany During World War II…* The Report was labelled a "preliminary study" since it focused on the case of Switzerland in the context of Nazi gold. In June 1998, a supplementary report was published, which provided a more comprehensive historical account of the handling of Nazi looted assets during and after the war and considered the cases of other neutral states: Argentina, Portugal, Spain, Sweden, and Turkey. This report was also critical of the Allied efforts to achieve the return of looted gold and other assets from neutral countries and of the assigning of these assets to the relief of Jewish refugees. See U.S. Department of State: *U.S. and Allied Wartime and Postwar Relations and Negotiations With Argentina, Portugal, Spain, Sweden, and Turkey on Looted Gold and German External Assets and U.S. Concerns About the Fate of the Wartime Ustasha Treasury…*". Although the reports were primarily concerned with the issue of looted assets and the role of the neutrals during the war, they were also, as the chief historian of the State Department who oversaw the completion of both Reports put it "a partial redress of the State Department's deplorable failures in recognizing and aiding Holocaust victims both during and after World War II". See Slany, William Z.: "The State Department, Nazi Gold, and the Search for Holocaust Assets…", p. 41.

89 See "Prepared Testimony of Ambassador Stuart E. Eizenstat. Undersecretary for International Trade. United States Department of Commerce" in U.S. Congress, Senate: *Swiss Banks and Attempts to recover Assets Belonging to the Victims of the Holocaust: Hearing before the Committee on Banking, Housing, and Urban Affairs.* 105th Congress, 1st Session, 15.05.1997. U.S. Government Printing Office: Washington, D.C. 1997, p. 59.
Interestingly, Eizenstat dedicated a substantial part of his speech to the disposition of heirless assets in the U.S. and the inadequate compensation provided to the Jewish Restitution Organization, calling for further investigation of dormant accounts in the U.S.

Holocaust victims, 3) the restitution of looted gold and other property after the war has not been completed, 4) the Allies, led by the U.S. were not sufficiently accomplished in their search for looted gold and stolen property.

The foreword to the Report was written by Stuart Eizenstat and placed the historical research in a political and moral context. Eizenstat specifically pointed out that under "the unique circumstances of World War II, neutrality collided with morality"[90] and the "vigorous trade" of the neutral states with the Third Reich "had the clear effect of supporting and prolonging Nazi Germany's capacity to wage war."[91] Eizenstat discussed the "very mixed"[92] role Switzerland played during World War II, its gold trade with the Nazis including trade in looted gold, its "business as usual"[93] attitude, and the indifference of Swiss bankers to the plight of Holocaust victims and their heirs. Eizenstat also asserted that the Swiss had no intention of ever implementing the 1946 Washington Accord. The report provided numerous historical facts, most of them not new to historians, but in a critical interpretation of these facts the Report boldly suggested that by concluding financial deals with Nazi Germany and acting as bankers for Hitler's regime the Swiss contributed to prolonging the war.

The involvement of the State Department in the Swiss bank scandal and the investigation of Swiss wartime conduct by such a broad panel of experts would not have been possible without the firm support of the President of the United States. The Clinton administration regarded restitution to victims as an important moral issue for the United States. In his statement upon signing the Holocaust Victims Redress Act, president Clinton emphasized his dedication to the Jewish cause: "My Administration has worked hard to bring whatever measure of justice might be possible to Holocaust survivors, their families, and the heirs of those who perished. We have pressed for restitution of property and for the full declassification of archives so that confiscated assets can be traced and restored to their rightful owners."[94]

---

90 U.S. Department of State: *U.S. and Allied Efforts To Recover and Restore Gold and Other Assets Stolen or Hidden by Germany During World War II...*, p. 5.

91 Ibid., p. 5.

92 Ibid., p. 6.

93 Ibid., p. 7.

94 Clinton, William J.: "Statement on signing the Holocaust Victims Redress Act, February 13, 1998". In: *Public Papers of the Presidents of the United States: William J. Clinton, 1998, Book I- January 1 to June 30, 1998*. Office of the Federal Register: Washington, D.C. 1999, p. 225. The Holocaust Victims Redress Act was a bill which provided redress for inadequate restitution of assets seized by the U.S. Government during world War

3.2.8 Swiss Reaction to the Eizenstat Report

The publication of the Report, which gained widespread media attention, further contributed to exacerbating the situation. In Switzerland, the Eizenstat Report was met with indignation and criticism. The strongly formulated foreword was especially perceived as being arbitrary and not reflecting the ideas of the full text. The Swiss Federal Council in its rather moderate response admitted that the report provided new facts which contributed to evaluating the conduct of Switzerland during World War II, and information which was not made public previously, however the Council expressed its criticism of the foreword of the report, whereby the representation of Switzerland as the banker of the Nazis was described by the Council as a "one-sided package judgement."[95] The Swiss Federal Council questioned the conclusion provided in the report, namely that the neutrals prolonged the war, as unsupported by facts. The Council vehemently rejected the notion that neutrality and morality contradict each other stating in response that owing to its neutrality Switzerland was able to persist as "an oasis of democracy and freedom in a totalitarian Europe," whereas "neutrality led to a difficult tightrope walk between adaptation and resistance."[96] Finally, the Federal Council pointed to the Bergier Commission, as the body which it erected to clarify the past, and which was granted access to all documentation normally protected by banking secrecy.[97]

The Swiss persistently resisted U.S. initiatives aimed at inducing an acknowledgement of Switzerland's wartime behavior and compensation of survivors. In addition, the approach taken by the U.S. media shocked the Swiss people, who felt that they were "under attack by the great American sister republic [...]"[98]

II which belonged to victims of the Holocaust, and allowed the U.S. to vote in favor of contributing a substantial part of the gold still under the supervision of the Tripartite Gold Commission to charity organizations assisting Holocaust survivors. The Holocaust Victims Redress Act authorized $20 million for U.S. restitution payments.

95 Federal Council: "Erklärung des Bundesrates zum Eizenstat-Bericht", Federal Council, Bern 22.05.1997, retrieved 27.02.2017, from https://www.admin.ch/cp/d/1997May22.093655.7790@idz.bfi.admin.ch.html.

96 Ibid.

97 Ibid.

98 This opinion was expressed by a Swiss historian Antione Fleury in relation to the U.S. enquiry into the Swiss conduct during World War II. See "Statement by Professor Antoine Fleury" in U.S. Department of State: *U.S. and Allied Wartime and Postwar Relations and Negotiations With Argentina, Portugal, Spain, Sweden, and Turkey on Looted Gold and German External Assets and U.S. Concerns About the Fate of the Wartime Ustasha Treasury...*", p. 79.

Undoubtedly, the publicity gained by the Eizenstat Report supported the effort of the American class action lawsuits, but it also put a strain on U.S. bilateral relations with Switzerland.

A powerful criticism of the Eizenstat Report came from the leader of the right-wing Swiss People's Party (Schweizerische Volkspartei – SVP), Christoph Blocher. In a speech addressing the Young SVP members Blocher called the foreword of the report "schoolmasterish, smug, and highly presumptuous"[99] and expressed his outrage at the fact that both Stuart Eizenstat and a foreign country he represents is pronouncing judgement on Switzerland. Blocher stressed his opinion that by conducting trade, including trade in gold, with Nazi Germany, by making available to Germany its railway alpine passages and its industry production Switzerland had an economic weapon and a position of strength with respect to the Nazis. He refuted basically every claim of the Eizenstat report including stating that the Germans never tried to integrate a large part of victim gold into international transactions and claiming that the United States "robbed our small country of the unproblematic access to a significant part of its own resources" by freezing Swiss assets in the U.S. in 1941. The gold transactions with Germany were a necessity for the Swiss as the gold acquired through such transactions paid for the supply of foreign raw materials and other imports crucial to the Swiss economy. In his conclusions, Blocher firmly stated that the Eizenstat Report "constitutes an attack on our state pillars of neutrality and sovereignty. It amounts to an inadmissible interference of a foreign state in our internal affairs."[100] Blocher called for the Swiss government to "clearly repudiate intentional slander and misrepresentation"[101] and asserted that the Swiss were being "threatened, ridiculed and blackmailed"[102] by the Jewish organizations and their representatives.

The pressure of Jewish organizations resulted in the Swiss government proposing the creation of a multibillion-dollar Swiss fund for solidarity, which would support victims of poverty and catastrophes, including Holocaust victims and which was to be financed from the assets of the Swiss National Bank. Blocher

99 Blocher, Christoph: "Switzerland and the Eizenstat Report: Speech given at a function organized by the Young SVP of Switzerland, the Young SVP of the Canton of Bern and the Young Future of Switzerland (JZS)". Christoph Blocher 21.06.1997, retrieved 15.09.2017, from http://www.blocher.ch/uploads/media/970621eizenstat_03.pdf.

100 Ibid., p. 17

101 Ibid., p. 19.

102 Ibid., p. 21

strongly opposed this concept, put forth by the Swiss President Arnold Koller in March 1997. He argued that to do so would mean to succumb to blackmail and to admit wrongdoing on the part of the Swiss.[103] He called for a popular vote on the erection of the fund, asserting that by giving the people a voice on this issue, Switzerland will exonerate itself.[104]

By June 1997, Blocher effectively mobilized public opinion against the U.S. and the WJC, brought down the proposal of the Swiss government to create the humanitarian fund and effectively precluded any involvement of the Swiss government in the negotiations with the United States.[105]

3.2.9 Holocaust Victims' Gold

The issue of Swiss gold trade during World War II and in particular that of victims' gold played a prominent part in the 1990s conflict. Although it was unrelated directly to the problem of dormant accounts, it was frequently mentioned together with other Swiss misdeeds during World War II and used as a powerful and appalling argument in the public debate surrounding these issues. The tracking down and estimating the value of Nazi gold transactions was the predominant problem referred to both in the Eizenstat Report and by the Bergier Commission.

The central questions to which answers were sought included two major issues, the first one being how many of the gold transactions executed by the Reichsbank and the German banks could be attributed to gold identified as Holocaust gold or gold belonging to victims of the Nazi regime, and the second one, how much of this gold finally found its way into the Swiss banking system, which in turn could only be assessed by analyzing and reconstructing every single delivery procedure. But providing credible answers to these questions proved to be a difficult task. As a U.S. National Archives study specified: "During the summer of 1948, most of the records of the Reichsbank's Precious Metals Department were microfilmed by the U.S. Army and, interestingly enough, turned over to Albert Thoms, who was working for the successor bank to the Reichsbank. These records have subsequently disappeared in Germany, and there has been a search for them the past two years in the belief they would shed light on how much non-monetary gold (e.g., dental gold) was melted down and mixed with the monetary

---

103 Ibid., p. 12 and p. 26.

104 Ibid., p. 27.

105 Codevilla, Angelo M.: *Between the Alps and a Hard Place. Switzerland in World War II and the Rewriting of History.* Regenery Publishing, Inc.: Washington, D.C., 2000.

gold (i.e., central bank gold) and thus indicate how much restitution still should be made to victims of Nazi persecution and their heirs."[106] Since the precise establishment of the amounts of victim gold seized by the Nazis, and the precise determination of the share of this gold which was included in the reserves of the Reichsbank and subsequently traded to the Swiss National Bank was in fact impossible, and this despite detective-like efforts undertaken by historians on both sides of the Atlantic, various estimates were used for this purpose.

As Stuart Eizenstat recalls in his memoir, a delay in the publication of the Report, the compilation of which he supervised, enabled to trace some of the gold belonging to the victims of the Holocaust, the so-called Melmer gold, back to the Swiss banking system.

Shortly after the war the U.S. army made a horrific discovery in the German Merkers Salt Mine – bags, trunks and boxes filled with gold, including 207 bags and containers filled with gold looted from concentration camp victims. In the mine, the U.S. army captured the chief of the Reichsbank's Precious Metals Department, who identified these 207 bags and containers as being part of the "Melmer" account of the SS at the Reichsbank.

Beginning in 1942, an SS captain named Bruno Melmer supervised 76 deliveries of valuables, including gold, to the Reichsbank for credit to an account of the SS revenue office. This so-called 'Melmer gold' consisted of personal items of inmates of Auschwitz and other concentration camps,[107] such as wedding rings, gold watches, spectacle-rims, jewelry, religious objects, and gold from dental work.

The estimates of the value of this gold vary widely from $2.9 million to $4 million.[108]

The Bergier Commission was able to confirm, on the basis of surviving microfilm of the records of the Reichsbank Precious Metals Department, that the

---

106 Bradsher, Greg: "Nazi Gold: The Merkers Mine Treasure". *Prologue Magazine* 31, No. 1, Spring 1999, National Archives and Records Administration, retrieved 28.02.2016, from https://www.archives.gov/publications/prologue/1999/spring/nazi-gold-merkers-mine-treasure.htmlhttps://www.archives.gov/publications/prologue/1999/spring/nazi-gold-merkers-mine-treasure.html. This paper also describes in detail the discovery process in the Merkers Mine.

107 The deliveries included valuables form the following camps: Belzec, Sobibr, Treblinka, Auschwitz-Birkenau, Lublin-Majdanek. See Independent Commission of Experts Switzerland – Second World War: *Switzerland and Gold Transactions…*, p. 43.

108 See Independent Commission of Experts Switzerland – Second World War, *Gold Transactions in the Second World War: Statistical Review with Commentary*, p. 8.

Reichsbank received at least \$2.9 million[109] in gold coins and bars only, directly from Melmer. This was a minimum estimate of the Melmer deliveries. Most probably, the Reichsbank received much more than this amount in gold coins and bars from the SS.[110] For example, in the final report on the Nazi Operation Reinhard the SS and Police Chief Odilo Globocnik reported that he shipped RM 9,883,658.12 or \$3,986,953.66 worth of gold bullion and coins to the SS in Berlin to be transferred to the Reichsbank. However, this gold, which was destined for the Melmer account, did not include the gold looted by the SS from inmates at Auschwitz and other concentration camps as well as slave labor camps outside the Lublin District in Poland.[111]

The testimonies of the Nuremberg Trial defendants including Emil Puhl,[112] Vice-president of the Reichsbank, and Melmer himself determined that the gold jewelry of concentration camp inmates, after its reception at the Reichsbank, was further transported to the Prussian Mint where it was recast and came back to the Reichsbank in bars. Therefore, the entry "Preußische Münze" (Prussian Mint) in the Reichsbank books could also point to victims' gold. In the Archives of the Prussian Mint the appropriate records are often missing but at the same time there are entries of gold deliveries to the Reichsbank, where a plausible chain of evidence could be established, as in the case of the nonrecurring entry of one gold bar, weighing 3,2 kg and with its origin specified as "RKK (Reichskredit-kasse) Stanislaus", which could refer to the delivery of gold after the massacre of more than 10,000 Jews in the pre-war Polish town of Stanislaus (Stanisławów), now in Ukraine.[113]

The "Melmer" gold did not include all the gold stolen in the concentration and extermination camps. The Bergier Commission also used the description 'Other Private Holdings' to indicate the sum of 7.3 million USD, which was calculated by the Bergier Commission as the residual balance necessary to equalize total credits and debits of the Reichsbank during the war. This sum included gold

109 This figure is provided in the report of Ibid., p. 31 and p. 43.

110 Ibid., p. 8.

111 White, Elisabeth: "The Disposition of SS-Looted Victim Gold During and After World War II". *American University International Law Review* 14, No. 1, 1998, p. 218.

112 Emil Puhl was sentenced to 5 years imprisonment as the person responsible for managing the assets of Holocaust victims within the Reichsbank, but he served not much more than half a year prison time, being released in time for Christmas, 1949. See LeBor, Adam: *Tower of Basel. The Shadowy History of the Secret Bank that Runs the World.* PublicAffairs: New York 2013, pp. 176–177.

113 Steinberg, Jonathan: *Die Deutsche Bank...*, p. 37.

seized from individuals through executive decrees, levies, laws not falling under the jurisdiction of the Four-Year Plan, and gold taken from concentration camp victims but not accounted for by other categories. In addition, gold was bought by Germany on the black market, in occupied Europe as well as in neutral countries including Switzerland, by selling other property, in particular diamonds, confiscated from the Jewish victims of persecution and referred to in German documents as Jewish jewelry or "Judenschmuck."[114] The German Foreign Office transferred the Judenschmuck to its German Legation in Bern in packages, which were passed on to a German agent, who exchanged them for currency or industrial diamonds, although the sale and export of industrial diamonds was banned under Swiss law at the time.[115]

In 1945, the U.S. occupation authorities in the course of their investigations established how the Reichsbank increased its gold reserves. Gold, silver bars and currency were bought by the Reichsbank at full value from the SS. Smaller items such as gold rings were sent to the Prussian Mint for re-smelting, larger pieces, including jewelry, were sent to the Municipal Pawnshop, which sold the more valuable items abroad in exchange for foreign currency and the rest was sent to Degussa[116] to be re-smelted. The company was allowed to keep a certain amount of gold for industrial purposes and the remaining amount was sold back to the Reichsbank.[117] The Reichsbank bought looted gold coins and bullion, as well as the ingots smelted by the Prussian Mint from dental gold and small gold items, as well as the gold smelted by Degussa and incorporated them into its gold reserves. The resmelted gold of victim origin, once it became part of the Reichsbank gold reserves, was not visibly distinguishable from genuine central bank gold reserves.

However, the American Foreign Exchange Depository, a section of the Office of the Military Government of the United States was able to identify specific smelting operations at the Prussian Mint, during which gold looted from the Netherlands was resmelted into gold bars. In case of one such operation there

---

114 Independent Commission of Experts Switzerland – Second World War: *Switzerland and Gold Transactions…*, p. 43.

115 U.S. Department of State: *U.S. and Allied Efforts To Recover and Restore Gold and Other Assets Stolen or Hidden by Germany During World War II…*, p. 166.

116 Degussa, an acronym for Deutsche Gold- und Silber-Scheideanstalt, was a German company specializing in the refinement of precious metals as well as the manufacture of chemicals.

117 U.S. Department of State: *U.S. and Allied Efforts To Recover and Restore Gold and Other Assets Stolen or Hidden by Germany During World War II…*, p. 161.

is evidence that 37 kilograms of gold purchased by the Reichsbank from the Melmer deliveries were added to the Dutch gold in the resmelting process. Out of the gold bars created in this way 83% were sold to the Swiss National Bank and the remaining 17 % to the Banca d'Italia and the Banco Commerciale Italiana. It is therefore clear, deduced the Eizenstat Report, that the bullion traded to Switzerland and other neutral countries did include a certain share of victim gold, but there is also no evidence that the countries which traded with the Reichsbank knowingly accepted victim gold.[118]

An analysis conducted by the Foreign Exchange Depository of another Prussian Mint smelting operation, whereby Dutch gold bars were resmelted to disguise their origin, found that six bars from the Melmer delivery with a weight of 56 kilograms were resmelted and renumbered at the same time. Therefore, the tracking of gold looted from the Netherlands allowed to identify the precise amounts of gold from SS shipments which were integrated into the Reichsbank's gold reserves in the process of smelting. Unfortunately, the immediate post war effort undertaken by the U.S. military authorities to identify specific gold bars form the Melmer account in the reserves of the Reichsbank was insufficient.[119]

At the Paris Conference on Reparations, held in 1945, the U.S. proposed to assign all the non-monetary gold to provide immediate assistance to stateless refugees, which included predominantly Jews, survivors of the Holocaust. The Paris Reparations Agreement did not provide precise definitions of "monetary gold" and "non-monetary gold."[120] During the Paris Conference it was nevertheless established that all "monetary gold" seized in Germany would be put together in a "gold pool" and distributed to the claimant countries according to their losses. This gold amounted to far less than all the gold looted from the German-occupied nations put together, and it was difficult to identify its origin. In 1946, a

118 Ibid., p. 161.

119 For a detailed description of the discovery process concerning gold looted by the SS from concentration camp inmates and the estimates of the value of this gold and its transition into Reichsbank reserves see U.S. Department of State: *U.S. and Allied Efforts To Recover and Restore Gold and Other Assets Stolen or Hidden by Germany During World War II…*, pp. 159–168. For an analysis of the process of collection and disposal of victim gold see the report of the Independent Commission of Experts Switzerland – Second World War: *Switzerland and Gold Transactions…*, pp. 30–36.

120 The problems which arose from the lack of such a precise definition of non-monetary gold are also extensively discussed in the Eizenstat Report, see U.S. Department of State: *U.S. and Allied Efforts To Recover and Restore Gold and Other Assets Stolen or Hidden by Germany During World War II…*, pp. 169–177.

Tripartite Commission for the Restitution of Monetary Gold was established by France, the United Kingdom and the U.S. to supervise the redistribution of the Gold Pool to the claimant countries.

In 1947, the United States Government finally defined "monetary gold" as "gold bars and coins, regardless of their origin". As a result of employing this definition the United States contributed to the gold pool all the gold coins and bullion in possession of the Reichsbank, including those coins and ingots that originated from the Melmer deliveries, this included 6,427 gold coins seized in the Melmer account at Merkers and 10.7 kilograms of gold bars that the United States military government had identified as constituting loot robbed by the SS from victims at the extermination and concentration camps.[121] The conclusion of the Eizenstat Report that both the Gold Pool administered by the Tripartite Gold Commission and the gold which was purchased by the Swiss National Bank included gold looted from victims of Nazi persecution is therefore not without concrete foundations.[122]

In December 1997, an international conference on Nazi gold was held in London at the initiative of the British Foreign Secretary, Robin Cook. This initiative was prompted by the Swiss banks scandal. Delegates from 41 countries participated in the London Gold Conference in an attempt to resolve the issue of the remaining reserves of Nazi gold which was taken from the national treasuries of the occupied countries and had not been distributed by the Tripartite Gold Commission. In 1997, the Commission was still in possession of 2% of the original gold, or 5.5 tones, an amount equal to $60 million. The conference was called in May 1997 in the wake of the Meili affair. France, the United Kingdom, and the U.S. proposed to establish a fund to help Holocaust victims, which was to be financed with the remaining gold. The Tripartite Gold Commission thereby completed its duty and was formally resolved.[123]

The issue of gold looted during World War II and in particular the problem of victims' gold was exploited to create another scandal surrounding the

---

121 Ibid., pp. 169–177.

122 The Tripartite Gold Commission was established to distribute the gold placed in the Gold Pool.

123 Goldman, Stuart D.: "Holocaust Restitution: Overview of the London Gold Conference". Jewish Virtual Library, 24.11.1999, retrieved 14.09.2017, from http://www.jewishvirtuallibrary.org/london-gold-conference, for the circumstances leading to the conference being held in London see "The Greatest Theft in History". *BBC News*, 01.12.1997, retrieved 23.05.2018, from http://news.bbc.co.uk/2/hi/special_report/1997/nazi_gold/35981.stm.

negotiations with the Swiss banks. It effectively served to link the Holocaust with Switzerland through a most horrid and at the same time a highly emotional association.[124]

3.2.10 Financial Sanctions

The political and diplomatic pressure during the settlement negotiations was exercised by the World Jewish Congress, Senator Alfonse D'Amato and the U.S. government represented by Stuart Eizenstat. However, it was the threat of financial sanctions, which was a critical component in the resolution of Holocaust related claims. The key advocate of the use of sanctions against European businesses in the Holocaust restitution process was Alan G. Hevesi, Comptroller and Chief Financial Officer of New York City, who formed a coalition of state and local government finance officers from across the United States, headed by the so-called Executive Monitoring Committee (known as the Hevesi Committee). During the conflict, the committee threatened to apply both regulatory and financial sanctions with respect to Swiss banks operating in the United States.

Economic sanctions have been a popular tool of American foreign policy, often employed with mixed results, however, the Holocaust restitution movement was an example of a successful application of sanctions against not countries but private corporations. Sanctions against Swiss banks were used despite opposition from the Clinton administration, which warned both state and local governments against imposing them.[125] Even Stuart Eizenstat, the author of the Report which stirred such controversy in Switzerland, was firmly opposed to applying sanctions against Swiss banks as a means of achieving progress in the negotiations. The Swiss government filed diplomatic protests, condemning the sanctions, but to no avail.[126]

---

124 See for example Bower, Tom: *Nazi Gold. The Full Story of the Fifty-Year Swiss-Nazi Conspiracy to Steal Billions from Europe's Jews and Holocaust Survivors.* Harper Perennial: New York 1998, p. 307.

125 In an interview on Swiss television Stuart Eizenstat stated that the Clinton Administration "feels very strongly that any sanctions at any level – Federal, state or local – are counterproductive." See Sanger, David E.: "As U.S. Urges Delicacy on Swiss Gold, New York City Hints at a Bold Stroke". *New York Times*, 25.08.1997, retrieved 04.03.2018, from http://www.nytimes.com/1997/08/25/world/as-us-urges-delicacy-on-swiss-gold-new-york-city-hints-at-a-bold-stroke.html.

126 Bazyler, Michael J.: *Holocaust Justice. The Battle for Restitution in America's Courts.* New York University Press: New York et al. 2003, pp. 21–22.

Alan G. Hevesi, the New York City Comptroller and H. Carl McCall the New York State Comptroller, as part of their duties both invested billions of dollars as the trustees of respectively the city and the state pension funds.[127] Hevesi threatened applying economic sanctions with respect to Swiss banks as early as 1996. The threat included withdrawing $1 billion of New York City's pension funds under Swiss management, selling $47 million worth of shares in Swiss banks, and withdrawing $150 million in overnight deposits. Further exacerbating these financial threats, by May 1997, six U.S. states drafted bills for the divestment of state funds under management by Swiss banks and the city council of Chicago considered introducing legislation which would bar city money from any financial institution which had a business relationship with Switzerland.[128]

H. Carl McCall, the New York State Comptroller blocked the execution of overnight investments via Swiss banks on January 30, 1997, this blockade lasted until February 26, 1997.[129]

In May 1997, Alan Hevesi visited Switzerland, where he met with senior government officials and bankers from the Swiss Federal Council, Swiss Federal Banking Commission and the Swiss National Bank, and upon his return called U.S. pension fund managers, state and local treasurers and comptrollers to come together and established an informal network consisting of state and local government public finance officers to support the initiative of the Jewish organizations to resolve Holocaust-era claims. This network grew to include some 800 public officers from across the United States. The office of the Comptroller demonstrated continuous commitment to the Jewish cause by publishing a quarterly bulletin, the "Swiss Monitor", distributed to over 4000 readers.[130]

127 The New York State pension fund is the third largest in the U.S. and amounts today to $178 billion. See Office of the New York State Comptroller: "New York State Common Retirement Fund". Retrieved 12.02.2017, from https://www.osc.state.ny.us/pension/.

128 These sanctions, were they to be actually applied, would have done much harm to the Swiss financial services sector. See Warner, Joan: "Raging At the Swiss. Will U.S. Anger Over Nazi Gold Lead to Damaging Sanctions?". *Bloomberg*, 26.05.1997, retrieved 02.04.2018, from https://www.bloomberg.com/news/articles/1997-05-25/raging-at-the-swiss.

129 World Jewish Restitution Organization: *Framework for Allocation Plan of Funds Received...*, p. 12.

130 U.S. Congress, Senate: *Current Developments in Holocaust Assets Restitution: Hearing before the Committee on Banking, Housing and Urban Affairs*, 105th Congress, 2nd Session, 22.06.1998, U.S. Government Printing Office: Washington, D.C.: 1999, p. 72.

Hevesi urged Swiss companies, the shares of which were held by New York City pension funds, to contribute to the Humanitarian Fund created by Swiss banks and the Swiss government.[131]

In October 1997, Alan Hevesi applied a sanction against Union Bank of Switzerland by banning it from participating in a routine billion-dollar bond offering to help finance the New York City's budget. The winning bid involved a syndicate of banks led by UBS. Hevesi stated that accepting the bid would have sent the wrong message to the Swiss bank and upon the request made by the New York City Comptroller UBS was replaced in the syndicate by two other banks. The sanction was implemented as a punishment for the Swiss bank for not fully cooperating in the investigations on its ties to Nazi gold. The action was immediately criticized by Stuart Eizenstat on behalf of the U.S. State Department, as it thwarted the efforts of the U.S. administration to come to terms with the Swiss. In the period preceding this sanction Hevesi also repeatedly criticized the bank and pressured UBS to release information on the documents rescued by Meili.[132]

In October 1997, California Treasurer, Matt Fong announced a moratorium on state investments and deposits in the three Swiss banks, which was effective since August of that year. The state of California liquidated $2 billion from the Swiss banks. This move was also strongly criticized by Stuart Eizenstat.[133]

On December 8, 1997, Alan Hevesi convened an International Conference on The Recovery of Dormant Holocaust-Related Swiss Bank Accounts and Hidden Assets. The conference was held in New York and Senator D'Amato was a guest speaker, as well as Edgar Bronfman and the plaintiffs' lawyers and on the Swiss side, the diplomat Thomas Borer. The public finance officers, prompted by Edgar Bronfman, decided to postpone implementing sanctions against Swiss banks. The 90-day moratorium was to last until March 31, 1998. During the conference an Executive Monitoring Committee was established to monitor the progress of the negotiations with the Swiss. The Committee consisted of five members, all public finance officers, headed by Alan G. Hevesi.[134]

---

131 Eizenstat, Stuart E.: *Imperfect Justice…*, p. 124.

132 Sanger, David E.: "New York Punishes Swiss Bank Over Nazi Gold". *New York Times*, 10.10.1997, retrieved 30.04.2018, from http://www.nytimes.com/1997/10/10/nyregion/new-york-punishes-swiss-bank-over-nazi-gold.html.

133 "Eizenstat Slams California for Moves Against Swiss Banks". *Jewish Telegraphic Agency*, 27.10.1997, retrieved 06.05.2018, from http://www.jta.org/1997/10/23/archive/eizenstat-slams-california-for-moves-against-swiss-banks-2.

134 The five members included Denise Ducharme, President of the National Association of Unclaimed Property Administrators, Matt Fong, Treasurer of the State of California,

On March 26, 1998, a hearing of the Executive Monitoring Committee took place. Upon this occasion a joint U.S.-Swiss statement opposing the sanctions was issued and presented by the State Department. The statement proclaimed that

> the Governments of the Swiss Confederation and the United States of America share a continuing commitment to addressing openly all issues related to the Holocaust, and bringing justice to its victims. Given the important initiatives and measures the Swiss have undertaken in this regard and the valuable bilateral relationship between the United States and Switzerland, our Governments believe that the calls for sanctions and boycotts from the US and recent echoes for countermeasures from Switzerland are unwarranted and counterproductive. Our governments urge all groups on both sides of the Atlantic to work together in a spirit of cooperation and moderation and to contribute to harmonious relations between our countries and peoples.[135]

The three Swiss banks: UBS, Swiss Bank Corporation and Credit Suisse issued a letter stating their dedication to resolve Holocaust era issues.[136] This appeased the Jewish representatives and again, both the WJC and Stuart Eizenstat asked the Hevesi Committee for another extension of the moratorium, and it was agreed that sanctions will be postponed until July 1, 1998.

The Swiss reacted by threatening with their own sanctions against U.S. companies seeking to do business in Switzerland. In March 1998, two interpellations were submitted to the Swiss Federal Council. The first interpellation, supported by 16 members of the Council of States, the upper house of the Swiss Federal Assembly, was issued on 18 March 1998 by Christine Beerli, whereby the parliament member asked the Swiss government whether it was ready to take a firm stance with respect to the U.S. and reject a global solution to the conflict involving

---

Barbara Hafer, Treasurer of the Commonwealth of Pennsylvania, and H. Carl McCall, Comptroller of the State of New York and Alan Hevesi as chairman of the Committee. See "Prepared Testimony of the Honorable Steven Newman, First Assistant Comptroller, City of New York, July 22, 1998" in U.S. Congress, Senate: *Current Developments in Holocaust Assets Restitution*, p. 73.

135 Federal Council: "Joint Swiss-American Statement on Sanctions", Bern 26.03.1998, retrieved 28.02.2017, from https://www.admin.ch/cp/d/1998Mar26.145548.9105@idz.bfi.admin.ch.html.

136 See Rickman, Gregg J.: *Swiss Banks and Jewish Souls*. Transaction Publishers: New Brunswick, New Jersey 1999, p. 215. The banks' letter addressed to Israel Singer, the Secretary General of the WJC encouraged the Jewish representatives to recommend another 90-day moratorium on sanctions. See World Jewish Restitution Organization: *Framework for Allocation Plan of Funds Received...*, p. 13.

the government, whether it was ready to intervene with the World Trade Organization concerning the U.S. sanctions against Swiss corporations and finally, whether it was prepared to introduce reciprocal means with respect to U.S. companies in Switzerland, if the sanctions against Swiss companies in the U.S. would actually be implemented.[137] The second interpellation was filed by Dick Marty on March 19, 1998 whereby he requested that the Swiss react to the U.S. threats with specific and adequate measures and requested the Swiss government to take action by delaying the forthcoming issue of telecommunication licenses for the Swiss market, which would effectively prohibit U.S. telecommunications companies from doing business in Switzerland.[138] This interpellation was supported by 37 out of 46 members of the Council of States. The Swiss government reacted to the interpellations by confirming that a "global solution" involving a contribution with the use of public funds was definitely out of the question and taking the issue to the World Trade Organization was a possibility, should other conflict resolution measures fail.[139] These threats were never implemented, but they did contribute to further straining the already heavily weakened bilateral relations.

By July 1, 1998, no agreement had been reached and Edgar Bronfman encouraged the Hevesi Committee to act in line with the issued warnings. The moratorium was lifted, and the Committee announced a system of rolling sanctions.[140]

In the meantime, in December 1997, two Swiss banks – UBS and Swiss Bank Corporation announced a plan to merge.

International financial institutions which operate in the U.S. are subject to both local and federal regulations and to be able to operate in the State of New York, both foreign and domestic banks need, as opposed to every other U.S. jurisdiction, the approval not only of the Federal Reserve Board in Washington, but also of the New York State Banking Department, which supervises all banks

137 Federal Assembly: "Interpellation: US-Boykottmaßnahmen: Reaktion der Schweiz: Eingereicht von: Christine Beerli", 18.03.1998, retrieved 26.02.2017, from https://www.parlament.ch/de/ratsbetrieb/suche-curia-vista/geschaeft?AffairId=19983116.

138 Federal Assembly: "Interpellation: Boykottdrohungen und eventuelle konkrete Vergeltungsmassnahmen: Eingereicht von Marty Dick", 19.03.1998, retrieved 26.02.2017, from https://www.parlament.ch/de/ratsbetrieb/suche-curia-vista/geschaeft?AffairId=19983129.

139 Federal Assembly: "Interpellation: US-Boykottmaßnahmen..."

140 See World Jewish Restitution Organization: *Framework for Allocation Plan of Funds Received...*, pp. 13–14 and Eizenstat, Stuart E.: *Imperfect Justice...*, p. 134 and pp. 158–160.

with agencies or branches in this state.[141] By making the announcement on the merger the Swiss banks gave U.S. officials an additional leverage. The New York Banking Commission began a costly investigation into the wartime accounts of New York branches of the three Swiss banks. The Jewish representatives and Senator D'Amato vehemently opposed the merger and intensely tried to convince the banking officials to block it.[142] Senator D'Amato turned to Alan Greenspan, the Chairman of the Board of Governors of the Federal Reserve System for support in opposing the merger of the two Swiss banks. In March 1998, the New York State Banking Department requested Alan Greenspan to disapprove the planned merger.[143]

Stuart Eizenstat, on the other hand, urged both Elisabeth McCaul, the New York bank superintendent, and the Federal Reserve authorities, including Alan Greenspan to rule on the merits of the case and not to succumb to the pressure of the WJC. Eizenstat insisted not to politicize the merger, which became the central bargaining issue in the negotiations with the Swiss banks throughout May, 1998.

June 4 was the deadline for the New York State to decide on the merger. The Swiss threatened that if it was not approved, there would be no settlement. Elisabeth McCaul finally approved the merger, stating that the banks made progress in "the recovery of records" and "settlement of claims", as well as the "reestablishment of the trust" between the two banks and the New York State Banking Department.[144]

On June 19, 1998, the two Swiss banks announced publicly their best offer to settle the claims, which they set at $600 million. The amount was much lower than what the plaintiffs' lawyers expected. This incensed Jewish leaders and on July 1, 1998 upon request made by Edgar Bronfman, the Executive Monitoring Committee lifted the moratorium on sanctions first introduced on December 8, 1997 and subsequently extended on March 26, 1998. At a press conference on July 2, 1998 Alan Hevesi together with the New York State Comptroller, H. Carl Mc Call announced a system of "rolling sanctions"[145] – instead of actually

141 Rickman, Gregg J.: *Swiss Banks...*, p. 206.

142 Eizenstat, Stuart E.: *Imperfect Justice...*, p. 145.

143 See Henry, Marilyn: "Fifty Years of Holocaust Compensation...," p. 36; and New York State Department of Financial Services: "New York State Banking Board Approves Application Which Furthers Merger Plan of Two Swiss Banks". 04.06.1998, retrieved 12.02.2017, from http://www.dfs.ny.gov/consumer/holocaust/hcpopr980604.htm.

144 Ibid.

145 This term is used with respect to the Hevesi sanctions by Michael J. Bazyler in Bazyler, Michael J.: *Holocaust Justice...*, p. 22.

imposing the sanctions, Hevesi threatened to gradually implement them according to the following procedure:

"If a settlement has not been reached by **September 1, 1998**, our office will bar overnight investments with Swiss banks, bar Swiss banks from new letter of credit arrangements and will bar Swiss investment firms and banks from underwriting or supporting new variable-rate debt transactions.

> By **November 15th**, if an agreement has not been reached, our office would recommend the New York City pension funds exclude Swiss investment managers from investment manager searches and bar our existing money managers from executing trades through Swiss brokerage and securities firms.
>
> By **January 1, 1999**, we would recommend the pension funds terminate contracts with Swiss money managers. We will also ask the New York State legislature and the New York City Council to pass laws barring Swiss companies from selling goods and services to the State and City of New York. I might add, that in contemplation of this request, Sheldon Silver, the Speaker of the New York State Assembly, announced on July 15th, plans for legislation that will enact such a sanction.
>
> By **July 1, 1999**, we would ask the City's $84 billion pension systems to consider divesting all holdings in Swiss stock. Presently, the City's pension funds own $735 million in stock in Swiss companies, including $136.7 million in the Swiss banks. The Silver bill provides for divestment as well.[146]

The Office of the New York City Comptroller justified the threat of sanctions by asserting that the diplomatic solution favored by the U.S. State Department had failed. The Comptroller's office also called upon the Swiss government to engage in the negotiations blaming the failure in reaching a global settlement and the necessity to impose the sanctions upon the lack of involvement of the Swiss authorities in the talks and upon its reluctance to participate in the financial burden of the settlement. The announced program of sanctions was a solution of "last resort" and a "drastic measure"[147] aimed at accelerating the settlement process, and was implemented as an alternative to traditional diplomatic tools of foreign policy.

In August 1998, the parties finally reached an agreement to settle the lawsuits for $1.25 billion.

It is perhaps surprising that sanctions worked so well in achieving a sufficient degree of pressure in the Swiss banks case, where they were applied with respect

---

146 See "Prepared Testimony of the Honorable Steven Newman, First Assistant Comptroller, City of New York, July 22, 1998" in Congress, Senate: *Current Developments in Holocaust Assets Restitution*, p. 74.

147 See Ibid.

to private institutions, whereas they usually do not work applied with respect to a foreign government. The banks made a rational choice that a settlement was a cheaper option than to continue fighting in court and to incur the substantial losses which would result from the sanctions. Governments on the other hand do not always follow a pattern of rational behavior.[148] Moreover, the economic and reputational cost of the sanctions was so high, that the banks chose to settle despite a high probability that the sanctions would have been ruled illegal by a U.S. court, had they been challenged by the banks in court on the grounds that the sanctions unconstitutionally violated the exclusive power of the federal government over foreign affairs.[149]

In Switzerland, the threats of economic sanctions were perceived as anti-Swiss and aimed at benefiting U.S. financial institutions on the global financial markets at the cost of weakening Swiss banks.

The investigations into Swiss banks backfired on U.S. banks when in January 1997 the New York bank superintendent Neil D. Levin launched investigations of banks which had business relationships with Swiss institutions between 1939 and 1941. The inquiry encompassed J.P. Morgan, Bank of New York, Bankers Trust, Chase Manhattan, and Citibank.[150]

3.2.11 The Involvement of the U.S. State Department: Mediation of the Settlement

Initially, the State Department perceived the litigation as an issue between private parties, however, as the crisis unfolded, the involvement of the U.S. government in the litigation of Swiss banks increased. The U.S. State Department acted both as a facilitator and a mediator in the talks between the different participants with the aim to alleviate the conflict and improve the U.S. relationship with Switzerland.[151]

---

148 For this argument Bazyler, Michael J.: *Holocaust Justice...*, p. 24.

149 Such a ruling was actually issued by the U.S. Supreme Court with respect to the so-called Massachusetts Burma Laws, whereby the agencies of the state of Massachusetts were restricted in their ability to purchase goods and services from companies conducting business with Myanmar (Burma). The court ruled that the law violated the Supremacy Clause of the U.S. Constitution and infringed upon the federal government's power over both foreign commerce and foreign affairs. See Ibid., p. 25.

150 Warner, Joan: "Raging At the Swiss..."

151 Bettauer, Ronald J.: "The Role of the United States Government in Recent Holocaust Claims Resolution". *Proceedings of the Annual Meeting (American Society of International Law)* 95, 2001, p. 38.

Stuart Eizenstat referred to the urgent need of pursuing negotiations with the Swiss, recounting the events in his memoir: "For the U.S. government it meant sailing into unchartered waters as a mediator with conflicting objectives – helping Holocaust victims and soothing U.S.-Swiss relations."[152] Eizenstat took over this role, believing that "the longer it took to resolve the cases, the greater the threat to U.S. relations with the Swiss."[153]

As the conflict aggravated, the mediation of the U.S. government appeared to be necessary to contain a potential international crisis. The situation was getting out of hand with threats from Alan Hevesi and the wave of negative public opinion in Switzerland which expressed hostility towards the United States.

Eizenstat's aim was to bring all the parties together: on the U.S. side the representatives of the WJC in cooperation with the class-action lawyers and on the Swiss side the Swiss government and the banks. The first step was to assure the involvement of the Swiss government. To achieve this purpose, on November 15, 1997, Eizenstat organized a meeting in Bern between Madeleine Albright, the first U.S. Secretary of State to visit Switzerland since 1961, and her Swiss counterpart, Flavio Cotti. Albright stressed her objection to state and municipal economic sanctions against Swiss banks and introduced Eizenstat as the leader of the U.S. team to resolve the class-action suits. But the Swiss government refused to engage in any the negotiations with the banks.[154]

On December 14, 1997, Stuart Eizenstat initiated a meeting with top Swiss bankers and the plaintiffs' lawyers. However, contrary to the lawyers' demands, the Swiss were willing to discuss sums related only to the documented dormant accounts.

Another meeting took place in January 1998, in the office of Stuart Eizenstat. The Undersecretary, with the power of the Clinton administration behind him, finally persuaded the Swiss to accept the principles of a settlement unrelated to the amount in the dormant accounts.

Eizenstat achieved a breakthrough when in April 1998 the negotiating parties agreed to a "Structure for Settlement of Swiss Bank Class Actions and Related Issues", which consisted of two separate parts. The first part of the settlement was to be related to the actual bank accounts belonging to Holocaust victims, as established by the Volcker audit, including interest and refund of fees. The second part of the settlement was to be a lump sum payment, a "rough justice amount"

---

152 Eizenstat, Stuart E.: *Imperfect Justice…*, p. 125.

153 Ibid., p. 126.

154 Ibid., p. 126.

which would cover the claims of class-action lawyers for looted assets and slave labor as well as any other claims against Swiss banks resulting from World War II.[155] This "rough justice amount" was the principal subject matter of further negotiations, as its value was determined only by the bargaining power of both parties, as opposed to any objective calculations.

Between April 27 and June 26, there were nine rounds of negotiations before the final agreement was reached. During this period Eizenstat made two additional attempts to secure the financial support of the Swiss National Bank and the Swiss government, however without success.

Despite a lack of evidence to back their demands, the class action lawyers' opening position was to request $5 billion from the Swiss banks, which in turn were prepared to offer $230 million for the rough justice amount.[156] Bringing both sides closer together proved to be quite a challenge. The class action lawyers and Jewish organizations' representatives were not able to justify their demands, therefore it was rather a matter of finding a figure upon which all parties would agree and then finding the arguments to support it.[157]

In July, Edward R. Korman, the Judge of the United States District Court for the Eastern District of New York took over as the leading mediator of the negotiations and in August 1998 the parties reached an agreement to settle the lawsuits for $1.25 billion.

Unfortunately, despite the fact that the key argument in the negotiations was the intention to provide justice to elderly Holocaust survivors and their heirs, for over three years after the agreement had been reached not a single dollar was distributed to the victims. The delay in the distribution of funds could be attributed to a number of factors, which would require a separate analysis, the key ones being the complexity of the allocation procedure and the dispute over how many of the accounts identified by the Volcker Committee as having a probable or a possible relationship to victims of the Nazis were to be made public.

In 2001, Stuart Eizenstat, in an interview with a Swiss magazine, apologized for any offence caused to the Swiss people and admitted that he did not do enough to emphasize the positive role of Switzerland during World War II. At

155 Ibid., p. 135.
156 Ibid., p. 141.
157 Ibid., p. 144.

the same time, he conveyed his disappointment with the Swiss government for its insufficient engagement in the plight of Holocaust victims.[158]

The active role played by the U.S. government in the settlement negotiations with Swiss banks differed from the traditional approach of the government in a claims settlement.[159] The Swiss banks settlement resolved claims not only for U.S. nationals, but also covered claims of persons who were not U.S. citizens at the time, when the claims arose, in particular in relation to worldwide classes of claimants regardless of their nationalities. Moreover, the U.S. government mediated negotiations between private parties: the plaintiffs, the Jewish organizations and the Swiss banks.

3.2.12 The Settlement

The final Settlement Agreement was signed on January 26, 1999, following months of negotiations of the details. The two leading Swiss banks, UBS AG and Credit Suisse Group, were to pay 1.25 billion USD into a Settlement Fund.[160]

In June 1998, a lawsuit was filed in the U.S. against the Swiss National Bank following the publication of the first interim report of the Bergier Commission, which concluded that the SNB had played a significant role in trading in Reichsbank's gold. The SNB refused to contribute to the settlement to avoid official involvement of Swiss authorities, but nevertheless the settlement provided that the lawsuit against the SNB was to be dismissed.[161]

The Swiss banks insisted that the settlement should resolve all outstanding financial obligations against all Swiss entities and the Swiss government arising from Holocaust-era misconduct,[162] an unprecedented nationwide release from responsibility for any type of Holocaust-era claim.

---

158 "Eizenstat Regrets that Holocaust Report Caused Offence to Swiss". *Swissinfo*, 27.04.2001, retrieved 07.05.2018, from https://www.swissinfo.ch/eng/eizenstat-regrets-that-holocaust-report-caused-offence-to-swiss/2007664.

159 Bettauer, Ronald J.: "The Role of the United States…," p. 38.

160 "Class Action Settlement Agreement". *Swiss Banks Settlement: In re Holocaust Victim Assets Litigation Official Website*, 26.01.1999, retrieved 28.05.2018, from http://www.swissbankclaims.com/Documents/Doc_9_Settlement.pdf.

161 Bazyler, Michael J.: *Holocaust Justice…*, pp. 25–26.

162 This included claims resulting from Swiss dormant accounts, Switzerland closing its boarders to refugees from Nazi controlled territories, laundering of slave labor proceeds, World War II forced labor for Swiss companies and the laundering of stolen Nazi assets.

The Swiss banks agreed to pay $1.25 billion in four installments over three years, with the last payment due in November 2001.

Following the conclusion of the settlement, the process of identifying and notifying all known Holocaust survivors and their heirs of the terms of the settlement began through a worldwide notice program, one of the most extensive ever pursued. The survivors and heirs had an option to object to the terms of the settlement, or opt out, and pursue their own claims individually. Judge Korman appointed Judah Gribetz, a New York City Attorney as the Special Master to develop a detailed plan of allocation and distribution of the settlement proceeds. Such a plan was presented in September 2000 and recommended allocating $800 million to bank account claims. The rest of the money was assigned to slave laborers, the poorest Holocaust survivors, and Jewish refugees.[163]

The settlement's weakness was in fact its distribution process: the court allowed up to $800 million for deposited assets claims and nothing for looted assets. However, this estimate of claims proved to be wrong and only $131 million was distributed to this class, but since the court had ruled that the funds could not be distributed to the looted assets subclass,[164] the money had to be finally allocated on a cy pres basis, a doctrine in class action law which states that any funds which cannot be distributed on a claims-made basis must be distributed for the benefit of the class members. The court was therefore involved in the largest cy pres distribution in judicial history, having to allocate around $800 million to nongovernmental organizations.

The settlement included not only Jews but also four other groups of victims persecuted by the Nazis: Romani, Jehovah's Witnesses, homosexual and physically or mentally disabled or handicapped persons.[165]

As of December 31, 2015, almost the total amount of the funds was allocated to 457 100 claimants.[166] The Deposited Assets Class included over 18 000

163 Neuborne, Burt: "Holocaust Reparations Litigation: Lessons for the Slavery Reparations Movement". *NYU Annual Survey of American Law* 58, 2003, pp. 615–622.

164 During the negotiations of the settlement, it was proposed to allocate $1 billion for looted assets, however the court ruled that the funds could not be distributed to the looted assets subclass, since it lacked standards to adjudicate the validity and the amount of the claims. See Swift, Robert A.: "Holocaust Litigation...," p. 55.

165 See the definition of Victim or Target of Nazi Persecution, "Class Action Settlement Agreement."

166 "Holocaust Victim Assets Litigation Case No. CV 96-4849: Swiss Banks Settlement Fund Distribution Statistics as of December 31, 2015 (Amounts Approved and Paid by the Court)". Swiss Banks Settlement: In re Holocaust Victim Assets Litigation Official

claimants who were allocated $719 million, $256 million was awarded to 236 128 persons falling under the Looted Assets Class and $280 million to 198 023 persons falling under the Slave Labor I Class.[167]

A crucial byproduct of the litigation is the historical research and documentation on Swiss complicity with the Nazi regime and the postwar unlawful behavior of banks: report of the Volcker Commission, report of the Bergier Commission, the Eizenstat report, the allocation proposal of the Special Master, and the survivor records collected by the Claims Resolution Tribunal, which provide valuable testimonies to the wartime fate of Holocaust victims.

The Swiss government refused to participate in the resolution process.[168]

3.2.13 The Political Power Game

An interesting and insightful, albeit a highly critical analysis of the political process leading to the settlement outcome for Swiss banks is presented by Angello Codevilla in his book "Between the Alps and a Hard Place". The arguments put forth in this book, although quite controversial, are worth mentioning in the context of the events described in this chapter. Codevilla claims that the publicity campaign, which was conducted by the Clinton administration and Edgar Bronfman, President of the World Jewish Congress, distorted the role of Switzerland during World War II. The campaign against Swiss banks, which was in fact a campaign against Switzerland, attacked the role of the Alpine country during the war, but did not provide any new facts besides a reinterpretation of what was already known. The Eizenstat Report made judgements which were rejected by the Roosevelt and Truman administrations and reversed the moral value assigned to Swiss conduct by the witnesses of the actual events of the war. Codevilla analyzed the policy of the Swiss during World War II and refuted most of the claims made in the Eizenstat Report as regards the shortcomings of Swiss conduct during World War II. The amount of $58 million to be paid by the Swiss as agreed upon in the Washington Agreement was in fact a "ransom,"[169] the Nazis never smelted the bulk of victim gold and therefore it never entered international

---

Website, retrieved 21.09.2016, from http://www.swissbankclaims.com/documents/distribution%20stats.pdf.

167 For details of this distribution see Ibid.

168 This approach is in stark contrast to the approach undertaken by the German government which actively participated in the resolution of claims against German industry in the 1990s.

169 Codevilla, Angelo M.: *Between the Alps and a Hard Place…*, p. 163.

circulation,[170] and the sole purpose of the Eizenstat Report was "to extort money from the Swiss"[171] without providing any merit for the claims put forth in the preface of the Report.

Codevilla further claims, that the outcome of the settlement with Swiss banks was the result of an international projection of domestic interest-group politics. American private actors used the power of the U.S. government to their advantage. The power of Edgar Bronfman and Jewish Organizations in the U.S. was to impose a settlement upon Swiss banks, whereby the final amount to be paid was not at all linked to the amounts documented on Swiss dormant accounts. This power resulted directly from the U.S. political process and the high-level connections which Bronfman enjoyed to the Democratic Party, and President Clinton in particular. Codevilla points to the fact, that Bronfman, a U.S. billionaire of Canadian origin and heir to the family beverage and media empire was the largest family donor to the U.S. Democratic Party, contributing $1,262,000 to the 1995–1996 Clinton – Gore election campaign.[172] In 1999, Bronfman was presented with the Presidential Medal of Freedom by President Bill Clinton.

The construct of the class action suit proved to be a mechanism conducive to the cause which Bronfman was pursuing. The class action suits allow judges and lawyers to exercise great power in cases where a class of plaintiffs represents millions of persons. The lawyers for such a class can exert pressure on the defendant to settle, without going to trial, typically paying out great sums. The judges contribute to this pressure by letting the defendants know during the negotiations stage what would be their final ruling. Class actions often involve public officials, who back the plaintiffs cause and benefit from the payoff.[173] Finally, the appealing aspect of class action suits is that by imposing a settlement they discharge public officials from responsibility for their actions on behalf of the plaintiffs, since all the parties have to "voluntarily" agree to a certain outcome – there is no court ruling. As Codevilla puts it, in case of Swiss banks the class action suits were "aimed at taxing a whole foreign country on behalf of a constituency of the U.S. Democratic Party."[174]

170 Ibid., p. 154.

171 Ibid., p. 169.

172 Ibid., p. 176.

173 For example, via donations made by the winning party. For a detailed discussion of the mechanism of class action suits and how they can benefit public officials see Codevilla, Angelo M.: *Between the Alps and a Hard Place…*, pp. 178–182.

174 Ibid., p. 182.

Bronfman and the WJC possessed superior political connections and therefore had the power to negotiate the agreement and to influence the process of the distribution of the proceeds. Their power resulted not so much from the influence of the U.S. Jewish community, as from the U.S. political process. And in fact, the Swiss side began to take the conflict seriously not immediately after the WJC joined it, but rather after Bronfman used his ties to the Clintons.

The negotiations process leading to a final settlement was backed by Democratic support. The final power game belonged to the Democratic New York City Comptroller, Allan Hevesi, whose threats confronted Swiss financial institutions with heavy costs. Judge Edward Korman was a Democrat. Undersecretary Eizenstat represented the Democratic Clinton Administration.

Codevilla bluntly states: "A powerful private party induced officials of the United States, as well as the American legal system, to force foreigners who do business here to pay a huge bribe."[175] The amount agreed upon in the final settlement had come down to how much two Swiss banks were willing to pay for the permission of the U.S. Democratic Party to conduct business on the territory of the United States. Moreover, this approach of "franchising foreign policy to interest groups"[176] compromised the standing of the United States on the international arena. The whole settlement was an informal process, without any judgement on the evidence.[177] The distribution of the proceeds occurred in line with the requirements put forth by the WJC.

The U.S. power politics served to appease the constituents and contributors to the Democratic Party. The Clinton administration extorted money from Swiss banks, relying on unfounded accusations of Switzerland's responsibility for the Holocaust, one of the greatest crimes of history, for the purpose of serving its contributors. Codevilla severely criticizes the U.S. settlement with Swiss banks and claims that the support given by the Clinton administration to its constituents "abused the U.S. legal system and was a foreign policy fiasco."[178] Codevilla points out, that such actions compromised the credibility of the righteousness of U.S. policy and weakened the "soft power", which the U.S. exerts upon other nations.[179]

---

175 Ibid., p. 10.

176 Ibid., p. 3.

177 Ibid., p. 190.

178 Ibid., p. 210.

179 Ibid., p. 221. For the concept of soft power see Nye, Joseph S.: "Soft Power". Foreign Policy, No. 80, Autumn 1990, pp. 153–171. The relative strength of a country measured by military power and conquest lost its relevance after the end of the Cold War

3.3 Holocaust Litigation: Its Distinctive Features and Historical Legacy

The Holocaust litigation, which initiated with Swiss banks, but subsequently expanded to include claims against financial institutions and private corporations in other countries, was criticized for providing inadequate compensation for victims, for distorting the historical representation of the Holocaust in the lawsuits and for targeting financial and industrial corporations according to their financial standing and international profile, rather than their relative fault. The fact that the lawsuits concentrated on monetary gains diverted attention from the core of the Holocaust crime: mass murder, and redirected it towards a much lesser crime of theft. Moreover, the approach undertaken within the legal construct of class action suits encouraged plaintiffs to distort history to submit a stronger complaint.

Leora Bilsky presents an opposing point of view on Holocaust litigation, which she perceives as bringing several positive effects to Holocaust research and the issue of responsibility for the fate of Jewish people during World War II. Whereas criminal law's focus is on individual intent, the U.S. construct of class action under civil procedure addressed the collective nature of bureaucratic and corporate misconduct, for the first time in history. No corporation has ever been charged for an international war crime and the civil lawsuits of the 1990s have in a certain way allowed to make corporations accountable for their wartime dealings. In addition to creating a new legal paradigm which addressed bureaucratic liability, Bilsky points to a new relationship between law and history created by Holocaust litigation, whereby private parties are assigned the control over litigation and historical enquiry which is pursued by independent historical commissions and not by the judges and courts.[180] This legal and historical legacy of Holocaust litigation and in particular the pioneering features of the Swiss banks' litigation are discussed in detail below.

---

and was replaced by the concept of soft power, whereby one country can impose its will upon another country not with the use of force but rather by getting other countries to follow its policies. Soft power can be defined by one country's ability to affect what other countries want by making its own political agenda, culture and ideology attractive to them, which in turn leads these countries to cooperate with the country which exercises soft power.

180 Bilsky, Leora: "The Judge and the Historian: Transnational Holocaust Litigation as a New Model". *History and Memory* 24, No. 2, Fall/Winter 2012, p. 119.

3.3.1 A Hybrid Legal Framework

In the course of the Swiss lawsuits, the plaintiffs alleged a violation of private law ("unjust enrichment") and international law (profiting from forced and slave labor). Two bodies of law were brought together in this litigation process: international criminal law and the U.S. class action. The international criminal law's legal constructs such as genocide and crimes against humanity can be tried under universal jurisdiction by third-party domestic courts. The U.S. courts had a history of permitting civil litigation for international human rights violations under the Alien Tort Statute and established that universal jurisdiction is not limited to the sphere of criminal law. The U.S. civil rights class action established a class of plaintiffs with a common interest, a group of victims from around the world. The lawsuits thus created a hybrid legal procedure – between private and public, domestic, and international law in order to, as Bilsky puts it, "abolish the de facto immunity of private corporations"[181] in their role in the Holocaust.

Criminal law, which was historically the dominant framework applied in Holocaust judgement, assessed the liability of individuals, class action lawsuits traditionally examined the liability of organizations. As opposed to international criminal law, where the control of the legal proceedings is handed over to an international body, in the Holocaust litigation of the 1990s the control of the legal process was granted to victims and their representatives, without the adherence to an international or national prosecutorial body. But this procedure also created the civil litigation's objective of monetary compensation and funding the litigation, which at some point distorted the motivation of the actors involved, and the need to achieve a historical narrative. In case of Holocaust litigation, the main objective was not to establish liability but rather to create sufficient pressure on the defendants to settle. The monetary aspect of the litigation, according to the critics of this approach, turned victims into anonymous members of a group whose claims are calculated by means of statistics. The lawsuits created a shift in the understanding of historical responsibility for Nazi crimes from the state and direct perpetrators (as for example in the Nuremberg trials) to a limited number of indirect perpetrators, the corporations. However, despite placing settlement and monetary compensation at their center, the lawsuits managed to provide a wholly new and previously unexplored historical narrative as regards the involvement of business corporations in the Nazi crimes.

181 Ibid., p. 121.

3.3.2 The United States as Jurisdiction

The lawsuits were brought before a U.S. court despite involving plaintiffs from all over the world and being targeted against foreign institutions.

There is a number of advantages to bringing a case before an American court: first of all, the discovery procedure unknown in Europe allows to develop the case during the pre-trial period, rather than having all the evidence available when filing a lawsuit, secondly, jury trials in civil cases render the financial success of a lawsuit more likely, since the juries are not uncomfortable with granting compensation in the range of millions or even billions of dollars, thirdly, the legal concept of a "class action" allows to file suit on behalf of similarly situated persons, which in turn further increases the possibility of a large compensation, and finally, American lawyers accept cases on a contingency basis, whereby the client pays success-based legal fees, expressed as a percentage of the payoff awarded to the plaintiffs. What is even more conducive to the suing party is that the losing side does not pay the attorney's fees of the successful litigant, unlike in most European countries. However, the most critical factor which made the litigation in the U.S. possible was the increased number of human rights cases brought to U.S. courts, whereby the acts complained of did not occur in the U.S. and where the plaintiff was not an American citizen. A number of such cases was successfully pursued in American courts it the 1980s, thereby paving the way for the Swiss banks' litigation in the mid-1990s.[1]

3.3.3 Litigation and Banking Secrecy

In the litigation against Swiss banks, the main obstruction with which the plaintiffs were confronted was banking secrecy. Banking secrecy was used by banks as justification with respect to Holocaust survivors and their descendants to support the withholding of information on their accounts. The claims of heirs of account holders were refused on the grounds of missing information regarding the exact number of the account and other identification details including providing death certificates for the deceased relatives. This rendered futile any potential individual requests and civil actions, were they to be brought before domestic European courts. The main advantage of bringing the cases before U.S. courts was the practice of broad and liberal rules of discovery in American law.[2] However,

1 Bazyler, Michael J.: "The Holocaust…", pp. 12–13.

2 Discovery is "the formal process of exchanging information between the parties about the witnesses and evidence they'll present at trial. […] Discovery enables the parties to know before the trial begins what evidence may be presented. It's designed to prevent

the judge presiding over the Swiss banks case, Edward R. Korman, refused to formally order discovery and allow the plaintiffs' experts to examine the records of Swiss banks. The judge instead applied pressure on the defendants to reveal the required information by chastising the banks for their noncompliance with the request to publish lists of dormant accounts. The Swiss banks under pressure of the court and the negative publicity connected with the litigation, finally agreed to form an independent commission – the Volcker Commission and perform an audit of dormant accounts. The U.S. civil procedure therefore allowed the plaintiffs to file claims despite a lack of evidence and forced the Swiss banks to lift the veil of Swiss banking secrecy.[3]

3.3.4 The Role of the Judge in Class Actions

Another specific feature of the American civil litigation in case of Holocaust claims was a new judicial role undertaken by the judge, who actively managed the case in each of its phases, including the implementation phase. Judge Korman actively encouraged the parties to settle, he also supervised the distribution of the settlement. But this broad role also resulted from the specific construct of the class action. In international criminal proceedings, the ultimate objective of the judge is to advance adjudication in order to reach judgement, in a class action it is to mediate and facilitate achieving a settlement. The historical narrative becomes a means to support the parties' legal claims and thereby produces a distorted account of the events. The managerial role of the judge in class action lawsuits creates the separation of legal and historical approaches in the legal proceedings. The gathering of historical information and providing a historical narrative is left not to the judge, but to other entities participating in the legal process.[4]

"trial by ambush," where one side doesn't learn of the other side's evidence or witnesses until the trial, when there's no time to obtain answering evidence. […]" Methods of discovery include among others "subpoenaing or requiring the other side to produce books, records or other documents for inspection (a subpoena is a written order issued by a court compelling a person to testify or produce certain physical evidence such as records); having the other side submit to a physical examination; or asking that a document be submitted for examination to determine if it is genuine". See "How Courts Work. Steps in a Trial, Discovery". American Bar Association, retrieved 21.10.2016, from http://www.americanbar.org/groups/public_education/resources/law_related_education_network/how_courts_work/discovery.html.

3 Bilsky, Leora: "The Judge…," pp. 123–126.

4 Ibid., pp. 127–128.

In international criminal trials the trial phase is central to the proceeding. In a class action the pre-trial and post-trial phases are more important. In the case of Swiss banks, the court relied on historical research, but also encouraged the gathering of information through victim questionnaires, the distribution plan, and the award process. The court appointed a Special Master who prepared a distribution plan. The settlement created various classes of claims including Slave Labor Class I – persons who performed slave labor for German entities with assets in Switzerland and Slave Labor Class II – persons who performed slave labor for Swiss entities. These classes were created not by historians, but by lawyers, with the aim to settle a lawsuit.

3.3.5 The Historical Legacy of Holocaust Litigation

By its very definition a settlement as a mechanism for the resolution of a dispute undermines the goal of determining legal and historical responsibility, by allowing the defendant to pay the settlement amount without the issue of liability being established, or without producing a historical judgement. But as Bilsky argues, the Holocaust litigation did allow to produce new historical narratives, most prominently about corporate involvement in the Nazi crimes, however it did so in a decentralized way.[5] The research conducted in the course of the lawsuits or by special historical commissions appointed by governments and private institutions supported the functionalist school approach, providing insight into the organizational, economic and social causes of the Third Reich's crimes, including the complicity of the elites and their role in sustaining the regime.[6]

The settlement provided incentives for Swiss corporations to admit to having used slave labor during World War II in exchange for obtaining a legal release from future claims.[7]

---

5 Ibid., p. 131.

6 Lenora Bilsky discusses two schools of thought to explain the phenomenon of Nazi crimes: the intentionalist or programmatist school – focused on Hitler and his intentional program of extermination of Jews and the functionalist or structuralist school which focuses on the structural factors which led to the crimes being committed. See Ibid., p. 131.

7 Among others the Swiss company Nestlé delivered a list with thousands of names of persons who worked for its entities during the War and might have performed slave labor. A full list of Swiss companies who provided information on this subject can be found on the official website of the Swiss Banks Settlement under: "Companies Which Seek a Release Under the Settlement Agreement by Identifying Themselves to the Special Master". *Swiss Banks Settlement: In re Holocaust Victim Assets Litigation*

In the course of his work, the Special Master established a list of German companies which owned assets in a Swiss company in order to come up with a list of persons belonging to Slave Labor Class II. He compared a list of German entities identified as using slave labor with the findings of the Volcker Committee, which identified German companies with a Swiss bank account. The surprising finding is that almost all German entities that used slave labor also held assets in Switzerland.[8]

A Claims Resolution Tribunal was set up in Zurich. The tribunal resolved over 100,000 claims. Each claim, which includes information on the family history and its wartime fate, constitutes in itself a valuable account of the history of World War II. In addition, the personal accounts of the victims' experience were told outside the courtrooms, in media campaigns.

Until the 1990s, the dominant way of dealing with the Holocaust in legal terms was either via a criminal law path, which focused on the guilt of individuals and presented the individual narratives of victims and perpetrators, or the reparations path which focused on numbers and money and represented state liability. The Holocaust litigation of the 1990s, which represented a hybrid approach, did reduce Nazi crimes in a certain way to numbers, or moreover to statistics – where data is formed in the language of probability as opposed to certainty.[9] But at the same time it allowed to address and investigate the involvement of organizations and their historical responsibility.

The new model of historical research which emerged from the Holocaust litigation included the creation of historical commissions, which played a special role in uncovering historical facts pertaining to the World War II history of the nations which appointed them. Following the Swiss example, at least 17 other nations established national commissions to study their history of World War II.[10]

The Bergier Commission is the best-known example of such a government-appointed commission. The findings of the Commission reported that during the war Swiss banks complied with German requests for transfers from Jewish accounts and supported the claim that after the war Swiss banks deliberately thwarted attempts by victims of the Holocaust to withdraw their assets. The banks used the amounts in the dormant accounts to earn income from them.

Official Website, 11.09.2000, retrieved 28.05.2018, from http://www.swissbankclaims.com/Documents_New/697505.pdf.

8 Bilsky, Leora: "The Judge...," p. 129 and p. 149.

9 Ibid., p. 132.

10 Henry, Marilyn: "Fifty Years of Holocaust Compensation...," p. 37.

The Bergier Commission had unprecedented power and resources, including the access to Swiss public archives, and the private archives of banks and insurance companies.[11]

Historians perceive the Holocaust litigation of the 1990s, which started with Swiss banks as a process, which by creating great pressure through public attention, ultimately led to European corporations voluntarily investigating their own history.[12] Private companies which participated in the Nazi war economy and profited directly or indirectly from the mistreatment of laborers as well as the looting and the misappropriation of their wealth for the first time ever opened up their wartime files for inspection by historians.

Private law covers a broader spectrum than criminal law, therefore the application of private law to Holocaust litigation allowed to encompass indirect participation in wrongdoing. The use of the civil class action mechanism allowed for an evaluation of the business corporation's responsibility by historians. The doctrine of unjust enrichment, without the requirement of subjective intent, allowed to hold corporations accountable for their wartime dealings and post war idleness and for the first time the responsibility of the bureaucratic machine was targeted.[13]

3.3.6 International Legacy

The Swiss banks' litigation triggered a surge in Holocaust lawsuits and inquiries into the wartime past of numerous countries. Even in the United States a number of initiatives were launched to clarify certain aspects of the U.S. wartime conduct. A special Presidential Commission on Holocaust Assets was established by President Clinton to undertake research into the fate of the assets of Holocaust victims in the possession of the U.S. Federal Government, including works of art, which became part of private collections and non-Federal government organizations, as well as to advise the President on restitution policies with respect to stolen property.[14]

After World War II, the value of heirless Jewish assets vested in the U.S. by the Alien Property Custodian during the war was estimated by Jewish

11 Bilsky, Leora: "The Judge…," pp. 133–134.

12 Ibid., p. 129 and p. 137.

13 Ibid., pp. 136–137.

14 U.S. Holocaust Assets Commission Act of 1998 (Pub.L. 105-186, 112 Stat. 611, 612, 613, 614, 615, 616 and 617, enacted J23.06.1998, H.R. 3662, codified at 5 U.S.C. 3109, 5314 and 5315 Chapter 53, 31 U.S.C. 1346, 105th Congress).

representatives at $3 million and this figure was submitted in the initial legislation proposal, which did not pass the legislative process. In October 1962, the Congress amended the Trading with the Enemy Act to designate $500,000 out of the War Claims Fund to the Jewish Restitution Successor Organization, which reluctantly accepted this amount as a lump sum settlement of all claims it made for unclaimed property vested in the Office of Alien Property Custodian. The Presidential Commission found this sum to be inadequate.

The Commission investigated the wartime plunder by U.S. soldiers of the so-called Hungarian Gold Train and shed light on what happened to assets stolen from Hungarian Jews by the Nazis. Following a report issued by the Commission in 2000,[15] a group of Hungarian Holocaust survivors sued the U.S. government in 2001. In 2005, a settlement was reached whereby $25.5 million was to be paid to various Jewish organizations for the benefit of Holocaust survivors.

The American company IBM was sued for its commercial dealings with the Nazis. IBM supplied Germany with punch cards and tabulating machines which enabled the Nazis to identify and categorize Jews during the war. Two other U.S. flagship companies were also sued – the Ford Motor Company and General Motors.[16]

The two U.S. leading banks, Chase Manhattan Bank and J.P. Morgan & Company, were accused of profiting from the Holocaust by seizing bank assets of Jewish customers in their French branches during the occupation of France by Germany and failing to return them after World War II.[17]

In Israel a commission was created to enquire about money deposited in banks in Palestine before the war by Jews who perished in Europe. The value of these dormant accounts was estimated at $40 million. The Israelis also conducted a search for landholdings which might have belonged to Holocaust victims and were estimated at a minimum value of $90 million.[18]

---

15 Presidential Advisory Commission on Holocaust Assets in the United States: *Plunder and Restitution: Findings and Recommendations of the Presidential Advisory Commission on Holocaust Assets in the United States and Staff Report*, The Commisssion: Washington, D.C. 2000.

16 Bazyler, Michael J.: "The Holocaust...", pp. 42–43.

17 J.P. Morgan decided to accept a settlement in 2000, paying $2.75 million. Chase Manhattan became a party in the so called Drai Commission's settlement together with other French banks. This settlement, contrary to the Swiss settlement did not introduce a cap on the amount to be paid but rather imposed an unlimited liability on the banks since the banks had to pay all awards issued by the Drai Commission. For an extensive description of the lawsuits see Ibid., pp. 181–201.

18 Ibid., pp. 43–44.

The Holocaust restitution movement which initiated in the U.S. in the 1990s with the purpose to determine the wartime financial misconduct of Swiss banks expanded to include numerous other European countries and corporations, as well as Israeli banks, and finally came back full circle and targeted the U.S. government and corporate America.

3.4 Silent Bystander, Willing Accomplice or Righteous Neutral: The Role of Switzerland During World War II in the Light of the Conflict

Swiss historian, Antoine Fleury, in his testimony before the U.S. Congress made the following statement: "[…] because of the wars, criminal acts, and the horrid things done by others, the Swiss have forged for themselves, rightly or wrongly, the image of a privileged people, one somewhat falsely heroic. The Swiss have also attributed to themselves the virtues of being a 'special case' – Sonderfall – for having been spared by the wars and their aftermath. As opposed to the neighboring countries, there were no crimes or shameful official behavior to be repressed or hidden."[1]

After World War II, the Allied stance stipulated that the neutrals have a moral obligation to contribute to reparations and the rehabilitation of the Nazi victims. This concept involved the notion of complicity of non-belligerents in Nazi crimes. Moreover, the neutral countries, including Switzerland, were not just silent bystanders, they were receivers and intermediaries, they facilitated the looting of assets by Germany in occupied countries and benefited directly from collaboration with the Nazi regime and its acts of expropriation and extermination of the Jewish people. This concept of shared responsibility of the neutrals for Nazi crimes, as supported by the Allies in the aftermath of the war and confirmed by the Paris Reparation Agreement of 1946,[2] was not accepted by the

---

1 See "Statement by Professor Antoine Fleury" in U.S. Department of State: *U.S. and Allied Wartime and Postwar Relations and Negotiations With Argentina, Portugal, Spain, Sweden, and Turkey on Looted Gold and German External Assets and U.S. Concerns About the Fate of the Wartime Ustasha Treasury…*", p. 256.

2 The Agreement specified that German assets in countries which remained neutral in the war were to be liquidated and the proceeds of liquidation made available to the Inter-Allied Reparation Agency for the purpose of reparations. A sum of 25 million dollars from the proceeds of liquidation of German assets in neutral countries was to be assigned to nonrepatriable victims of Germany. The heirless assets in neutral countries were to be assigned for the same purpose. See Distribution of Reparation, Establishment of Interallied Reparation Agency, and Restitution of Monetary Gold

Swiss government, on the contrary, the Swiss clearly refuted this notion of responsibility. The provisions of the Washington Accord pertaining to the liquidation of German assets and the transfer of 50% of the proceeds to the reparations fund designated for the rehabilitation of stateless Nazi victims were declared by the Swiss as voluntary and humanitarian contributions.[3] The first installment, 20 million Swiss francs, out of a total of 50 million, was received by the International Refugee Organization responsible for administering the rehabilitation funds only in July 1948. The remaining sum was paid four years later. The issue of heirless assets was simply ignored.

In the mid-1990s, the Swiss were again accused of enrichment as a result of World War II and of prolonging the war by providing financial services to the Nazis and trading with Germany. The Swiss public perceived these allegations as outrageous, but they were not new at all, they simply reaffirmed the Allied stance expressed during the war. Switzerland was again perceived as the middleman between Nazi crimes, a country which provided economic advantages for the German war machine. But how is this economic participation linked to the Holocaust? Holocaust assets found their way to Swiss banks and companies because they were directly deposited in Switzerland by individuals, who fell victim to Nazi extermination policy, or they found their way to the Swiss economy in the form of flight capital accumulated by the Nazis as a result of expropriation, plunder, and murder. The Swiss, by providing the Nazis with financial services created and sustained favorable circumstances for their criminal policy. Switzerland fulfilled the following needs of Nazi Germany: it continued trading with Germany in goods and services, supplied it with strategic electricity power, allowed Germany to use its railway system, it acted as a broker for all sorts of financial transactions and business activities, from trade in Nazi gold[4] to facilitating Nazi capital flight, receiving and trading in stolen goods and cloaking German financial transactions. Finally, by providing its hallmark of credibility, the Swiss facilitated the laundering of assets of questionable provenance.[5] Swiss

---

in "Agreement on Reparation from Germany, on the Establishment of an Inter-Allied Reparation Agency and on the Restitution of Monetary Gold".

3 For an argument along these lines see Ludi, Regula: "'Why Switzerland?'…," pp. 182–186 and p. 197.

4 Almost 80% of Reichsbank's gold transactions during the war were processed via Switzerland.

5 In 1942, almost 80% of the Swiss industrial capacity directed towards warfare production was devoted to fulfilling German orders. The Swiss import credits granted to Nazi

companies operating in Germany applied for forced and slave laborers just like German companies did. The Allies perceived Swiss financial and other economic services as an important factor, which contributed to the German military power, and building on this presumption linked the financing of reparations after the war to the liquidation of German external assets in neutral countries. The Swiss refused to acknowledge any wartime guilt or liability for indemnification.

In the 1990s, the traditional approach which centered on the nation-state was replaced by a new approach to wartime history and Holocaust research. The focus of analysis was shifted towards the ethical aspect of the response to Nazi genocide, special emphasis was placed on questions of moral responsibility and political accountability. In the case of Switzerland, this trend was reflected in abandoning the Swiss self-representation of its wartime policy, which was prevalent since the end of the war and was based on the notion of unconditional survival of the country during World War II, stressing the role of Switzerland as a potential victim of Nazi aggression, which had to succumb to Nazi demands in order to preserve its independence. The idealized concept of neutrality gave way to the idea of "Holocaust bystander", which introduced a different quality of moral judgement to the interpretation of Swiss wartime history, whereby the policy of ensuring national survival at any cost was deemed morally, politically, and legally ambiguous.

The Bergier report critically evaluated the wartime role of Switzerland, in line with this trend: "The question which arises is not whether Switzerland should or could have maintained its business contacts and foreign trade with the warring powers in the first place, but rather how far these activities went: in other words, where the line should be drawn between unavoidable concessions and intentional collaboration. After 1945 Switzerland found itself, unharmed by war, in a relatively favorable position: its intact manufacturing resources, retained markets and political stability, the latter particularly remarkable in a world so marked by the upheaval and destruction of war, assured it a leading position in post-war Europe. This, together with the effects of the Cold War, meant that in Switzerland hardly any critical questions were posed regarding the past, not to mention the fact that self-criticism of any kind would not have been permitted at the time. Generally speaking, recollections were colored by positive aspects of the war period and lent credence to a one-sided view of history. The problem with this idealized collective memory is not the impression it gives of having

---

Germany within a bilateral clearing agreement amounted to over $1 billion by 1945. See Ludi, Regula: "'Why Switzerland?'…," p. 188.

been entirely made up of "phony" elements, and any criticism is not intended to belittle the contribution made by the soldiers, women and men who made tremendous efforts in different places for worthwhile causes and wanted to resist the Nazi regime. But after 1945, this view of history, which highlighted resistance whilst ignoring conformist tendencies, served only to eschew important questions. And in this view of history there was room neither for the victims of the Nazi regime nor the economic and financial network which linked Switzerland to the Third Reich, and thus the country where these victims underwent persecution, deprivation and annihilation. Towards the end of the twentieth century, the positive historical image which had dominated since 1945 came in for ever-increasing criticism."[6]

However, it was not the publication of the Bergier report which led to restitution measures or the settlement outcome, since the settlement of the lawsuits preceded the Bergier Report by four years. The critical evaluation of Switzerland's wartime conduct featured in the Report came too late. The official and the popular representation of wartime history in Switzerland which denied collaboration with Nazi Germany and cultivated a certain myth of resistance did not in effect support the recognition of claims of the victims of the German regime.

This representation of history was questioned by the U.S. administration in the 1990s by the publication of the Eizenstat Report. The Swiss reacted to the Report and the lawsuits against Swiss banks by reexamining their own history primarily by establishing the Bergier commission which was explicitly assigned with dealing with this task. The Bergier historical commission made a major contribution to the reevaluation of the wartime role of Switzerland and of the way in which Swiss neutrality served the interests of Nazi Germany, leading to a revision of the Swiss myth of heroic resistance to the Germans, facilitated by geography in the form of its alpine boundary, and the strength of its army. But in fact, it took a major banking scandal and a conflict with the U.S. in the 1990s to force this systematic reevaluation upon the Swiss.[7]

The Swiss have established a special identity for the Swiss people, cultivating the image of Switzerland as being a neutral, peace-loving nation. Kastner and Jedermann called this vision of Swiss identity a "tale of neutral, peace loving, pastoral banality."[8] The Swiss wartime national narrative was that of Swiss

---

6 Independent Commission of Experts Switzerland – Second World War: *Switzerland, National…*, pp. 497–498.

7 Berenbaum, Michael: "Confronting History…," p. 45.

8 Kastner, Elizabeth/Jedermann, Laurent: "Hitler's Willing Bankers". *German Politics & Society* 15, No. 2 (43), Summer 1997, p. 96.

resistance to the Hitler regime: defending independence, helping refugees, and not participating in the atrocities of World War II, it is a myth of purity and neutrality. Kastner and Jedermann stated: "For fifty years to be Swiss has meant not to be German – not to live in the Land der Täter (country of perpetrators)." As opposed to Germany the Swiss have not processed their wartime experience.

The banking scandal of the 1990's shattered this perceived image of Switzerland to pieces. The first Swiss reactions to the revelations exhibited a high degree of denial. There were voices, including those coming from top Swiss politicians, that the foreign campaign against Swiss banks was conducted to damage Switzerland as a financial center. The Swiss expected the investigations into the country's wartime past to exonerate them and regarded the media campaign as a spectacle directed against Switzerland by Jewish organizations. In the period preceding the U.S. elections the attacks on Switzerland were considered to be a part of the U.S. campaign rhetoric aimed at winning the Jewish voters. The Swiss rejected the attacks as directed against their banks, the root of the Swiss economy.[9]

In an article published in 2012, Joseph Jung, a Swiss historian, provided numerous examples of Swiss banks' misdeeds. In the 1930s, and the 1940s Swiss banks participated in the aryanization of Jewish assets. Jewish businesses in Germany were to be either liquidated or aryanized, that is bought up by German companies. Swiss banks had a large credit exposure in Germany and therefore they were directly confronted with the Nazi aryanization policy – as Jewish companies were driven to bankruptcy, the loans remained unpaid. The banks were faced with a choice of either writing off the loans or transferring them to the new owners. As Joseph Jung notes – Swiss banks operating in Germany had no choice but to comply and transfer the loans to avoid huge losses. The Swiss banks also followed the instructions received from owners in Germany and transferred securities and other assets to the designated accounts in Germany. Some of these money orders were made under duress, as Germany detected and sought to repatriate flight capital. Again, the question remains whether the bank customers would have been better off had the transfer instructions been ignored. A decision to transfer the funds might have resulted in saving the customer's life or it might have deprived the customer of funds, depending on the circumstances. Some Swiss banks also participated in transactions in stolen securities on behalf of German interests, despite knowing that some of the assets they were handling were acquired through theft. Many customers requested compensation after the war for the assets they lost as a consequence of the practices of forced transfers

9 Ibid., pp. 103–105.

and transactions in looted assets. The Swiss banks failed to respond to these requests adequately. Since the Swiss banks became involved in the Nazi policy of expropriation, did it make them equally complicit? In any case their response could have been more accommodating towards the victims of these policies after the war.[10]

Admitting that there existed evidence to the blatant complicity of Swiss banks with the Nazi regime Joseph Jung stated: "Even though, with a few exceptions, the Swiss banks had always met their legal obligations, they now had to admit that they had not been sensitive enough with regard to the psychological and emotional aspects of the dormant accounts issue."[11] At the same time Jung criticized the research conducted by the ICE claiming it to be inadequate and the interpretation of facts provided by the Commission as being superficial.[12] Jung further criticized the ICE Report pointing out that it "ignores the fact that as the examples of the USA and the UK and Israel show – dormant assets belonging to Shoah victims were in no way a specifically Swiss problem" and called the Swiss Banks agreement exemplary and generous.

To the very end, the Swiss media and politicians failed to provide an objective and honest response or the will to confront the past. Only the pressure coming from a foreign power was able to persuade the Swiss to confront the accusations. The Swiss Parliament did as much as to lift banking secrecy rules to allow for an examination of dormant accounts, which in a country where banking secrecy is the fundamental value behind its economic success, represented a concession not to be undervalued. In a speech made by President Arnold Koller, he called for a confrontation of the Swiss past and the creation of a humanitarian fund. However, even this fund was presented to the public as a gesture cultivating the Swiss humanitarian tradition, in line with the Swiss self-image of a righteous people. This conciliatory approach was annihilated by a speech made by Christoph Blocher, who repeated the prevailing view of Switzerland being the righteous neutral, which only defended its independence against Germany, and was now being attacked by Jewish organizations in the name of extortion out of financial motives. Finally, the Swiss felt that it was only their country, which was singled out for attacks.[13]

---

10 See Jung, Joseph: "Swiss Banking in World War II". In: Vogler, Robert U. et al. (eds.): *Financial Markets of Neutral countries in World War II*. Neue Zürcher Zeitung: Zurich 2012, pp. 207–244 pp. 226–230 for a discussion of these issues.

11 Ibid., p. 229.

12 Ibid., pp. 226–229 and p. 231.

13 Kastner, Elizabeth/Jedermann, Laurent: "Hitler's Willing…," pp. 105–111.

3.5 The Debate on the Moral Ambiguity and Validity of Holocaust Restitution: How Legitimate Was the Final Outcome of the Conflict?

The Jewish Organizations' demands for compensation in the mid-1990s evoked awkward material and moral questions. In the period immediately following the war Jewish representatives were concerned that the compensation payments would be confused with the expiation of the perpetrators. In the context of the settlements of the 1990s they were concerned that the successors to the Nazi era perpetrators and their collaborators would refuse to acknowledge their moral debt for the crimes committed during World War II.

But for the Jewish community as a whole, the debate concerning the effectiveness and validity of Holocaust restitution centers around the primary question of whether victims of the Holocaust should accept compensation payments at all. In the 1950s, following the restitution negotiations with West Germany, the payments were called "blood money" and both supporters and opponents of the restitution took to the streets in Israel, to defend their opinion.[14] A similar controversy, albeit not as vehement, reemerged after the 1990s movement. As Michael Berenbaum points out, there is a risk, that "the final word of the Holocaust will not be justice, nor education, nor remembrance, but money. For the monetary nature of the compensation reinforces 'the deepest anti-Semitic stereotypes in the European mind.'"[15]

The Swiss Holocaust litigation triggered a wave of criticism stemming not only from the banks and the Swiss public, but also from the survivors themselves and their heirs, who perceived economic compensation as morally degrading. Their line of argument asserted that since it is impossible to provide compensation which corresponds to the loss and the suffering of the victims, accepting any amount at all would reduce the value of their suffering.[16]

An American-Jewish author and son of Holocaust survivors, Norman Finkelstein in the second edition of his provocative book which included the case of Swiss banks litigation, formulated these concerns in a powerful statement: "The current campaign of the Holocaust industry to extort money from Europe in the

---

14 Ibid., p. 38.

15 Berenbaum, Michael: "Confronting History: Restitution and the Historians". In: Bazyler, Michael J./Alford, Roger P. (eds.): *Holocaust Restitution. Perspectives on the Litigation and Its Legacy*. New York University Press: New York et al. 2006, pp. 43–49.

16 Weiss, Melvyn I.: "A Litigator's...," p. 109.

name of 'needy Holocaust victims' has shrunk the moral stature of their martyrdom to that of a Monte Carlo casino."[17] Finkelstein claims that the Swiss bank litigation fulfilled the personal, financial and political interests of the "Jewish-American establishment" and served the purpose of an extortion campaign.[18] He notes that Swiss banks were recognized as being highly vulnerable to economic pressure from the U.S., and therefore a perfect target for the Jewish organizations, which insisted on reaching a settlement before any findings of the special commissions created to investigate the facts were made public. Finkelstein claims that this was an intentional strategy – if the outcome of the investigations had not proven sufficient Swiss involvement, the case against Swiss banks would have lost credibility.[19] The Jewish organizations used the argument that the Holocaust survivors were passing away and the financial aid from the Swiss settlement, which was supposed to reach them would arrive too late, however once the settlement was reached, there was no actual distribution and no distribution plan for the funds for over a year.[20]

Finkelstein points out that the Volcker Committee listed the United States as a primary safe haven destination for transferable European Jewish assets alongside Switzerland. He quotes the testimony of Seymour Rubin, who was assigned the task of investigating dormant accounts in U.S. banks in the 1950s. Rubin stated before the House Banking Committee that the U.S. took "only very limited measures to identify heirless assets" and despite the finding of heirless Jewish accounts valued at $6 million following a rudimentary audit, the Congress decided to make only $500,000 available to the needy Holocaust victims.[21] Moreover, the U.S. was never made accountable for its policy of refusing Jewish refugees, or for the fact that the German subsidiaries of U.S. companies employed slave labor, obviously profiting from it.[22] What the U.S. demanded of the European nations, in particular Switzerland, namely the honest confrontation and documentation of their wartime financial dealings and other questionable conduct and complicity with the Nazis, it failed to do with respect to its own wartime policy.

17 Finkelstein, Norman G.: *The Holocaust Industry…*, p. 8. Finkelstein goes as far as to claim that the "Holocaust industry" is a greater threat to the memory of the Holocaust, than Holocaust deniers.

18 Ibid., p. 219.

19 Ibid., p. 90, p. 97, and p. 99.

20 Ibid., p. 107.

21 Ibid., pp. 115–116.

22 See Bazyler, Michael J.: "The Holocaust…", pp. 260–261, for these arguments.

Finkelstein's opponents claim that the financial component of the Holocaust litigation was only one dimension of the restitution process, the other being the acknowledgement of the wrongdoing during and after the war, which resulted from the profit-oriented complicity with the Nazi regime.

Other critics of the Holocaust settlements in the 1990s argue that the restitution process promoted only Jewish interests. However, non-Jews were in fact included in the Swiss settlement, and in case of the German settlement constituted the vast majority of the settlements' beneficiaries.[23]

Others have argued that the monetary compensation provided by the settlements was miserably inadequate compared to the personal and financial losses suffered by the Holocaust victims.[24] This argument misses the moral implications of the restitution effort, whereby the perpetrators were obliged to acknowledge their behavior, providing Holocaust survivors with emotional closure and legal justice. In this respect, the settlements proved that the American legal system is capable of protecting human rights and the rule of law.[25] Moreover, not seeking financial restitution would imply allowing an unjust enrichment of the corporations which profited from funds and labor of victims and reinvested these funds over a period of more than fifty years. Without having to pay financial compensation such companies would escape any liability for their unjust financial gains.[26]

A comprehensive and most critical analysis of the pursuit of restitution by Jewish organizations was provided by Gabriel Schoenfeld in an article published in a Jewish magazine *Commentary*.[27] His arguments centered around the question whether the claims made on Swiss banks and other European companies were legitimate and whether they were pursued in a legitimate manner. Schoenfeld

23 Ibid., p. 24.

24 The actual payments received by the claimants were in the range of $7,500– $50,000. See Ibid., p. 41. In case of slave or forced laborers the payout was around $1500.

25 Weiss, Melvyn I.: "A Litigator's…," pp. 110–111.

26 For an extensive discussion of the ethical considerations concerning the Holocaust restitution movement, but also other reparation efforts such as to African-American descendants of slaves, the Aborigines and other classes of victims of mistreatment and discrimination see Masci, David: "Reparations Movement: Should Payments Be Made for Historical Wrongs?". In: *Issues in Race, Ethnicity, Gender, and Class. Selections from CQ Researcher*. Sage Publications, Inc.: Los Angeles 2010, pp. 95–115.

27 Schoenfeld, Gabriel: "Holocaust Reparations – A Growing Scandal". *Commentary*, 01.09.2000, retrieved 17.09.2017, from https://www.commentarymagazine.com/articles/holocaust-reparations-a-growing-scandal/.

argued that the restitution effort of the 1990s was detrimental to Jewish interests, honor, and the perception of history of World War II and accused it of distorting the historical truth. In addition, the Nazi gold and dormant accounts controversy gave rise to anti-Semitic sentiments in Switzerland including hate mail, death threats and physical harassment of Jews. Schoenfeld questioned the tactics employed in the negotiations of the settlements, he questioned the lawyers' personal enrichment, and the historical representation of wartime history of European states, as portrayed by the restitution movement.

Schoenfeld pointed out that the issue of looted gold was settled from a legal point of view by the Washington Accord and that Switzerland, if it would have put itself in a position of military conflict with Germany, by refusing to cooperate in economic matters, would have been of no use to the Allies. He expressed his criticism of the approach taken up by the U.S. administration, and pointed out that "to reprove Swiss neutrality from an office in Washington five decades after the fact, without considering the alternative and what it would have entailed, is to indulge in the worst kind of armchair moralizing."[28] History cannot be molded to suit even the worthiest cause.

The article provides a defense of Swiss banks. Their main fault lied in their inability to resolve an expanding scandal. For years they were faced with an extraordinary situation which they sought to resolve, applying their standard procedures of conduct. The fundamental cause of the problem was the legal framework of the Swiss banking system based upon secrecy provisions[29] and the lack of escheat legislation.

The bad behavior of banks was limited to only a small number of banks and happened years ago. In fact, as the Volcker Committee pointed out "there is ample evidence of many cases in which banks actively sought out missing account holders or their heirs, including Holocaust victims, and paid the account balances of dormant accounts to the proper parties."[30] Schoenfeld points to the questionable validity of the dormant accounts claims, and the fact that following the settlement, 80% of the submitted claims were rejected.

Further, the restitution effort pursued by Jewish organizations might harm the security of Israel, as the threats and bad press incensed Germany, The Netherlands and Switzerland – all Israel's supporters. The accusations made against

---

28 Ibid.

29 Schoenfeld makes the common mistake of attributing the origins of Swiss banking secrecy provisions to the necessity of protecting the assets of persecuted German Jews.

30 See Independent Committee of Eminent Persons: *Report on Dormant Accounts…*, p. 14.

these countries have not only caused anti-Semitic reactions on the far Right, but also damage in the center of the political spectrum. By offending traditional allies of Israel moral and political capital was wasted.

Schoenfeld, along lines similar to the argumentation of Angelo Codevilla, asserts that the Jewish organizations have allied with politicians, and both have exploited the Holocaust to their needs: the Jewish organizations to win their case, and the politicians to win popularity and support of the voters, as well as campaign contributions. This behavior is considered by Schoenfeld to be immoral.

The article in *Commentary* was strongly criticized by Judge Korman, who oversaw the class-action settlement with Swiss banks. Korman attempted to refute Schoenfeld's arguments in his essay entitled "Rewriting the Holocaust History of the Swiss Banks" published in "Holocaust Restitution. Perspectives on the Litigation and Its Legacy."[31] Korman points out that the Volcker Committee was comprised of accountants, who were not after the historical truth, but were primarily interested in identifying bank accounts that might have belonged to victims of the Holocaust. The accounting companies had long term relationships with the banks as their customers and this conflict of interest might have influenced their work. Korman quotes numerous findings of the Bergier Commission, including the fact that the banks transferred money to accounts in Germany, upon Nazi orders, which were extracted by force from banks' customers. The present value of these forced transfers would amount to $1.7 billion, much more than the Swiss banks settlement figure.[32] By yielding to Nazi requests the banks violated their fiduciary duties. Korman refers to the benefits reaped by banks from holding on to unclaimed accounts, as discussed in the report of the Bergier Commission, moreover, as he points out, the policy of stonewalling was a concerted and persistent strategy on the part of the banks. The strict adherence to bank secrecy regulations was only profit driven. A clear proof of this was provided by the disclosure agreements signed with Poland and Hungary after the war. It was possible for the banks to pursue internal investigations and come up with lists of dormant accounts, which were passed to the governments of Poland and Hungary – in these two cases neither banking secrecy nor private property rights provided any obstructions. Banks engaged in the practice of routine document destruction and account erasure. This must have distorted the results of the Volcker Committee's search. Records have been found for only 60% of the accounts opened in the period between 1933 and 1945. For 40% of bank accounts

31 Korman, Edward R.: "Rewriting the Holocaust…," pp. 115–134.
32 Ibid., p. 120.

opened in Swiss banks during this period there is no remaining record. Both the Bergier Commission and the Volcker Committee did confirm that banks destroyed records older than ten years. Korman invokes the doctrine of spoliation against Swiss banks, whereby the law infers that the destroyed evidence was detrimental to the party which destroyed it. He argues that the destruction of the documents constituted in fact the destruction of evidence, since the banks knew that these documents could be relevant to legitimate claims made by Nazi victims and their heirs and would expose the banks to liability. In his final comment Judge Korman states: "The class action against Swiss banks is based on continuing conduct and rests principally on the notion that a bank is a fiduciary to its account holders. If a bank complied with a transfer request made under duress, that bank is legally liable for the transfer. If a bank failed to pay the proceeds of an account to the account holder or its heirs, that bank is legally liable. These facts have nothing to do with the morality of Swiss behavior during the war."[33]

3.6 Conclusions

In this chapter, the detailed examination of the developments of the U.S.-Swiss conflict over heirless assets and dormant accounts in the 1990s was undertaken, beginning with the background to the events, rooted in the Holocaust restitution efforts after World War II, and concluding with the evaluation of the Swiss banks' litigation and the historical and moral legacy of this conflict.

The fact that the Swiss had failed to constructively resolve the issue of Holocaust-related claims during the Cold War era resulted in an outburst of the conflict with the U.S. over this issue in the 1990s.

The initial Swiss response to the crisis was completely failed. The diplomatic blunders further fueled international outrage. However, once the gravity of the situation became apparent to the Swiss, the Swiss Bankers Association finally reacted and agreed to form the Independent Committee of Eminent Persons, responsible for coordinating a comprehensive audit of all Swiss banks in search of dormant accounts. The search was conducted at the expense of the banks. A historical commission was created by the Swiss government to examine the conduct of Switzerland during World War II. The Swiss viewed their efforts as sufficient and a sign of good will. The establishment of these two commissions was perceived by the Swiss as "an extraordinary commitment to national

33 Ibid., p. 132.

self-examination"[34] and the commissions produced uncompromising reports. The Swiss banks created a $200 million Humanitarian Fund for Holocaust victims and entered into settlement negotiations, despite maintaining the position that the lawsuits filed against them should be dismissed on legal grounds.

These efforts, however, proved insufficient to fend off bitter resentment and conflict, which could be blamed on two factors – the first one being the internal divisions among the Jewish community, which hindered reaching a comprehensive agreement with all the parties. The various factions were aggressively attacking the banks in public and making extreme financial demands. From the Swiss perspective, to be able to credibly settle the dispute, the Jewish side had to overcome its own divisions and speak in one voice. The second factor was the critical attitude of the U.S. towards the Swiss, which incensed the Swiss public. The major figure behind a Swiss-bashing campaign was Senator D'Amato. The Eizenstat Report which concluded "with little factual basis"[35] that the Swiss contributed to prolonging the war was another issue which upset the Swiss public opinion. The final blow was the threat made by Jewish groups to block the merger between Union Bank of Switzerland and Swiss Bank Corporation. The Swiss public resented the American accusations and moved towards defending its principles of neutrality and integrity, and the Swiss government withdrew from the conflict altogether, leaving the task of resolving it to Swiss private banks.[36]

---

34 Witten, Roger M.: "How Swiss Banks and German Companies Came to Terms with the Wrenching Legacies of the Holocaust and World War II: A Defense Perspective". In: Bazyler, Michael J./Alford, Roger P. (eds.): *Holocaust Restitution. Perspectives on the Litigation and Its Legacy*. New York University Press: New York et al. 2006, p. 82.

35 Ibid., pp. 80–91.

36 See for example an article by Faith Whittlesey, former U.S. Ambassador to Switzerland: "From the cover of Time to front pages across the country, Switzerland has been the defendant in an American media trial. The tiny nation, a noncombatant in World War II, has been accused by Senator D'Amato and others of collusion with Nazi Germany. A speedy verdict has been rendered by the press, and reparations demanded. Reacting to press and congressional pressure, the US Department of State has also rushed to issue a report, self-admittedly 'preliminary and therefore incomplete' (as stated in the Report's Foreword) but no less starkly judgmental in its conclusions and highly critical of Switzerland's role in World War II, which seeks to reevaluate the State Department's postwar agreements with Switzerland. Others, filing unprecedented class-action lawsuits, seek sums so large that they threaten to tear the political fabric of Europe's most enduring democracy. [...] To charge the Swiss with wholesale plunder of assets of murdered people is simply false". See: Whittlesey, Faith: "Switzerland on Trial". American Swiss Foundation, retrieved 24.09.2017,

During congressional hearings conducted by U.S. Senator Alfonse D'Amato on the issue of dormant accounts of Holocaust victims in Swiss banks, the agreement concluded after World War II between Switzerland and the Polish communist regime was also brought to light. In line with this agreement Swiss citizens were to be compensated for the nationalized Polish assets belonging to them by using money from dormant accounts which most likely belonged to Polish-Jewish Holocaust victims. A similar agreement was signed with Communist Hungary. These two agreements pointed to a selective application of Swiss banking secrecy, which was not restrictively abided by when it came to compensating Swiss citizens, and they caused international outrage and condemnation as unethical and unlawful, since inheritance procedures were not carried out with respect to the liquidated heirless assets in these two cases.

Once the World Jewish Congress mobilized the support of Senator D'Amato and the White House, the issue of Jewish dormant accounts was no longer a controversy between Swiss banks and nongovernmental organizations. In fact, in the course of the negotiations the U.S. government took on the task of mediating a private settlement between American lawyers and Jewish representatives on the one side and the Swiss Banks on the other. However, upon the insistence of the banks, the agreement which was finally reached included the Swiss government, protecting it from further lawsuits pertaining to its refugee policy and the Swiss National Bank, protecting it from claims and lawsuits pertaining to its gold trade with Nazi Germany. The final settlement, whereby the Swiss banks had to pay $1.25 billion to a Holocaust victims' fund, allowed the Swiss banks to continue business as usual on the American market.

A long and complicated distribution process followed for the victims and Jewish organizations. The settlement could be seen only as a suboptimal solution to a problem, which could not have been resolved in a more precise way due to the erosion of documents, devaluation of assets, and most claimants no longer being alive. The compensation payments were perceived as an "approximation of justice" and as a symbolic measure to bring justice to the victims and to hold Swiss multinational corporations accountable for doing business with the Nazi regime. The outcome of the conflict was reminiscent of the outcome of the Washington negotiations in 1946, whereby Switzerland ultimately bought its way out of diplomatic and economic isolation.[37]

from http://www.americanswiss.org/assets/1/7/Switzerland_on_Trial.pdf, p. 1 and p. 5.

37 For this last argument see Ludi, Regula: "'Why Switzerland?'...," pp. 202–203.

The four sources of pressure on Swiss banks throughout the conflict were: 1) the hearings of the U.S. Senate Commission led by Senator Alfonse d'Amato, 2) the negative PR campaign with respect to Switzerland, resulting from Swiss diplomatic blunders and the largest Swiss bank UBS being caught red-handed shredding World War II documents, 3) the Eizenstat Report, which criticized Switzerland for its World War II policy with respect to the Nazis, prepared by U.S. historians under the supervision of the Department of State, and 4) the threats of economic sanctions made by state and local U.S. governments.

This final measure, namely the threat of financial and economic sanctions, was by all means the decisive factor in coercing the Swiss banks into agreeing to the terms of the Settlement.

The conflict with Swiss banks was not only emotionally charged but also had profound political implications, leading to a wide multinational inquiry – not only on restitution and reparations but also on issues of morality and neutrality. The financial demands of Jewish organizations were combined with moral demands for a public acknowledgement of guilt and responsibility for wartime misconduct. The Swiss national narrative with respect to its role during World War II was questioned. However, it was the threat of damage to commercial and economic interests rather than a moral epiphany, which induced the Swiss to investigate and reevaluate their wartime history.

One side effect of the conflict was the dissection of the Washington Accord and the documents related to the question of German assets in neutral countries. The Washington Accord was not widely known after the war, in fact it was "rediscovered" and became a subject of renewed analysis only in the 1990s, after the revelations about Jewish dormant accounts in Switzerland gained publicity.

Another side effect was the international legacy of the conflict, which triggered inquiries into the wartime past of other countries, including the United States. The increased scrutiny of the attitude of the U.S. towards the Jews during World War II led to calls for the recognition of its meager role in saving Jewish refugees and the establishment of the Presidential Commission on Holocaust Assets, which investigated the fate of the property of Jewish victims taken over by the United States Federal government.

There are numerous criticisms with respect to Holocaust litigation of Swiss banks, including that it failed to produce a historical narrative, which typically is an outcome of traditional criminal procedures. However, it can be argued that although it failed to produce a historical judgement in the traditional sense, nevertheless Holocaust litigation did produce a number of historical findings through the workings of the historical commissions, which were established during the conflict and the settlement distribution process, and which required the claimants to present the personal accounts of their or their family's wartime experience. The civil lawsuits in the form of class actions, through their specific features and the fact that they addressed bureaucratic liability, as opposed to the criminal procedure, and its focus on individual intent, allowed to make corporations accountable for their business dealings with the Nazis during World War II and their corporate misconduct thereafter.

The U.S. achieved its aim in making vast financial resources available for the compensation of Holocaust victims, but the conflict strained U.S.-Swiss relations to the extent which surpassed all prior tensions between these two countries. From the media to the politicians and the public at large – the damage was difficult to contain. The U.S. administration's involvement in the settlement negotiations resulted among other factors from the need to alleviate the conflict, fueled by the unprecedented involvement of U.S. state and local officials and their initiative of imposing economic sanctions against Swiss banks.

The fact that the final agreement was not directly tied to the amounts found in dormant accounts, but instead involved a "rough justice amount", raised questions about the legitimacy of the settlement, adding to numerous voices critical of the Jewish demands to any Holocaust compensation at all. Some have gone as far as to call the strategy of Jewish organizations in the negotiations blackmail.

The conflict with Swiss banks over dormant accounts and unclaimed assets was followed by a series of actions directed against companies in other European countries. As soon as an agreement with the Swiss banks had been reached, already in August 1998, the Jewish Organizations turned to Germany with a strategy quite similar to that employed with respect to Swiss banks. The same three legal teams launched class-action lawsuits against German private companies with demands for compensation as high as $20 billion. Alan Hevesi was also involved in casting threats of economic sanctions. The settlements concluded between 1998 and 2001 with the aid of the U.S. government and before U.S. judges amounted to between $8 and $11 billion, depending on the applied method of calculation.[38] Despite this financial achievement, only 3% of unpaid Holocaust

---

38 Michael Bazyler puts this figure between $8 and $11 billion, whereas Sidney Zabludoff estimates the amount actually paid to Jewish survivors or their heirs to be equal to $4 billion. The difference presumably stems from the fact that not all of the settlement proceeds went to Jewish victims, but rather benefited other categories of eligible survivors. See Bazyler, Michael J.: "At Issue: Suing Hitler's Willing Business Partners: American Justice and Holocaust Morality". *Jewish Political Studies Review* 16 (3/4), "Emerging Anti-Semitic Themes", Fall 2004, p. 172 and Zabludoff, Sidney: "Restitution of Holocaust-Era Assets…," p. 11.

assets were restored in the ten-year period following 1995, when the scandal surrounding Jewish dormant accounts in Swiss banks erupted.[39]

The conflict between the U.S. and Switzerland over dormant accounts and Holocaust assets in the mid-1990s was the first of such magnitude and such profound consequences between the two countries.

The confrontation with the U.S. weakened the Swiss "Sonderstatus", questioned its national myth of World War II resistance and forced Switzerland to reexamine its past, however unwelcome this task of rediscovering the uncomfortable truth was in the Swiss media and society.

In spite of this, over twenty years after the initial conflict erupted, Switzerland still did not have a federal escheat law to settle the dormant accounts issue and no statute of limitations. The treatment of dormant accounts is further left to the discretion of the banks.[40]

Banking secrecy was the main culprit blamed for failure to resolve the issue of heirless Jewish assets immediately after the war. However, although Swiss banking secrecy was for the first time actually lifted by a governmental order to allow for inspections of Swiss banks by international accounting firms in the process governed by the Volcker Commission, and subsequently lifted to allow for the examination by the Bergier Commission, it remained intact in its core. The legal foundations of Swiss banking secrecy and its practical implementation were neither questioned nor weakened.

39 Zabludoff, Sidney: "Restitution of Holocaust-Era Assets…," p. 11.

40 For a review of the lawmaking attempts in this regard see Jung, Joseph: "Swiss Banking…," pp. 238–239.

Concluding Remarks

The main purpose of this book was to investigate the impact of Swiss banking secrecy on U.S.-Swiss relations during the period from World War II until the end of the 1990s in the context of Holocaust claims. The book examined how the U.S. exploited its superpower status to influence Swiss internal policy using not only diplomatic, but mainly economic pressure. In the analyzed conflicts between the two countries the argument of moral superiority was also raised by both sides and the conflict often evolved into a public relations war. These channels of influence proved to be effective and allowed the U.S. to achieve its political and economic goals.

Chapter 1 of the book discussed the origins, foundations, and legal implications of Swiss banking secrecy.

Switzerland is not the only country in the world to protect banking secrecy by law, however it is considered a pioneer in this respect. The comprehensive legal protection granted to banking secrecy in Switzerland, as well as the strong attachment to this principle by both Swiss banks and the Swiss society are unrivalled among secrecy jurisdictions worldwide. In Switzerland banking secrecy is perceived as a reflection of the right to privacy in the financial sphere and one of the basic guarantees of personal liberty.

Although the term "banking secrecy" lacks a formal definition in Swiss law, this concept is protected by various provisions within the Swiss legal framework, including the Swiss Constitution, internal bank codes of conduct, cantonal laws, the Swiss Civil Code, the Swiss Code of Obligations and the Swiss Criminal Code. The connection to criminal law was made by encoding a provision pertaining to banking secrecy in the Federal Act on Banks and Savings Banks, commonly known as the Banking Act of 1934. In line with Article 47 of this law, the breach of banking secrecy was made a state crime and explicitly coupled with criminal sanctions. Two key principles result from the legal protection granted to banking secrecy: the first states that a Swiss banker is punishable for any violation of bank secrecy whether it occurs in Switzerland or abroad and the second that only Swiss judicial authorities are endowed with the power to lift Swiss banking secrecy.

The foundations of Swiss banking secrecy are much older than commonly perceived. Secrecy was a customary practice of Swiss banks which have been associated with discretion with respect to their customers from the beginning of the formation of the Swiss banking sector and Switzerland has often served as a safe haven for foreign assets escaping the excessive fiscal burdens and monetary perturbations of the neighboring countries. In particular, the turmoil of World War I and World War II and the uncertainty of the interwar period contributed to the establishment of Switzerland as a banking center, which offered political, legal and economic stability, currency convertibility, and low taxation. The Swiss Banking Act of 1934 merely consolidated and fortified regulations pertaining to banking secrecy, which were traditionally practiced within the Swiss banking sector.

A common misperception prevails about the origins of Swiss banking secrecy. It refers to laws passed in 1933 in Germany, which forced domestic residents to disclose all their foreign assets and enabled the confiscation by the Nazi regime of foreign-held assets of Jewish residents. Banking secrecy law was introduced in 1934 supposedly to protect Jewish money deposited in Swiss banks, as a result of capital flight from Nazi Germany. This misperception was fabricated by the Swiss banks themselves in the 1960s, however, it is still widespread, both in popular and scientific publications. Swiss historians have dispelled this myth following an increased interest in the topic because of the conflict with the U.S. over Holocaust assets. They have pointed to the fact that the timing of the emergence of the myth coincides with increased attacks on Swiss banking secrecy in the United States. The humanitarian aspect of the myth, namely the need to protect Jewish assets from Hitler's regime, provided both legitimacy and respectability to the notion of Swiss banking secrecy and the Swiss correctly assumed that it would be much harder to attack a practice which was invented to support such an honorable cause.

The abolition of Swiss banking secrecy would require the approval both by the Swiss parliament and Swiss voters in the form of a positive outcome in a public referendum. In 1984, the Swiss overwhelmingly rejected an initiative to limit banking secrecy and as surveys show, the support for this tradition is still strong among the Swiss society today.

The protection of banking secrecy in Switzerland stands in stark contrast to the status that banking secrecy enjoys in the United States, where banks have to disclose information about accounts and customer transactions if compelled to do so by the U.S. government, the U.S. tax authorities, or U.S. courts.

After World War II, as the expansion of Swiss banks on international financial markets took off, Switzerland gradually rose to become the world's leading financial center. Today, the banking sector, which accounts for about 10% of Swiss GDP, is a major source of prosperity for the Swiss economy. Two largest Swiss banks are recognized as global systematically important banks and the big bank UBS is one of the largest financial institutions in the world. Swiss banks occupy the number one position globally in terms of private banking and wealth management. In 2014, Switzerland managed $2.7 trillion worth of offshore financial assets, while its GDP amounted to $701 billion.

Chapter 2 of the book examined Swiss banking secrecy during World War II and the first major conflict of Switzerland with the United States.

During World War II Swiss banks facilitated the settlement of transactions, the transfer of gold, currencies, and commodities for Nazi Germany, thereby acting as clearinghouses within the wartime financial system. This was due to the fact that the Swiss franc remained the only internationally convertible currency throughout the whole war. The Nazi regime required a steady supply of foreign currency to furnish exports essential for maintaining Germany's war effort and this was provided for by exchanging Reichsbank's gold for Swiss francs in Switzerland. The gold that the Reichsbank accumulated at its disposal came from various sources, including sources outside of Germany, from the national gold reserves of the occupied countries. Since the early 1930s, the German government pursued a policy intended to increase its gold holdings by restricting the possession, or by confiscating privately owned gold of both German citizens and the citizens of occupied states. The Reichsbank delivered in total $444.1 million worth of gold to Swiss banks, making Switzerland the most important recipient of German gold, which was sold mainly to the Swiss National Bank, but also directly to Swiss commercial banks.

At the same time when the German Reichsbank conducted its gold affairs, individual Germans and German corporations prepared for the imminent defeat in the war by allocating their assets in foreign countries, thereby protecting them from seizure by the Allies. The Swiss financial sector served either as an intermediary, or the ultimate destination for the assets of German citizens.

The U.S. government feared a revival of German aggression resulting from German economic power. The assets looted in occupied countries by the Nazis and safely located abroad would have served this purpose well. In order to prevent such a resurgence of Nazi Germany a special Safehaven Program was devised in Washington to track down German assets in neutral countries and prevent them from being re-used by the Nazis. Switzerland was perceived as one of the key fields of German financial expansion and targeted by the Allies in the course of the attempted implementation of the Safehaven program. The German assets found in Switzerland were to be put under Allied control and later used to provide reparation payments and reconstruction funds for war-ravaged countries.

In August 1945, the U.S. government requested the right of ownership or control of all German assets in Switzerland, which was to be held by the Allied

Control Council as the de facto government of Germany. The Swiss Federal Council declined the request, on the grounds that it had no legal foundations. In October 1945, the Allied Control Council established a German External Property Commission, which was granted all titles and rights to German property outside of Germany, owned by German citizens. However, the Swiss Federal Council further refused to recognize the rights of ownership or control of the Allies over German property in Switzerland. Finally, the U.S. Government proposed a meeting in Washington to discuss the disputable issue. The negotiations initially planned for one week lasted for over two months and concluded on May 25, 1946, with the signing of the Washington Accord, which aimed to regulate three major issues: the acquisitions of gold by the Swiss National Bank from the German Reichsbank, the German assets in Switzerland, and the abolition of wartime economic restrictions, which the Allies implemented against Switzerland. The Swiss proposal to make a complete census of German assets located in Switzerland or in the hands of Swiss companies and subsequently to expropriate them anonymously was rejected. The Swiss banks were obliged to disclose the names of the German asset holders and communicate them to the Allies, thereby lifting banking secrecy, however, Switzerland managed to secure that a Swiss-controlled organ, the Swiss Compensation Office, should carry out the liquidation of German property. On the other hand, the provisions of the Accord, pertaining to the release of Swiss assets frozen in the U.S. during the war, made no mention of an obligatory disclosure of the names of the asset holders. This allowed to protect the owners of these assets and was an issue of major importance for the Swiss. In this respect the Accord was a partial success for the Swiss negotiators with respect to banking secrecy laws.

The Swiss public perceived the Accord to be a great injustice, to which Switzerland was compelled as a result of U.S. pressure, and political and economic dominance in the post-war world. The Accord violated foreign property rights and encroached upon Swiss sovereignty. In addition, the Washington commitment to list and liquidate German assets was a violation of Swiss banking secrecy. Swiss politicians refused to assume any moral or legal obligation with respect to Swiss wartime conduct, instead justifying the payments to the Allies as a contribution to the economic recovery of Europe and an act of good will. It was a sacrifice which Switzerland simply had to make in order to restore good political and economic relations with the Allies.

Although, following the conclusion of the Washington Accord, the U.S. released the assets of the Swiss government and the Swiss central bank, it refused to unblock the assets of certain Swiss private companies in cases where doubts existed in relation to the true ownership of these assets. The U.S. perceived the

Swiss structures to serve as fronts for German operations. The most prominent such case of the U.S.-Swiss custodial conflict was examined in detail in Chapter 2 and pertains to a Swiss company, Interhandel. The legal battle over Interhandel's U.S. based assets was driven by the persistent Swiss adherence to banking secrecy and poisoned U.S.-Swiss relations well into the post-war period. The case was finally resolved in the 1960s by the Kennedy administration.

The wartime economic sanctions against Switzerland were lifted completely with the exception of certain private assets by 1948. But the liquidation of German assets by the Swiss was never actually carried out. In line with the provisions of the Washington Accord, the German owners were to be compensated for their assets, although in the course of the negotiations the Allied side demanded a liquidation of these assets without any compensation at all. The German assets were to be sold in Swiss francs, and the German owners compensated in German currency. Unfortunately, the rate of exchange for this conversion had not been determined by the Washington negotiations, and using this as an excuse, Switzerland managed to delay the fulfillment of the settlement by a few years. The increasing importance of the economic rehabilitation of Germany in the face of the Cold War contributed to further moderating the approach of the U.S government towards the issue of German assets and eventually in 1952 the Accord was replaced by three separate agreements, concluded between Switzerland and the Allies and Switzerland and Germany. By the provisions of these agreements Switzerland, instead of turning over the proceeds from the liquidation of German assets, paid a lump sum amount to the Allies, which was reimbursed to the Swiss by the German Federal Republic, which in turn was compelled to repay its wartime debt to Switzerland, and ultimately the German asset owners were allowed to retrieve their property allocated in Swiss banks. Through this revision of the Washington Accord, in the end Switzerland managed to protect banking secrecy with respect to German assets, and to secure its own economic interests.

Unfortunately, neither the Washington Accord, nor the agreements concluded in 1952 settled all wartime disputes between the U.S. and Switzerland. The way the Swiss authorities handled the implementation of the provisions of the Accord and the subsequent insufficient effort of the Swiss to clarify and deal with the controversies of the country's wartime economic conduct, especially with respect to the financial sector, had overwhelming consequences for the dispute of Switzerland with the United States in the 1990s and, as a result of this dispute, for the international image of Switzerland.

In Chapter 3 of the book, the conflict which evolved around Holocaust-related claims in the 1990s was investigated.

The failure of immediate post-war restitution of Jewish assets and the failure to make a census of heirless assets and to provide them for relief and rehabilitation purposes as declared in the Washington Accord allowed the problem to be raised again 50 years after the end of World War II. The issue of Holocaust related claims resurfaced after over half a century as the result of the end of the Cold War. During the Cold War period the ideological division between the East and the West suppressed any potential controversies over ethical principles. Neutral Switzerland was by implication a member of the Western camp and although the Western decision makers were well aware of Switzerland's wartime conduct, they preferred to ignore the issue for political reasons.

The unsettled question of Switzerland's wartime financial dealings opened the door to Holocaust related claims which exploded in a legal, political and economic conflict with the U.S. of unprecedented scale. Again, the concept of banking secrecy was fundamental to the understanding of this controversy. The preparation of a census of such assets would have violated Swiss banking secrecy, and was resisted by Swiss banking circles, despite the high probability that a scrupulous census of heirless property and the allocation of the proceeds to organizations supporting the designated cause would have most likely prevented a conflict with the U.S. over this issue.

The preliminary initiative in this conflict was taken by Jewish organizations, subsequently supported by the U.S. Government. The campaign started by Edgar Bronfman, the President of the World Jewish Congress was backed by powerful politicians within the U.S. Senate and the Clinton administration.

In the debate concerning Holocaust-related claims, two different matters have been raised: the first was the problem of the so called "dormant accounts" that is the accounts belonging to war victims, which were not claimed by their heirs, or access to these accounts was denied by the bankers and these assets were therefore left at the disposal of Swiss banks, and the second issue concerned the so called "Victim gold", which was stolen from Holocaust victims by the Nazis during World War II.

At the time of the conflict Switzerland had neither escheat laws nor a statute of limitations on bank deposits. This meant that if the deposits were unclaimed, they remained with the bank forever. In accordance with Swiss law the heirs are entitled to all assets of the deceased deposited in a bank, however, in order to prevent any potential fraud, the heirs are required to furnish three obligatory documents: a death certificate, the name of the depositor's bank, and a bank account number. The fulfillment of these requirements was not possible in the case of Holocaust victims for obvious reasons – concentration camps simply did not issue such certificates. As a result, many heirs were rejected by the Swiss banks, which refused to assist claimants, who provided deficient documentation. Between the end of World War II and 1995, several attempts were made to resolve the issue of dormant accounts.

In 1995, in reaction to international press publications referring to the possibility of the existence of Swiss dormant accounts belonging to Holocaust victims, the Swiss Bankers Association (SBA) issued its Guidelines on the Treatment of Dormant Accounts, Custody Accounts, and Safe-Deposit Boxes Held in Swiss Banks. As a result of this regulation already in February 1996 additional 776 heirless accounts were identified, with assets of 38.7 million Swiss francs. But this action came too late, as the issue of dormant accounts in Switzerland was already brought before the United States Senate Committee on Banking, chaired by Alfonse D'Amato, a republican senator from New York, who endorsed the campaign of Jewish organizations.

On May 2, 1996, the Independent Committee of Eminent Persons was established, to conduct the largest bank audit in the history of world finance. The Swiss Federal Banking Commission provided a legal basis for the investigation to avoid a potential violation of banking secrecy by Swiss banks, which were required to make public the names and other information on accounts defined as dormant since 1945. The Committee finally concluded its findings in December 1999. The total number of accounts with probable or possible relationship to Holocaust victims equaled 53 886, with an estimated current value of these accounts amounting to between $643 million and $1.36 billion.

In October 1996, class action suits against Swiss banks were filed by Jewish plaintiffs in the United States.

The U.S. announced its own investigation into the matter of dormant accounts and Nazi Gold. The investigation was led by U.S. Undersecretary of State, Stewart Eizenstat. As a counteraction to these investigations, the Swiss Parliament established in December 1996 an Independent Committee of Experts, under the chairmanship of Swiss professor and historian Jean François Bergier. The aim of the Bergier Commission, as it was called, was to provide detailed findings on the involvement of the SNB and Swiss banks in international gold transactions, currency trade, looted goods, and art dealings during World War II and in its immediate aftermath.

In October 1997 the New York City Comptroller, Alan G. Hevesi, banned the Union Bank of Switzerland from participating in a billion-dollar bond offering to help finance the City's budget. Members of the U.S. Congress threatened to delay or prevent the merger of UBS and Swiss Bank Corporation. An informal network of state and local government public finance officials led by Hevesi supported the initiative of the Jewish organizations and threatened to impose economic sanctions upon Swiss banks. The program of rolling sanctions was an efficient alternative to traditional tools of foreign policy, such as diplomatic pressure. The sanctions were announced despite official opposition from the U.S. administration, which favored a more lenient approach and at that point was worried about a further deterioration of relations with Switzerland, where the sanctions were perceived as aimed at increasing the competitiveness of U.S. financial institutions at the expense of Swiss banks.

Although the State Department initially perceived the litigation as an issue between private parties, as the conflict aggravated, the mediation of the U.S. government appeared to be necessary to contain a potential international crisis. The situation was getting out of hand with threats from Alan Hevesi and a wave of negative public opinion building up in Switzerland towards the United States and in the U.S. with respect to Switzerland. Stuart Eizenstat was assigned the role of a mediator between the parties. Eizenstat persistently sought the involvement of the Swiss government, but to no avail. The internal debate in Switzerland and the negative stance of the public towards the conflict, in particular resulting from a campaign pursued by the right-wing Swiss People's Party prevented the Swiss government from any engagement in the conflict.

The final Settlement Agreement was signed on January 26, 1999. It involved an unprecedented amount of $1.25 billion to be covered by two largest Swiss banks, UBS and Credit Suisse. In fact, the U.S. government mediated a private settlement between American lawyers and the Swiss banks. The settlement would not have been possible without the backing of the Clinton administration and the high-level connections, which Bronfman maintained to the Democratic Party. However, the U.S. succeeded in achieving the desired outcome in the negotiations with Swiss banks only as a result of threats of economic boycotts and sanctions. By agreeing to the U.S. demands the Swiss banks in fact "bought" their way out of an impasse and this payoff effectively allowed them to continue business as usual on the American market. Swiss banks rationally chose to settle with the Jewish organizations and incur lower costs than those, which would have resulted from a court fight, or the substantial losses from economic sanctions.

The persistent Swiss adherence to banking secrecy lost credibility in the light of the revelations about the Swiss agreement with the Polish government, whereby Swiss citizens were to be compensated for their nationalized Polish assets by using money from dormant accounts of Polish-Jewish Holocaust victims. The Swiss-Polish agreement was inconsistent with the arguments raised by the Swiss government in relation to the issue of heirless Holocaust claims in the immediate aftermath of the war and the position assumed by Swiss banks, which quoted secrecy provisions when enquired by claimants about their inheritance throughout the post-war period.

The integrity of the Swiss banking industry was tattered by revelations about its role in handling victim gold looted by the Nazi regime, the participation of Swiss banks in forced transfers of money from accounts in Switzerland to Germany upon Nazi orders, and the details of the Washington Accord, as well as the Swiss-Polish Agreement. Although these facts were not entirely new to historians, the context in which they were depicted further exacerbated the conflict. The affair surrounding Christoph Meili, a security guard who found shredded documents dating to the period before and during World War II in the premises of the bank UBS and the diplomatic blunders of the Swiss officials added to the tensions and the negative portrayal of Switzerland in the U.S. press.

Although, in the light of international law, Switzerland cannot be held accountable for its wartime conduct, the conflict with the U.S. in the 1990s has led to a thorough reexamination of its dealings with Germany and a reassessment of the Swiss wartime policy on moral grounds.

The U.S. raised the argument of moral ambiguity of Swiss neutrality during World War II and, in the course of this conflict, challenged a pervasive myth, which the Swiss have nurtured about their wartime virtue and innocence, forcing Switzerland to reexamine its wartime past. As a result, the "pastoral banality" of Swiss wartime self-representation was shattered to pieces. But the U.S. conduct during World War II and in its immediate aftermath also came under scrutiny. The U.S. failed to accommodate Jewish refugees during the war, return Jewish property vested by the Alien Property Custodian, and adequately search for dormant accounts belonging to Holocaust victims in U.S. banks. The Holocaust litigation, which followed with respect to other European countries and corporations within the 1990s restitution movement also resulted directly from the legal legacy of the conflict with Swiss banks.

The Holocaust litigation of Swiss banks was severely criticized for being an extortion campaign, supported by the U.S. political process, and aimed at winning the popularity and support of the voters, as well as campaign contributors. The final amount of the settlement was perceived by its critics as excessive and out of proportion to the actual amounts found in the dormant accounts and the distribution process as extensively delayed and inadequate.

In the litigation against Swiss banks, the main obstruction with which the plaintiffs were confronted was Swiss banking secrecy that precluded them from obtaining information on their accounts. The specific features of the U.S. civil procedure and the construct of class action suits in fact allowed the plaintiffs to file claims despite a lack of evidence and forced the Swiss banks to lift the veil of Swiss banking secrecy for the purpose of examining the dormant accounts by the Volcker Committee. However, although Swiss banking secrecy was lifted for the first time by a government order to allow for inspections of Swiss banks in an external audit by international accounting firms, as the result of pressure which originated in the United States, and subsequently lifted to allow for the examination by the Bergier Commission, its principles remained preserved. The legal foundations of Swiss banking secrecy were neither questioned nor weakened throughout this conflict.

The practice of banking secrecy is deeply rooted in the Swiss banking sector and the Swiss authorities have firmly stood behind this principle. Switzerland has vehemently defended its own national and financial interests and rejected U.S. requests in order to protect its own citizens and its corporations. The myth of Swiss banking secrecy as a means of providing a safe haven for persecuted peoples or their assets serves only as a facade to mask commercial interests and promote Swiss banking. Private banking and wealth management constitute an important source of wealth for the Swiss and the banking secret is first and foremost a foundation of the Swiss market economy based on the protection of individual property rights and an important instrument of retaining a competitive advantage of the Swiss financial center on the international level.

The U.S. on the other hand has rejected Swiss secrecy laws because they prejudiced U.S. interests.

This book provides arguments that the U.S. has effectively used its economic and political power to curtail Swiss banking secrecy in many of the discussed cases. The U.S. was determined to enforce its law and repeatedly resorted to unilateral measures to achieve its goals. Ultimately, however, the U.S. was not able to impose its policy upon Switzerland whenever banking secrecy came into question, without adhering to economic sanctions and Switzerland conceded to U.S. pressure only after credible threats of sanctions were made by the United States.

The U.S. legal and economic measures against Swiss banks reflect the U.S. determination to enforce its law with respect to a sovereign country such as Switzerland. The Swiss in turn have perceived these actions as an attack on their independence and the personal values which have been incorporated into their economy and their collective consciousness for centuries. The continued U.S. pressure on Switzerland and its persistent condemnation of Swiss banking secrecy was perceived in Switzerland as an arrogant projection of the political and, in particular, economic power of the United States.

During the U.S.-Swiss conflicts over banking secrecy, moral arguments were put forward in support of the economic and commercial interests on both sides, but on numerous occasions the U.S. has played the moral higher ground trump card, condemned Swiss policy and strained the international reputation of Swiss banks, but also that of Switzerland itself. This was clearly detrimental to Swiss interests and was an effective means of exerting influence. Moreover, the US pressured Switzerland for both financial and moral accountability. As a result, Switzerland was forced to undergo a radical reappraisal of its wartime history and cover substantial restitution claims. The demise of Swiss banking secrecy occurred together with the fall of Swiss "myths" such as its role as a neutral, its attitude during World War II and its role as a refugium for persecuted people and their assets. The U.S. has played an important role in exposing these myths.

The conflict analyzed in this book provides an example of a rupture in international relations between two countries which share common values, have similar democratic traditions and institutions, as well as free market economies and in this context the analysis presents US policy towards Switzerland as a case of projection of US economic, as opposed to military power.

The process through which the U.S.-Swiss conflict over Holocaust claims forced Switzerland to reevaluate its history is an interesting example of a case, whereby bilateral relations between countries, which were strained due to financial issues, have influenced the national identity of one of them. In the light of international relations theory, and in particular constructivism, this process shows a transformation of a national identity of a country as a result of external pressure.

Throughout the course of U.S.-Swiss conflicts Switzerland was forced to make numerous concessions and the Swiss banks have paid a high price for consequently adhering to banking secrecy. The controversies involving banking secrecy also had a devastating effect on the international image of Switzerland. Although Swiss banking secrecy is considered a highly controversial practice by the international community, it still constitutes the basis of the Swiss financial system and is highly regarded by Swiss citizens, who pride in the historical role their country has played in protecting individual rights from powerful governments. The conflict with the U.S. over banking secrecy, which among other findings unveiled the conduct of the Swiss during World War II, has shed light on the true nature of this phenomenon. With roots in civil, commercial, criminal and banking law, the concept of banking secrecy was not designed to encourage illegal behavior but it undoubtedly contributed to facilitating such practices among foreign nationals.

Although in the course of the US- Swiss conflict over Holocaust claims the U.S. did not manage to fully dismantle Swiss banking secrecy, it certainly was an important step towards achieving this outcome and the success of the U.S. strategy in this case paved the way for further actions aimed at weakening the

Swiss determination to defend its key banking principle. The conflict over Holocaust claims was resolved once and for all, but the most recent U.S. policy with respect to Swiss banking secrecy and related to tax issues, financial crimes and money laundering has led to further conflicts between the two countries well into the twenty-first century.[1]

1 The conflicts between the U.S. and Switzerland in the context of tax related matters, money laundering and financial crimes will be the subject of a separate publication.

Summary

Throughout much of history the relations between the United States and Switzerland could be described as friendly. Often referred to as "sister republics" the two countries shared common democratic values, historical experiences, and institutional features, as well as a sense of uniqueness with respect to their republican governments.

Despite these strong common foundations, the relations between the U.S. and Switzerland encompassed periods of strong tensions, which commenced during World War II and continued throughout the whole postwar period.

In each case when these tensions could be observed in the relations between the U.S. and Switzerland, they took place in an economic context and were related to the role played by Swiss banks and their strict adherence to Swiss banking secrecy, which is defined in a most rigorous way compared to international standards practiced among developed countries worldwide and firmly and comprehensively protected within the Swiss legal framework.

The first serious conflict between the two countries erupted during World War II and continued in its immediate aftermath. The rupture resulted from U.S. attempts to trace German funds thought to be hidden in Swiss banks and the rejection of Swiss participation in the Safehaven program, which was designed to track down and block German assets and looted property in neutral countries, thereby preventing a potential resurgence of Nazi Germany via an economic recovery. The U.S. planned to use these funds for post war reparations.

However, the Swiss persistently refused to provide any information on German assets to the Allies, on the grounds that doing so would constitute a breach of trust and a violation of banking secrecy.

Throughout the war the Swiss also continued to purchase gold from the Reichsbank. The U.S. claimed that this gold was looted from the occupied countries, and by conducting gold transactions with Germany, Switzerland supported the Nazis by providing them with foreign currency necessary to pay for the imports of raw materials essential for the German war effort.

Following lengthy negotiations and a severe amount of pressure, the Swiss finally agreed to block German assets and provide a census of all German property in Switzerland. In May 1946, the Washington Accord was signed, whereby the Swiss government conceded to a number of provisions aimed at resolving the impasse. Nevertheless, the fulfillment of this agreement was carried out only partially and in 1952 a different solution was implemented.

The repercussions of the involvement of Switzerland in the purchasing of Reichsbank's gold and the safekeeping of German assets as well as the assets of the victims of Nazi Germany had profound consequences for U.S.-Swiss relations fifty years later, fueling a major conflict between the two countries in the 1990s. In this period the issues pertaining to the U.S.-Swiss wartime conflict resurfaced with renewed force when Jewish organizations raised questions about dormant Swiss bank accounts which belonged to Holocaust victims and heirless assets on the books of Swiss financial institutions. The campaign for the restitution of these assets, assisted by the U.S. administration, not only resulted in a billion-dollar settlement financed by two largest Swiss banks, but also induced the Swiss to reexamine and reevaluate the wartime history of their country.

This book will examine in detail the development and the mechanisms of these two conflicts between the United States and Switzerland in relation to the concept of Swiss banking secrecy.

Bibliography

International Treaties, Conventions, Agreements and Documents, Reports and Web Pages of Intergovernmental and International Organizations

"Agreement on Reparation from Germany, on the Establishment of an Inter-Allied Reparation Agency and on the Restitution of Monetary Gold" opened for signature at Paris, 14.01.1946, United Nations Treaty Series, No. 8105.

"Addressing SIFIs". Financial Stability Board, retrieved 12.06.2017.

Financial Stability Board (FSB): *Reducing the moral hazard posed by systemically important financial institutions: FSB Recommendations and Time Lines*, 20.10.2010, retrieved 15.06.2016.

Financial Stability Board (FSB): *2015 Update of list of globally systematically important banks (G-SIBs)*, 03.11.2015, retrieved 13.09.2017, http://www.fsb.org/wp-content/uploads/2015-update-of-list-of-global-systemically-important-banks G SIBs.pdf.

International Monetary Fund (IMF): "Spillovers in International Corporate Taxation". IMF Policy Paper, International Monetary Fund: Washington, D.C. 09.05.2014, retrieved 24.11.2017.

"Inter-Allied Declaration against Acts of Dispossession Committed in Territories under Enemy Occupation of Control (with covering Statement by His Majesty's Government in the United Kingdom and Explanatory Memorandum issued by the Parties to the Declaration) London, January 5. 1943". London Declaration, H. M. Stationery Office: United Nations 1943.

Keen, Michael: "Peer Pressure: Tax competition and developing economies". 07.11.2017, retrieved 13.09.2017, https://blogs.worldbank.org/governance/peer-pressure-tax-competition-and-developing-economies

"Switzerland". World Bank, retrieved 30.09.2017, http://data.worldbank.org/country/switzerland.

U.S. Domestic Documents

1. Legal Acts and Documents of U.S. Judiciary

Roosevelt, Franklin D.: "Executive Order 8785 Freezing the Assets of Certain European Countries", 14.06.1941.

Rule 23 – Class Actions, Federal Rules of Civil Procedure, retrieved 25.09.2017, https://www.federalrulesofcivilprocedure.org/frcp/title-iv-parties/rule-23-class-actions/.

U.S. Holocaust Assets Commission Act of 1998 (Pub.L. 105-186, 112 Stat. 611, 612, 613, 614, 615, 616 and 617, enacted J23.06.1998, H.R. 3662, codified at 5 U.S.C. 3109, 5314 and 5315 Chapter 53, 31 U.S.C. 1346, 105th Congress).

12 U.S. Code § 3409 – Delayed Notice.

28 U.S. Code § 1331 – Federal question.

28 U.S. Code § 1332 – Diversity of citizenship; amount in controversy; costs.

28 U.S. Code § 1350 – Alien's action for tort.

Article 28 of the Swiss Civil Code of 10.12.1907 (Status as of 01.01.2018), Federal Council, retrieved 03.05.2018, https://www.admin.ch/opc/en/classified-compilation/19070042/2018-01010000/210.pdf.

Federal Act on the Amendment of the Swiss Civil Code (Part Five: The Code of Obligations) of 30.03.1911 (Status as of 01.07.2015), Federal Council, retrieved 28.10.2017.

1. U.S. Executive Branch Documents

Bradsher, Greg: "Nazi Gold: The Merkers Mine Treasure". *Prologue Magazine* 31, No. 1, Spring 1999, National Archives and Records Administration, retrieved 28.02.2016, https://www.archives.gov/publications/prologue/1999/spring/nazi-gold-merkers-mine-treasure.htmlhttps://www.archives.gov/publications/prologue/1999/spring/nazi-gold-merkers-mine-treasure.html.

Clinton, William J.: "Statement on signing the Holocaust Victims Redress Act, February 13, 1998". In: *Public Papers of the Presidents of the United States: William J. Clinton, 1998, Book I- January 1 to June 30, 1998*. Office of the Federal Register: Washington, D.C. 1999

"Records of the Foreign Economic Administration". National Archives, retrieved 02.04.2016.

New York State Department of Financial Services: "New York State Banking Board Approves Application Which Furthers Merger Plan of Two Swiss Banks". 04.06.1998, retrieved 12.02.2017, http://www.dfs.ny.gov/consumer/holocaust/hcpopr980604.htm.

Office of the New York State Comptroller: "New York State Common Retirement Fund". Retrieved 12.02.2017, https://www.osc.state.ny.us/pension/.

Presidential Advisory Commission on Holocaust Assets in the United States: *Plunder and Restitution: Findings and Recommendations of the*

Presidential Advisory Commission on Holocaust Assets in the United States and Staff Report, The Commisssion: Washington, D.C. 2000.

P. Steury, Donald: "The OSS and Project SAFEHAVEN: Tracking Nazi Gold". *Studies in Intelligence*, No. 9, Central Intelligence Agency, Center for the Study of Intelligence: Summer 2000, retrieved 27.02.2016, https://www.cia.gov/library/center-for-the-study-of-intelligence/csi-publications/csi-studies/studies/summer00/art04.html.

U.S. Department of State: "Policy Statement Prepared in the Department of State, Washington, August 17, 1950: Switzerland". In: *Foreign Relations of the United States, 1950, Western Europe, Volume III*. U.S. Government Printing Office: Washington, D.C. 1977. Office of the Historian Website, retrieved 17.12.2016, https://history.state.gov/historicaldocuments/frus1950v03/d694.

U.S. Department of State: "Report by Mr. Randolph Paul Concerning Allied – Swiss Negotiations on German External Assets in Switzerland. Section V, Final Agreement: Washington, June 3, 1946". In: *Foreign Relations of the United States, 1946, the British Commonwealth, Western and Central Europe, Volume V*. U.S. Government Printing Office: Washington, D.C. 1969. Office of the Historian Website, retrieved 17.12.2016.

U.S. Department of State: *U.S. and Allied Efforts to Recover and Restore Gold and Other Assets Stolen or Hidden by Germany During World War II. Preliminary Study*. Coordinated by Eizenstat, Stuart E., prepared by Slany, William Z.. Department of State, Washington, D.C. May 1997.

"U.S. Department of State, U.S. and Allied Wartime and Postwar Relations and Negotiations with Argentina, Portugal, Spain, Sweden, and Turkey on Looted Gold and German External Assets and U.S. Concerns About the Fate of the Wartime Ustasha Treasury". Supplement to Preliminary Study on U.S. and Allied Efforts to Recover and Restore Gold and Other Assets Stolen or Hidden by Germany During World War II. Coordinated by Eizenstat, Stuart E., prepared by Slany, William. U.S. Government Printing Office: Washington, D.C. 1998, p. 251

U.S. Department of State: "National Security Council Staff Study: The Position of the United States with Respect to Switzerland: Washington, November 20, 1951". In: *Foreign Relations of the United States, 1951, Europe: Political and Economic Developments, Volume IV, Part 1*. U.S. Government Printing Office: Washington, D.C. 1985. Office of the Historian Website, retrieved 17.12.2016, https://history.state.gov/historicaldocuments/frus1951v04p1/d414.

2. U.S. Legislative Branch Documents

U.S. Congress, House of Representatives: *Legal and Economic Impact of Foreign Banking Procedures on the United States: Hearing Before the Committee on Banking and Currency*, 90th Congress, 2nd Session, 09.12.1968, U.S. Government Printing Office: Washington, D.C. 1968, p. 6.

U.S. Congress, House of Representatives: *The Eizenstat Report and Related Issues Concerning United States and Allied Efforts to Restore Gold and Other Assets Looted by Nazis During World War II: Hearing Before the Committee on Banking and Financial Services*, 105th Congress, 1st Session, 25.06.1997, U.S. Government Printing Office: Washington, D.C. 1997, p. 82.

U.S. Congress, Senate: *Swiss Banks and Attempts to recover Assets Belonging to the Victims of the Holocaust: Hearing before the Committee on Banking, Housing, and Urban Affairs*. 105th Congress, 1st Session, 15.05.1997. U.S. Government Printing Office: Washington, D.C. 1997, p.59.

U.S. Congress, Senate: *Current Developments in Holocaust Assets Restitution: Hearing before the Committee on Banking, Housing and Urban Affairs*, 105th Congress, 2nd Session, 22.06.1998, U.S. Government Printing Office: Washington, D.C.: 1999, p. 72.

U.S. Congress, Senate: *Committee on Homeland Security and Governmental Affairs, Permanent Subcommittee on Investigations, Offshore Tax Evasion: The Effort to Collect Unpaid Taxes on Billions in Hidden Offshore Accounts: Majority and Minority Staff Report*. 113th Congress, 2nd Session, 26.02.2014, retrieved 15.08.2017, https://www.hsgac.senate.gov/imo/media/doc/REPORT%20-%20OFFSHORE%20TAX%20EVASION%20(Feb%2026%202014,%208-20-14%20FINAL).pdf, p. 9.

U.S. Department of State: "Concern of the United States over enemy attempts to secrete funds or other assets in neutral countries: Inception of the Safehaven program: Circular Telegram: The Acting Secretary of State to Certain Diplomatic and Consular Officers, Washington, February 22, 1944" by Stettinius Jr., Edward. In: *Foreign Relations of the United States: Diplomatic Papers, 1944, General: Economic and Social Matters, Volume II*. U.S. Government Printing Office: Washington, D.C. 1967. Office of the Historian Website, retrieved 17.12.2016.

U.S. Department of State: "Memorandum by the Secretary of State to President Roosevelt, Washington, December 29, 1944" by Edward Stettinius Jr. In: *Foreign Relations of the United States: Diplomatic Papers, 1944, General: Economic and Social Matters, Volume II*. U.S. Government Printing Office: Washington, D.C. 1967. Office of the Historian Website, retrieved 17.12.2016, https://history.state.gov/historicaldocuments/frus1944v02/d108

U.S. Congress, Senate: *Committee on Homeland Security and Governmental Affairs, Permanent Subcommittee on Investigations, Permanent Subcommittee on Investigations. Historical Background,* retrieved 02.08.2017, https://www.hsgac.senate.gov/download/?id=95277F6F-E3C7-4ADF-B106-70CE060134C5.

Swiss Domestic Documents

1. Legal Acts

Swiss Criminal Code of 21.12.1937 (Status as of 01.01.2017), Federal Council, retrieved 03.05.2018, https://www.admin.ch/opc/en/classified-compilation/19370083/201701010000/311.0.pdf.

Bundesgesetz über die Banken und Sparkassen (Bankengesetz, BankG) vom 8. November 1934 (Stand am 1. January 2016), Federal Council, retrieved 28.10.2017, https://www.admin.ch/opc/de/classified-compilation/19340083/201601010000/952.0.pdf.

(See Article 13) "Right to privacy" of the Federal Constitution of the Swiss Confederation, of 18.04.1999 (Status as of 14.06.2015), Federal Council, retrieved 15.08.2016, **Error! Hyperlink reference not valid.**.

Documents of the Swiss Government

Federal Assembly: "Chronology: Switzerland and the Second World War", retrieved 27.02.2017, https://www.parlament.ch/centers/documents/en/do-ch-wk2-chronologie-e.pdf.

Federal Assembly: "Einfache Anfrage: Herrenlose Vermögenswerte: Eingerecht von: Otto Piller", 06.12.1994, retrieved 17.04.2017.

Federal Assembly: "Einfache Anfrage: Ziegler Jean: Vermögenswerte von Holocaust Opfern", 07.03.1995, Federal Department of Foreign Affairs, retrieved 17.04.2017.

Federal Assembly: "Federal Decree Concerning the Historical and Legal Investigation of the Fate of Assets Which Reached Switzerland as a Result of National Socialist Rule of December 13, 1960." In: Independent Committee of Eminent Persons: *Report on Dormant Accounts of Victims of Nazi Persecution in Swiss Banks.* Stämpfli Verlag AG: *Bern* 1999, Appendix F: Report of the Independent Committee of Eminent Persons, retrieved 14.04.2018, http://www.swissbankclaims.com/Documents/DOC_4_bergier_.pdf, pp. A-21–A-28.

Federal Assembly: "Interpellation: Boykottdrohungen und eventuelle konkrete Vergeltungsmassnahmen: Eingereicht von Marty Dick", 19.03.1998, retrieved 26.02.2017.

Federal Assembly: "Interpellation: US-Boykottmaßnahmen: Reaktion der Schweiz: Eingereicht von: Christine Beerli", 18.03.1998, retrieved 26.02.2017.

Federal Assembly: "Motion: Herrenlose Vermögen auf Schweizer Banken: Eingereicht von Otto Piller", 12.06.1995, retrieved 17.04.2017.

Federal Assembly: "Motion Piller-Plattner: Herrenlose Vermögen auf Schweizer Banken: Eingereicht am 12.06.1995", *Amtliches Bulletin der Bundesversammlung*, 20.12.1995, Federal Department of Foreign Affairs, retrieved 17.04.2017,

Federal Assembly: "Parlamentarische Initiative: Herrenlose Vermögen von Opfern Nationalistischer Verfolgungen: Eingereicht von Verena Grendelmeier", Dossier 95.407, 24.03.1995, retrieved 28.04.2018.

Federal Chancellery: "Schweizerische Stiftung für Solidarität", Press Release, Federal Council, 05.03.1997, retrieved 27.02.2017.

Federal Council: "Erklärung des Bundesrates zum Eizenstat-Bericht", Federal Council, Bern 22.05.1997, retrieved 27.02.2017.

Federal Council: "Joint Swiss-American Statement on Sanctions", Bern 26.03.1998, retrieved 28.02.2017.

Federal Council: "Switzerland's Political System", retrieved 28.09.2016, https://www.admin.ch/gov/en/start/federal-council/political-system-of-switzerland.html

Federal Council: "The Federal Department of Foreign Affairs (FDFA)", retrieved 29.09.2016.

Villiger, Kaspar: "Gedanken zum Kriegsende vor 50 Jahren, Sondersession", speech by Kaspar Villiger, President of the Swiss Confederation, 07.05.1995, retrieved 27.02.2017, https://www.admin.ch/cp/d/1995May9.165750.4088@idz.bfi.admin.ch.html.

Documents and Reports of Special Commissions Established to Analyze Swiss Policy and The Conduct of Swiss Banks During World War II and in Its Aftermath

Independent Commission of Experts Switzerland – Second World War, retrieved 02.02.2017, https://www.uek.ch/en/.

Independent Commission of Experts Switzerland – Second World War: *Gold Transactions in the Second World War: Statistical Review with Commentary: A Contribution to the Conference on Nazi Gold London, 2–4 December 1997*, Bern December 1997, retrieved 04.02.2017.

Independent Commission of Experts Switzerland – Second World War: *Switzerland and Gold Transactions in the Second World War, Interim Report*, Bern July

1998, retrieved 12.01.2017, https://www.uek.ch/en/publikationen1997-2000/golde.pdf, p. 39 and p. 44.

Independent Commission of Experts Switzerland – Second World War: *Switzerland, National Socialism and the Second World War. Final Report*, Pendo Verlag: Zürich 2002.

Independent Committee of Eminent Persons: *Report on Dormant Accounts of Victims of Nazi Persecution in Swiss Banks*. Stämpfli Verlag AG: Bern 1999.

Reports, Documents and Websites of Non-governmental Organizations and Other Institutions

Centre for Applied Research, Norwegian School of Economics Global Financial Integrity, Jawaharlal Nehru University Instituto de Estudos Socioeconômicos, Nigerian Institute of Social and Economic Research: "Financial Flows and Tax Havens: Combining to Limit the Lives of Billions of People". Global Financial Integrity: December 2015, retrieved 05.11.2017, http://www.gfintegrity.org/wp-content/uploads/2016/12/Financial_Flows-final.pdf,

Crettol, Vincent/Halbeisen, Patrick: *Monetary policy background to the gold transactions of the Swiss National Bank in the Second World War*. Zürich, Swiss National Bank, May 1999, retrieved 05.05.2017, p. 24.

Henry, James S.: "The Price of Offshore Revisited. New Estimates for "Missing" Global Private Wealth, Income, Inequality, and Lost Taxes". Tax Justice Network, July 2012, p. 5, retrieved 12.10.2017.

Herkenrath, Mark/Longchamp, Olivier/Missbach, Andreas: "Steuern und Entwicklung. Wie die Steuerflucht die Entwicklung behindert – und was die Schweiz daran ändern kann", Alliance Sud und Erklärung von Bern, June 2012, retrieved 25.10.2017, p. 6.

"Key Figures". Swiss Bankers Association, retrieved 11.10.2017, http://www.swissbanking.org-/en/financial-centre/key-figures.

"Memorandum of Understanding between The World Jewish Restitution Organization and the World Jewish Congress representing also the Jewish Agency and Allied Organizations and the Swiss Bankers Association". New York 02.05.1996, *Swiss Banks Settlement: In re Holocaust Victim Assets Litigation*, retrieved 28.05.2017, http://www.swissbankclaims.com/Documents/DOC_1_memo_of.pdf.

"Portrait". Swiss Bankers Association, retrieved 15.10.2017, http://www.swissbanking.org/en/bankers-association/about-us/mission.

"Survey 2015: Banks make significant reputational gains, protection of privacy central, but bank-client confidentiality in Switzerland viewed in differentiated manner". Swiss Bankers Association, 26.03.2015, retrieved 26.10.2017, http://www.swissbanking.org/en/medienmitteilung-20150326.

Swiss Bankers Association: *2015 Banking Barometer. Economic Trends in the Swiss Banking Industry*. September 2015, retrieved 14.06.2016, http://shop.sba.ch/1100003_e.pdf.

Swiss Bankers Association: *The Financial Centre: Engine of the Swiss Economy*. April 2016, retrieved 15.09.2017, http://www.swissbanking.org/en/20130715-fp_motor_der_schweizer_wirtschaft.pdf.

Swiss Bankers Association: *2015 Financial Centre Strategy*. 2010, retrieved 02.10.2016,

Vogler, Robert: *The Swiss National Bank's gold transactions with the German Reichsbank from 1939 to 1945*. Swiss National Bank, 1984, retrieved 08.01.2017, http://www.snb.ch/en/mmr/reference/snb_gold_ww2_vogler/source/snb_gold_ww2_vogler.en.pdf.

World Jewish Restitution Organization: *Framework for Allocation Plan of Funds Received in Global Settlement with the Swiss Banks & Others. Proposal to the Court. Swiss Banks Settlement: In re Holocaust Victim Assets Litigation Official Website*, October 1999, retrieved 28.05.2017.

Monographs and Collective works

Adams, Maurice/Heirbaut, Dirk: *The Method and Culture of Comparative Law. Essays in Honour of Mark von Hoecke*. Hart Publishing: Oxford and Portland, Oregon 2014.

Bär, Hans J./Albrecht Daniel U.: *The Banking System of Switzerland*. Schulthess Polygraphischer Verlag AG: Zurich 1975, pp. 10–12.

Bauer, Hans/Blackman, Warren J.: *Swiss Banking: An Analytical History*. Macmillan Press: Basingstoke 1998, pp. 10–13.

Bazyler, Michael J./Alford, Roger P. (eds.): *Holocaust Restitution: Perspectives on the Litigation and Its Legacy*. New York University Press: New York and London 2006.

Bazyler, Michael J: *Holocaust Justice. The Battle for Restitution in America's Courts*. New York University Press: New York et al. 2003, pp. 21–22.

Bourgeois, Daniel: *Le Troisième Reich et la Suisse 1933–1941*. Éditions de la Baconnière: Neuchatel 1974.

Bower, Tom: *Nazi Gold. The Full Story of the Fifty-Year Swiss-Nazi Conspiracy to Steal Billions from Europe's Jews and Holocaust Survivors*. Harper Perennial: New York 1998, p. 307.

Braillard, Philippe/Schwamm, Henri: *Place financière Suisse. L'autre stratégie.* Éditions Slatkine: Genève 2006.

Buechenbacher, Christoph: *Tatsachen über das schweizerische Bankgeheimnis.* Nova-Press AG: Zürich et. al. 1977, pp. 77–80

Castelmur, Linus von: *Schweizerisch – Allierte Finanzbeziehungen im Übergang vom Zweiten Weltkrieg zum Kalten Krieg. Die Deutschen Guthaben in der Schweiz zwischen Zwangsliquidierung und Freigabe 1945–1952.* Chronos: Zürich 1992,

Codevilla, Angelo M.: *Between the Alps and a Hard Place. Switzerland in World War II and the Rewriting of History.* Regenery Publishing, Inc.: Washington D.C. 2000.

Durrer, Marco: *Die schweizerisch – amerikanischen Finanzbeziehungen im Zweiten Weltkrieg. Von der Blockierung der schweizerischen Guthaben in den USA über die "Safehaven" – Politik zum Washingtoner Abkommen (1941–1946).* Paul Haupt Verlag: Bern et al. 1984.

Eizenstat, Stuart E.: *Imperfect Justice. Looted Assets, Slave Labor, and the Unfinished Business of World War II.* PublicAffairs: New York 2004.Faith, Nicolas: *Safety in Numbers. The Mysterious World of Swiss Banking.* Hamish Hamilton: London 1982, pp. 73–80.

Fehrenbach, T.R.: *The Gnomes of Zurich.* Leslie Frewin Publishers Limitcd: London 1966.

Finkelstein, Norman G.: *The Holocaust Industry. Reflections on the Exploitation of Jewish Suffering.* Verso: London et al. 2003.

Fleury, Antione/Möller, Horst and Schwarz, Hans-Peter (eds.): *Die Schweiz und Deutschland 1945–1961.* Oldenbourg Verlag: München 2004, pp. 125–126.

Hutson, James H.: *The Sister Republics. Switzerland and the United States from 1776 to the Present.* Library of Congress: Washington 1991, p. 66.

Iklé, Max: *Switzerland: An International Banking and Finance Center.* Dowden, Hutchinson & Ross Inc.: Stroudsburg (Pa.) 1972, p. 19

König, Mario: *Interhandel. Die schweizerische Holding der IG Farben und ihre Metamorphosen – eine Affäre um Eigentum und Interessen (1910–1999).* The Chronos Verlag: Zürich 2001, p. 33.

LeBor, Adam: *Tower of Basel. The Shadowy History of the Secret Bank that Runs the World.* PublicAffairs: New York 2013, pp. 176–177

Lorenz-Meyer, Martin: *Safehaven: The Allied Pursuit of Nazi Assets Abroad.* University of Missouri Press: Columbia, Missouri 2007, p. 42.

Luescher M.: *Das Schweizerische Bankgeheimnis in Strafrechtlicher Sicht.* Schulthess Polygraphischer Verlag: Zürich 1972, p. 5.

Meier, Heinz K.: *Friendship Under Stress. U.S. Swiss Relations 1900–1950.* Herbert Lang & Co: Bern 1970, p. 291.

Meier, Henri B./Marthinsen, John E./Gantenbein, Pascal A.: *Swiss Finance. Capital Markets, Banking, and the Swiss Value Chain.* John Wiley & Sons, Inc.: Hoboken, New Jersey 2013.

Novick, Peter: *The Holocaust in American Life.* Mariner Books: Boston 2000.

Palan, Ronen/Murphy, Richard/Chavagneux, Christian: *Tax Havens: How Globalization Really Works.* Cornell University Press: Ithaca and London 2010.

Rickman, Gregg J.: *Swiss Banks and Jewish Souls.* Transaction Publishers: New Brunswick, New Jersey 1999, p. 215.

Roosevelt, Franklin D.: *The Public Papers and Addresses of Franklin D. Roosevelt, Compiled with Special Material and Explanatory Notes by Samuel I. Rosenman: 1944–1945 Volume: Victory and the Threshold of Peace.* Harper & Brothers Publishers: New York 1950, pp. 255–259.

Schapiro, Jane: *Inside a Class Action: The Holocaust and the Swiss Banks.* University of Wisconsin Press/Terrace Books: Madison, Wisconsin 2003, p. 131.

Shaxon, Nicolas: *Treasure Islands. Tax Havens and the Men who Stole the World.* Vintage Books: London 2012.

Steinberg, Jonathan: *Die Deutsche Bank und ihre Goldtransaktionen während des Zweiten Weltkrieges.* C.H. Beck Verlag: München 1999, p. 17.

Toniolo, Gianni/Clement, Piet: *Central Bank Cooperation at the Bank for International Settlements, 1930–1973.* Cambridge University Press: Cambridge 2005, p. 249.

Vogler, Robert U.: *Swiss Banking Secrecy: Origins, Significance, Myth.* Association for Financial History: Zurich 2006, p. 76.

Chapters in Edited Books

Berenbaum, Michael: "Confronting History: Restitution and the Historians". In: Bazyler, Michael J./Alford, Roger P. (eds.): *Holocaust Restitution. Perspectives on the Litigation and Its Legacy.* New York University Press: New York et al. 2006, pp. 43–49.

Bradfield, Michael/Sak, Pamela: "Swiss Law on the Treatment of Dormant Accounts: A Comparison with European and U.S. Law". In: *Current Developments in Monetary and Financial Law.* Volume 2. International Monetary Fund: Washington, D.C. 2003.

Cassis, Youssef: "Swiss International Banking 1890–1950". In: Jones, Geoffrey (ed.): *Banks as Multinationals.* Routledge: New York 2012, pp. 160–170.

Guex, Sébastien: "Le secret bancaire a-t-il un avenir?". In: Froidevaux, Dominique (ed.): *La Suisse dans la constellation des paradis fiscaux*. Éditions d'en bas et COTMEC: Lausanne and Genève 2002, pp. 171–182.

Guex, Sébastien: "Place financière Suisse et secret bancaire au XXe siècle: ombres at pénombres". In: Froidevaux, Dominique (ed.): *La Suisse dans la constellation des paradis fiscaux*. Éditions d'en bas et COTMEC: Lausanne and Genève 2002, pp. 54–79.

Henry, Marilyn: "Fifty Years of Holocaust Compensation". In: Singer, David/ Grossman, Lawrence (eds.): *The American Jewish Yearbook*. American Jewish Committee: New York 2002, pp. 3–84 and pp. 4–5.

Hopkin, Jonathan: "The Comparative Method". In: Marsh, David/Stoker, Gerry (eds.): *Theory and Methods in Political Science*. Palgrave Macmillan: New York 2010.

Hug, Peter: "Steuerflucht und die Legende vom antinazistischen Ursprung des Bankgeheimnisses: Funktion und Risiko der moralischen Überholung des Finanzplatzes Schweiz". In: Tanner, Jakob/Weigel, Sigrid (eds.): *Gedächtnis, Geld und Gesetz, Vom Umgang mit der Vergangenheit des Zweiten Weltkrieges*. Hochschulverlag: Zürich 2002, pp. 269–322.

Hug, Peter: "Unclaimed Assets of Nazi Victims in Switzerland: What People Knew and what else They Ought to Know". In: Kreis, Georg (ed.): *Switzerland and the Second World War*. Frank Cass Publishers: London 2000, pp. 81–102.

Jung, Joseph: "Swiss Banking in World War II". In: Vogler, Robert U. et al. (eds.): *Financial Markets of Neutral countries in World War II*. Neue Zürcher Zeitung: Zurich 2012, pp. 207–244 pp. 226–230.

Korman, Edward R.: "Rewriting the Holocaust History of Swiss Banks: A Growing Scandal". In: Bazyler, Michael J./Alford Roger P. (eds.): *Holocaust Restitution. Perspectives on the Litigation and Its Legacy*. New York University Press: New York et al. 2006. pp. 115–134.

Ludi, Regula: "'Why Switzerland?' Remarks on a Neutral's Role in the Nazi Program of Robbery and Allied Postwar Restitution Policy". In: Dean, Martin/ Goschler,Constantin/Ther, Phillip (eds.): *Robbery and Restitution. The Conflict over Jewish Property in Europe*. Berghan Books: New York et al. 2008, pp. 182–210 and p. 195.

Masci, David: "Reparations Movement: Should Payments Be Made for Historical Wrongs?". In: *Issues in Race, Ethnicity, Gender, and Class. Selections from CQ Researcher*. Sage Publications, Inc.: Los Angeles 2010, pp. 95–115.

Slany, William Z.: "The State Department, Nazi Gold, and the Search for Holocaust Assets". In: Bazyler, Michael J./Alford, Roger P. (eds.): *Holocaust*

Restitution: Perspectives on the Litigation and Its Legacy. New York University Press: New York and London 2006, p. 34.

Swift, Robert A.: "Holocaust Litigation and Human Rights Jurisprudence". In: Bazyler, Michael J./Alford, Roger P. (eds.): *Holocaust Restitution: Perspectives on the Litigation and Its Legacy*. New York University Press: New York and London 2006, p. 54.

The State of Israel: International Relations". In: Oron, Yitzhak (ed.): *Middle East Record*. Volume Two. Israel Program for Scientific Translations: Jerusalem, Israel 1961, p. 317.

Vromen, Ariadne: "Debating Methods: Rediscovering Qualitative Approaches". In: Marsh, David/Stoker, Gerry (eds.): *Theory and Methods in Political Science*. Palgrave Macmillan: Basingstoke, UK 2010, pp. 249–266.

Weder, Beatrice/Weder, Rolf: "Switzerland's Rise to a Wealthy Nation: Competition and Contestability as Key Success Factors". In: Fosu, Augustin K. (ed.): *Development Success Historical Accounts from More Advanced Countries*. Oxford University Press: Oxford 2013, pp. 192–215.

Weiss, Melvyn I.: "A Litigator's Postscript to the Swiss Banks and Holocaust Litigation Settlements". In: Bazyler, Michael J./Alford, Roger P. (eds.): *Holocaust Restitution. Perspectives on the Litigation and Its Legacy*. New York University Press: New York and London 2006, p. 113.

Witten, Roger M.: "How Swiss Banks and German Companies Came to Terms with the Wrenching Legacies of the Holocaust and World War II: A Defense Perspective". In: Bazyler, Michael J./Alford, Roger P. (eds.): *Holocaust Restitution. Perspectives on the Litigation and Its Legacy*. New York University Press: New York and London 2006, p. 82.

Articles in Scholarly Journals

Aubert, Maurice: "The Limits of Swiss Banking Secrecy under Domestic and International Law". *Berkeley Journal of International Law* 2 (2), Fall 1984, pp. 273–297.

Bazyler, Michael J.: "At Issue: Suing Hitler's Willing Business Partners: American Justice and Holocaust Morality". *Jewish Political Studies Review* 16(3/4), "Emerging Anti-Semitic Themes", Fall 2004, p. 172.

Bazyler, Michael J.: "The Holocaust Restitution Movement in Comparative Perspective". *Berkeley Journal of International Law* 20 (1), 2002, p. 12.

Bettauer, Ronald J.: "The Role of the United States Government in Recent Holocaust Claims Resolution". *Proceedings of the Annual Meeting (American Society of International Law)* 95, 2001, p. 38.

Bilenker, Stephanie A.: "In Re Holocaust Victims' Assets Litigation: Do the U.S. Courts Have Jurisdiction Over the Lawsuits Filed by Holocaust Survivors Against the Swiss Banks?". *Maryland Journal of International Law* 21 (2), 1997, p. 140.

Bilsky, Leora: "The Judge and the Historian: Transnational Holocaust Litigation as a New Model". *History and Memory* 24 (2), Fall/Winter 2012, p. 119.

Blau, Gisela: "Switzerland". *The American Jewish Yearbook* 98, 1998, p. 296.

Capitani, Werner de: "Banking Secrecy Today". *University of Pennsylvania Journal of International Business Law* 10 (1), 1988, pp. 60–61.

Cowell, Alan: "Switzerland's Wartime Blood Money". *Foreign Policy* 107, Summer 1997, p. 140.

Eggenberger, Katrin/Emmenegger, Patrick: "Economic Vulnerability and Political Responses to International Pressure: Liechtenstein, Switzerland and the Struggle for Banking Secrecy". *Swiss Political Science Review* 21(4), 2015, pp. 491–507.

Eldridge, James E.: "The Bank Secrecy Act: Privacy, Comity, and the Politics of Contraband". In: *North Carolina Journal of International Law and Commercial Regulation* 11 (3), 1986, p. 681.

Emmenegger, Patrick/Eggenberger, Katrin: "State Sovereignty, Economic Interdependence, and U.S. Extraterritoriality: The Demise of Swiss Banking Secrecy and the Re-Embedding of International Finance". *Journal of International Relations and Development* 21 (3), 2018, pp. 146–164.

Emmenegger, Patrick: "The Long Arm of Justice: U.S. Structural Power and International Banking". *Business and Politics* 17(3), 2015, pp. 473–493.

Emmenegger, Patrick: "Swiss Banking Secrecy and the Problem of International Cooperation in Tax Matters: A Nut too Hard to Crack?". *Regulation & Governance* 11 (1), 2017, pp. 24–40.

Emmenegger, Patrick: "The Politics of Financial Intransparency: The C.ase of Swiss Banking Secrecy". *Swiss Political Science Review* 20(1), 2014, pp. 146–164.

Ganz, Jodi Berlin: "Heirs Without Assets and Assets Without Heirs: Recovering and Reclaiming Dormant Swiss Bank Accounts". *Fordham International Law Journal* 20 (4), 1996, p. 1322.

Grassi, Paolo S./Calverese, Daniele: "The Duty of Confidentiality of Banks in Switzerland: Where It Stands and Where It Goes – Recent Developments and Experience – The Swiss Assistance to, and Cooperation with the Italian Authorities in the Investigation of Corruption among Civil Servants in Italy (The "Clean Hands Investigation): How Much Is Too Much". *Pace International Law Review* 7 (2), April 1995, pp. 331–334.

Guex, Sébastien: "The Origins of the Swiss Banking Secrecy Law and Its Repercussions for Swiss Federal Policy". *The Business History Review* 74 (2), Summer 2000, p. 244.

Heilig, Karen: "From the Luxembourg Agreement to Today: Representing a People". *Berkeley Journal of International Law* 20 (1), 2002, p. 176.

Jones, C. Todd: "Compulsion Over Comity: The United States' Assault on Foreign Bank Secrecy." *Northwestern Journal of International Law and Business* 12 (3), Winter 1992, pp. 459–464.

Kastner, Elizabeth/Jedermann, Laurent: "Hitler's Willing Bankers". *German Politics & Society* 15, No. 2 (43), Summer 1997, p. 96.

King, Nat B.: "An Innovation in international Arbitral Tribunals -- The Swiss – Allied Accord". *The American Journal of International Law* 46, No. 3, July 1952: p. 481.

Lamont, Kathryn H.: "Banking Secrecy Lifted: The Swiss Act to Counter Attacks Launched as a Result of Their Banks' Actions During World War II and Thereafter". *Penn State International Law Review* 16, No. 1, p. 239.

Meier, Walter: "Banking Secrecy in Swiss and International Taxation". *The International Lawyer* 7,no. 1, January 1973, p. 19.

Meyer, Bernhard F.: "Swiss Banking Secrecy and Its Legal Implications in the United States". *New England Law Review* 14, 1978.

Meyer, Hermine Herta: "Banking Secret and Economic Espionage in Switzerland". George Washington Law Review, No. 23, 1955, p. 288.

Mueller, Kurt: "The Swiss Banking Secret: From a Legal View". *The International and Comparative Law Quarterly* 18, No. 2, April 1969, pp. 363–364.

Neuborne, Burt: "Holocaust Reparations Litigation: Lessons for the Slavery Reparations Movement". *NYU Annual Survey of American Law* 58, 2003, pp. 615–622.

Nye, Joseph S.: "Soft Power". Foreign Policy, No. 80, Autumn 1990, pp. 153–171.

Rutledge, G. Philip.: "Bank Secrecy Laws: An American Perspective". *Dickinson Journal of International Law* 14 (3), p. 607.

"Secret Swiss Bank Accounts: Uses, Abuses, and Attempts at Control". *Fordham Law Review* 39, No. 3, 1971, p. 505.

Rubin, Seymour J.: "The Washington Accord Fifty Years Later: Neutrality, Morality, and International Law". American University International Law Review 14 (1), 1998, p. 68.

Ruth, Arne: "Postwar Europe: The Capriciousness of Universal Values". *Daedalus* 126, no. 3, Summer 1997, p. 270.

Sagalowitz, Benjamin: “Switzerland”. *The American Jewish Year Book* 65, 1964, p. 234.

Stauter, Robert Louis: “Swiss Bank Secrecy Laws and the U.S. Internal Revenue Service – Are the Swiss to Blame for Tax Dollars That the U.S. Internal Revenue Service Cannot Collect When U.S. Citizens Hide Their Money in Swiss Banks”. *Case Western Reserve Journal of International Law* 20 (2), 1988, pp. 623–641.

Studer, Roman: “When did the Swiss Get so Rich. Comparing Living Standards in Switzerland and Europe, 1800–1913”. *Journal of European Economic History* 37 (2), January 2008, pp. 405–452.

Weinberg, Gerhard L.: “German Plans and Policies Regarding Neutral Nations in World War II with Special Reference to Switzerland”. *German Studies Review* 22, No. 1, February 1999, pp. 99–103.

White, Elisabeth: “The Disposition of SS-Looted Victim Gold During and After World War II”. *American University International Law Review* 14, No. 1, 1998, p. 218.

Vagts, Detlev F.: “Switzerland, International Law and World War II”. *The American Journal of International Law* 91, No. 3, July 1997, p. 469.

Weber, Rolf H.: “Holocaust-Related Claims and Liability of Swiss Banks – Political and Legal Implications”. *The International Lawyer* 36, No. 4, Winter 2002, p. 1221.

Zabludoff, Sidney: “Restitution of Holocaust-Era Assets: Promises and Reality”. *Jewish Political Studies Review* 19, No. 1/2, Spring 2007, pp. 3–14 and p. 4.

Newspapers, Magazines and News Agencies’ Press Releases

Allen, Matthew:“History bites back at Swiss private banking”. *Swissinfo*, 22.02.2013, retrieved 14.11.2017, http://www.swissinfo.ch/eng/roots-of-wealth_history-bites-back-at-swiss-private-banking/35033852.

Amsden, David: “Building the First Slavery Museum in America”. *New York Times*, 26.02.2015, retrieved 30.09.2017, http://www.nytimes.com/2015/03/01/magazine/building-the-first-slave-museum-in-america.html

“Banking secrecy loosing ‘sacred’ status among Swiss public”. *Swissinfo*, 14.09.2000, retrieved 03.12.2017, http://www.swissinfo.ch/eng/banking-secrecy-losing--sacred--status-among-swiss-public/1657958.

“Christoph Meili Returns – as Hero or Villain?”. *Swissinfo*, 09.04.2009, retrieved 20.10.2017.

"Clinton Backs Efforts to Track Bank Accounts of Nazi Victims". Jewish Telegraphic Agency, 05.05.1996, retrieved 23.05.2018, http://www.jta.org/1996/05/05/archive/clinton-backs-efforts-to-track-bank-accounts-of-nazi-victims.

Cosgrave, Jenny: "UBS, Morgan Stanley private bank assets swell past $2trillion: Report". *CNBC*, 08.07.2015, retrieved 21.11.2017, http://www.cnbc.com/2015/07/08/ubs-morgan-stanley-see-private-bank-assets-pass-2t.html.

"Eizenstat Regrets that Holocaust Report Caused Offence to Swiss". *Swissinfo*, 27.04.2001, retrieved 07.05.2018, https://www.swissinfo.ch/eng/eizenstat-regrets-that-holocaust-report-caused-offence-to-swiss/2007664.

"Eizenstat Slams California for Moves Against Swiss Banks". *Jewish Telegraphic Agency*, 27.10.1997, retrieved 06.05.2018, http://www.jta.org/1997/10/23/archive/eizenstat-slams-california-for-moves-against-swiss-banks-2.

"Former Swiss President Apologizes". *Chicago Tribune*, 15.01.1997, retrieved 04.04.2018, http://articles.chicagotribune.com/1997-01-15/news/9701160323_1_world-jewish-congress-nazi-victims-swiss-government.

Gumbel, Peter: "Secret Legacies: Heirs of Nazis' Victims Challenge Swiss Banks On Wartime Deposits – Do Vaults Still Hold Jewelry or Cash in Accounts Dating to the Holocaust? – Pressure for Full Disclosure". *Wall Street Journal*, 21.06.1995, p. A1.

Hug, Peter: "Eclairage. Les vraies origins du secret bancaire, démontage d'un mythe". *Le Temps*, 28.04.2000, retrieved 09.12.2017, https://www.letemps.ch/opinions/eclairage-vraies-origines-secret-bancaire-demontage-dun-mythe.

"Numbered Accounts Profit from Bank Crisis". *Swissinfo*, 08.02.2010, retrieved 02.12.2017, http://www.swissinfo.ch/eng/numbered-accounts-profit-from-bank-crisis/8256858.

Nguyen, Duc-Quang: "Is Switzerland really the country of bankers?". *Swissinfo*, 18.09.2014, retrieved 20.10.2017, http://www.swissinfo.ch/eng/by-the-numbers_is-switzerland-really-the-country-of-bankers-/40473658.

Rising,David: "Germany Increases Reparations for Holocaust Survivors". *The Times of Israel*, 16.11.2012, retrieved 20.10.2017, http://www.timesofisrael.com/germany-increases-reparations-for-holocaust-survivors/.

Rosenbaum, Ron: "Eichmann and the Banality of Evil". *The Observer*, 23.08.1999, retrieved 23.05.2018, http://observer.com/1999/08/eichmann-and-the-banality-of-the-banality-of-evil/

Sanger, David E.: "As U.S. Urges Delicacy on Swiss Gold, New York City Hints at a Bold Stroke". *New York Times*, 25.08.1997, retrieved 04.03.2018, http://www.nytimes.com/1997/08/25/world/as-us-urges-delicacy-on-swiss-gold-new-york-city-hints-at-a-bold-stroke.html

Sanger, David E.: “D’Amato Threatens Action Against Swiss Banks in Shredding Case”. *New York Times*, 31.07.1997, retrieved 20.05.2018.

Sanger, David E.: “New York Punishes Swiss Bank Over Nazi Gold”. *New York Times*, 10.10.1997, retrieved 30.04.2018, http://www.nytimes.com/1997/10/10/nyregion/new-york-punishes-swiss-bank-over-nazi-gold.html.

Sanger, David E.: “Swiss Envoy to U.S. Resigns After His Report on Holocaust Dispute is Disclosed”. *New York Times*, 28.01.1997, retrieved 14.03.2018.

Schoenfeld, Gabriel: “Holocaust Reparations – A Growing Scandal”. *Commentary*, 01.09.2000, retrieved 17.09.2017.

Sheehan, Neil: “White House Backs Curbs On Use of Swiss Accounts”. *New York Times*, 03.03.1970, retrieved 12.03.2018.

“Swiss President Says Pleas for a Holocaust Fund Are ‘Blackmail”. *Reuters*, 01.01.1997, retrieved 30.03.2018.

“The Greatest Theft in History”. *BBC News*, 01.12.1997, retrieved 23.05.2018.

Warner, Joan: “Raging At the Swiss. Will U.S. Anger Over Nazi Gold Lead to Damaging Sanctions?”. *Bloomberg*, 26.05.1997, retrieved 02.04.2018.

Internet Sources

Beardsley, Brent et al.: “Global Wealth 2015: Winning the Growth Game”. Boston Consulting Group, 15.06.2015, retrieved 21.05.2017, https://www.bcgperspectives.com/content/articles/financial-institutions-growth-global-wealth-2015-winning-the-growth-game/?chapter=2.

Blocher, Christoph: “Switzerland and the Eizenstat Report: Speech given at a function organized by the Young SVP of Switzerland, the Young SVP of the Canton of Bern and the Young Future of Switzerland (JZS)”. Christoph Blocher 21.06.1997, retrieved 15.09.2017.

“Class Action Settlement Agreement”. *Swiss Banks Settlement: In re Holocaust Victim Assets Litigation Official Website*, 26.01.1999, retrieved 28.05.2018, http://www.swissbankclaims.com/Documents/Doc_9_Settlement.pdf.

“Companies Which Seek a Release Under the Settlement Agreement by Identifying Themselves to the Special Master”. *Swiss Banks Settlement: In re Holocaust Victim Assets Litigation Official Website*, 11.09.2000, retrieved 28.05.2018.

“Currencies Traded in the Forex Market”. ForexTraders, 03.11.2016, retrieved 15.03.2017.

“Escher: The Founder of Modern Switzerland”. Credit Suisse, retrieved 02.02.2016, https://www.credit-suisse.com/us/en/articles/articles/news-and-expertise/2014/01/en/escher-the-founder-of-modern-switzerland.html.

"Established 1863". SwissRe, retrieved 02.02.2016, http://www.swissre.com/about_us/swissre_group/our_history/established_1863/?syr=1860&eyr=1869.

Goldman, Stuart D.: "Holocaust Restitution: Overview of the London Gold Conference". Jewish Virtual Library, 24.11.1999, retrieved 14.09.2017.

"Holocaust Victim Assets Litigation Case No. CV 96-4849: Swiss Banks Settlement Fund Distribution Statistics as of December 31, 2015 (Amounts Approved and Paid by the Court)". *Swiss Banks Settlement: In re Holocaust Victim Assets Litigation Official Website,* retrieved 21.09.2016, http://www.swissbankclaims.com/documents/distribution%20stats.pdf.

"How Courts Work. Steps in a Trial, Discovery". American Bar Association, retrieved 21.10.2016, http://www.americanbar.org/groups/public_education/resources/law_related_education_network/how_courts_work/discovery.html.

"John F. Kennedy's Favorite Quotations: Dante's Inferno". John F. Kennedy Presidential Library and Museum, retrieved 23.05.2018, https://www.jfklibrary.org/Research/Research-Aids/Ready-Reference/JFK-Fast-Facts/Dante.aspx.

Junz, Helen B.: "Confronting Holocaust History: The Bergier Commission's Research on Switzerland's Past". Jerusalem Center for Public Affairs, 01.05.2003, retrieved 15.06.2017.

"List of Holocaust memorials and museums". Wikipedia, retrieved 04.02.2018.

"Gestez über die Einziehung volks- und staatsfeindlichen Vermögen vom 14. Juli 1933", (Reichsgesetzblatt 1, 1933, p. 479). Official Website of the Claims Resolution Tribunal of the Holocaust Victim Assets Litigation against Swiss Banks and other Swiss Entities, retrieved 18.05.2017, http://crt-ii.org/_nazi_laws/_lpdfs/19330714.pdf.

"Our Company". Credit Suisse, retrieved 12.06.2016, https://www.credit-suisse.com/corporate/en/our-company.html.

"Standing Law and Legal Definition". USLegal, retrieved 22.03.2017.

Whittlesey, Faith: "Switzerland on Trial". American Swiss Foundation, retrieved 24.09.2017, p. 1 and p. 5.

Index of Names

Adams, Maurice 21, 246
Albrecht, Daniel U. 37-39, 41, 55, 246
Albright, Madeleine 192
Alford, Roger P. 24, 118, 161, 165, 173, 213, 219, 246, 248-250
Alighieri, Dante 77
Allen, Matthew 35, 253
Amsden, David 146, 253
Andersen, Arthur 157
Arendt, Hannah 137
Aubert, Maurice 50-55, 69, 250
Auboin, Roger 100

Bär, Hans J. 37-39, 41, 55, 246
Bartoszewski, Władysław 166
Bauer, Hans 29, 34, 246
Bazyler, Michael J. 24, 118, 144, 161, 162, 165, 173, 184, 189, 191, 194, 201, 206, 213, 214, 219, 222, 246, 248-250
Beardsley, Brent 36, 255
Beerli, Christine 187, 188, 244
Berenbaum, Michael 210, 213, 248
Bergier, Jean François 24, 166, 231
Bettauer, Ronald J. 191, 194, 250
Bilenker, Stephanie A. 139, 151, 162, 164, 165, 172, 251
Bilsky, Leora 199, 202, 203, 204, 205, 251
Blackman, Warren J. 29, 34, 246
Blau, Gisela 148, 151, 155, 157, 165, 168-171, 251
Blocher, Christoph 172, 177, 178, 212, 255
Borer, Thomas 165, 186
Bourgeois, Daniel 120, 246
Bower, Tom 184, 246
Bradfield, Michael 144, 248
Bradsher, Greg 179, 240
Braillard, Philippe 22, 247
Bronfman, Edgar 138, 152, 154, 155, 173, 186, 188, 189, 196, 197, 230
Buechenbacher, Christoph 57, 63, 247
Burlamaqui, Jean Jacques 13

Calverese, Daniele 41, 46, 47, 49 54, 251
Calvin, John 29
Capitani, Werner de 40, 41, 73, 251
Cassis, Youssef 35, 248
Castelmur, Linus von 107, 109-111, 113, 117, 247
Chavagneux, Christian 40, 61, 64, 248
Clement, Piet 99, 248
Clinton, William J. 175, 240
Codevilla, Angelo M. 178, 196, 197, 198, 217, 247
Constantin, Goschler 147, 249
Cosgrave, Jenny 36, 254
Cotti, Flavio 192
Cowell, Alan 138, 251
Crettol, Vincent 86, 245

D'Amato, Alfonse 152, 155, 156, 184, 220, 221, 231
de Vattel, Emmerich 13
Dean, Martin 147, 249
Delamuraz, Jean-Pascal 170, 171
Ducharme, Denise 186
Durrer, Marco 23, 81, 83-86 90, 91, 93-95, 97, 100, 102-104, 106, 107, 247

Eichmann, Adolf 137, 150
Eldridge, James E. 44, 251
Emmenegger, Patrick 68, 251
Esche, Alfred 31

Faith, Nicholas 57, 61, 129, 247
Fehrenbach, T.R. 24, 27, 29, 31-33, 60, 65, 126, 127, 247
Finkelstein, Norman G. 25, 213, 214, 247
Fleury, Antione 121, 123, 176, 207, 247
Fong, Matt 186
Fosu, Augustin K. 31, 250
Froidevaux, Dominique 22, 249
Funk, Walther 81, 95

Gantenbein, Pascal A. 22, 34, 35, 38-40, 45, 48, 56, 61, 63, 72, 145, 148, 248
Ganz, Jodi Berlin 145, 160, 164, 251
Goldman, Stuart D. 183, 256
Grassi, Paolo S. 41, 46, 47, 49, 54, 251
Greenspan, Alan 189
Grendelmeier, Verena 153, 244
Greutert, Eduard 124, 125, 127, 128
Grossman, Lawrence 141, 249
Guex, Sébastien 14, 22, 33, 41, 56, 61, 62, 64-67, 73, 84, 106, 249, 252
Gumbel, Peter 154, 254

Hafer, Barbara 187
Halbeisen, Patrick 86, 245
Harley M. Kilgore 95, 117
Heilig, Karen 142, 143, 252
Heirbaut, Dirk ark von Hoecke 21, 246
Henry, Marilyn 141, 142, 155, 156, 165, 189, 204, 249
Hevesi, Alan G. 184-190, 192, 198, 222, 231, 232
Hirs, Alfred 101, 102
Hopkin, Jonathan 21, 249
Hug, Peter 22, 58-62, 67, 75, 150, 249, 254
Hull, Cordell 84, 124

Iklé, Max: 32, 247

Jagmetti, Carlo 170
James, Harold 166
Jedermann, Laurent 210-212, 252
Jefferson, Thomas 13
Johnston, Ohlin D. 59
Jones, C. Todd 40, 252
Jones, Geoffrey 35, 248
Jung, Joseph 211, 212, 223, 249
Junz, Helen B. 167, 256

Kastner, Elizabeth 210-212, 252
Kennedy, John F. 77, 256
Kennedy, Robert F. 129
King, Nat B. 116, 252
Koller, Arnold 172, 178, 212
König, Mario 126, 127, 129, 130, 247
Korman, Edward R 118, 193, 195, 198, 202, 217, 218, 249
Kreis, Georg 150, 249

Lamont, Kathryn H. 155, 252
Landmann, Julius 64
Lauchlin Currie 92
LeBor, Adam 180, 247
Levin, Neil D. 191
Lorenz-Meyer, Martin 90, 247
Luescher, Martin 42, 247

Mania, Andrzej 20
Marsh, David 20, 21, 249, 250
Marshall, George 134
Marthinsen, John E. 22, 34, 35, 38-40, 45, 48, 56, 61, 63, 72, 145, 148, 248
Marty, Dick 188, 243

Masci, David 215, 249
McCall, H. Carl 185, 187, 189
McCaul, Elisabeth 189
McKittrick, Thomas 99
Meier, Heinz K. 15, 22, 23, 83, 87, 90-97, 106-108, 115, 118, 121, 124, 135, 248
Meier, Henri B. 22, 34, 35, 38-40, 45, 48, 56, 61, 63, 72, 145, 148, 248
Meier, Walter 48, 50, 252
Meili, Christoph 168, 169, 233, 253
Melmer, Bruno 179
Meyer, Bernhard F. 42, 51, 53, 55, 70, 252
Meyer, Hermine Herta 48, 56, 57, 252
Möller, Horst 121, 247
Morgenthau, Henry 78, 84, 85,
Morgenthau, Robert M. 59, 60,
Mueller, Kurt: 53, 145, 252
Murphy, Richard 40, 61, 64, 248

Neuborne, Burt 195, 252
Nguyen, Duc-Quang 36, 254
Novick, Peter 146, 248
Nye, Joseph S. 198, 252

Oron, Yitzhak 149, 250

Palan, Ronen 40, 61, 64, 248
Patman, Wright 60
Paul, Randolph 104, 241
Pfenninger, Rudolf 103
Picard, Jacques 166
Piller, Otto 152-154, 243, 244
Pugacewicz, Tomasz 20

Rabin, Yitzhak 154
Regula, Ludi 147, 208, 209, 220, 249
Rickman, Gregg J. 187, 189, 248
Roosevelt, Franklin D. 83, 91, 124, 196, 239, 242, 248
Rosenbaum, Ron 137, 254
Ruth, Arne 141, 252
Rutledge, G. Philip. 44, 252

Sagalowitz, Benjamin 148, 253
Sak, Pamela 144, 248
Sanger, David E. 169, 171, 184, 186, 254, 255
Schaefer, Alfred 58
Schapiro, Jane 169, 248
Schmidt, Orvis A. 96
Schmitz, Hermann 124-127, 130
Schoenfeld, Gabriel 215-217, 255
Schwamm, Henri 22, 247
Schwarz, Hans-Peter 121, 247
Seymour Rubin J. 104, 116, 214, 252
Shaxon, Nicholas 24, 25, 248
Sigrid, Weigel 22, 249
Singer, David 141, 249
Slany, William Z., 19, 23, 123, 173, 174, 241, 249
Stauter, Robert Louis 44, 253
Steinberg, Jonathan 80, 82, 180, 248
Stettinius Jr., Edward 89, 91, 242
Steury, Donald P. 89, 92, 98, 102, 241
Stoker, Gerry 20, 21, 249, 250
Stuart Eizenstat 19, 23, 24, 123, 155-157, 161, 168, 170, 172-175, 177, 179, 184, 186-189, 192, 193, 241, 247
Stucki, Walter 102-104, 118
Studer, Roman 30, 253
Swift, Robert A. 165, 195, 250

Tanner, Jakob 22, 249
Ther, Phillip 147, 249
Thoms, Albert 178
Toniolo, Gianni 99, 248
Truman, Harry S. 117, 196

Vagts, Detlev F. 119, 121, 253
Villiger, Kaspar 154, 244
Vinson, Fred M. 59

Vogler, Robert U 59, 63, 65, 70, 103, 212, 246, 248, 249
Volcker, Paul 18, 19, 23, 24, 139, 157, 158, 160, 166, 192, 193, 196, 202, 204, 214, 216, 217, 218, 223, 234
Vromen, Ariadne 20, 250

Warner, Joan 185, 191, 255
Weber, Rolf H. 102, 151, 152, 253
Weder, Beatrice 30, 250
Weder, Rolf 30, 250
Weinberg, Gerhard L. 121, 122, 253
Weiss, Melvyn I. 161, 213, 215, 250
White, Elisabeth 180, 253
Whittlesey, Faith 219, 256
Wiesel, Elie 137
Witten, Roger M. 219, 250

Zabludoff, Sidney 141, 143, 144, 222, 223, 253
Ziegler, Jean 153, 243
Zwingli, Ulrich 29

INTERNATIONAL RELATIONS IN ASIA, AFRICA AND THE AMERICAS

Edited by Andrzej Mania & Marcin Grabowski

Vol. 1 Olga Barbasiewicz (ed.): Postwar Reconciliation in Central Europe and East Asia. 2018.

Vol. 2 Adam Nobis: A Short Guide to the New Silk Road. 2018.

Vol. 3 Radka Havlová (ed.): Untangling the Mayhem: Crises and Prospects of the Middle East. 2018.

Vol. 4 Marcin Grabowski / Paweł Laidler (eds.): Global Development Policy in the 21st Century. New Challenges. 2018.

Vol. 5 Andrzej Mania / Marcin Grabowski / Tomasz Pugacewicz (eds.): Global Politics in the 21st Century. Between Regional Cooperation and Conflict. 2019.

Vol. 6 Marcin Grabowski / Tomasz Pugacewicz (eds.): Application of International Relations Theories in Asia and Africa. 2019.

Vol. 7 Адам Нобис. Краткий путеводитель по Новому Шелковому Пути. 2019.

Vol. 8 Olga Barbasiewicz / Marcin Grabowski / Ewa Trojnar (eds.): Security Dilemmas and Challenges in 21st Century Asia. 2020.

Vol. 9 Marcin Gabryś / Magdalena Marczuk-Karbownik / Magdalena Paluszkiewicz-Misiaczek (eds.): Canadian Political, Social and Historical (Re)visions in the 20th and 21st Centuries. 2020.

Vol. 10 Agata Wiktoria Ziętek / Grzegorz Gil (eds.): ASEAN in a Changing World. 2021.

Vol. 11 Maciej Kurcz: Urban Now. A Human in the Face of Borderliness and Urbanisation in Juba, South Sudan. 2021.

Vol. 12 Olga Barbasiewicz / Maciej Pletnia (eds.): Internal and External Aspects of Japanese Security. 2021.

Vol. 13 Olga Barbasiewicz / Michał Lipa / Karolina Rak (eds.): Historical and Collective Memory in the Middle and Far East. 2021.

Vol. 14 Tomasz Pugacewicz / Marcin Grabowski (eds.): Great and Small Games in Central Asia and the South Caucasus. 2022.

Vol. 15 Anna Pruska: Swiss Banking Secrecy and the US-Swiss Conflict Over Holocaust Claims. 2022.

www.peterlang.com

www.ingramcontent.com/pod-product-compliance
Ingram Content Group UK Ltd.
Pitfield, Milton Keynes, MK11 3LW, UK
UKHW041825031026
15587UKWH00002B/561

9 783631 872819